Introspective Voyager

Introspective ❧ Voyager

THE POETIC DEVELOPMENT OF WALLACE STEVENS

A. Walton Litz

1972
Oxford University Press
New York

Preface

When Marius Bewley surveyed the existing criticism of Wallace Stevens' poetry in 1949, he discovered a "persistent bias" in favor of Stevens' first volume of verse, *Harmonium* (1923), and a corresponding neglect of the later work. The poems of *Harmonium* were still taken by most readers as the center of Stevens' poetic achievement, and the major poetry which followed *The Man with the Blue Guitar* (1937) had scarcely been assimilated. Today the opposite bias prevails: the later poetry has become the focus of critical attention, and the poetry of 1914–37 is in danger of being arbitrarily absorbed into the "grand poem" of the last years. This emphasis on the later poetry is easy to explain, and in its way appropriate. The publication of *The Necessary Angel* in 1951, *Collected Poems* in 1954, and *Opus Posthumous* in 1957 made evident the coherence and power of Stevens' final "poetic." Beginning with *Parts of a World* (1937–42) and *Notes toward a Supreme Fiction* (1942), he constructed a self-contained poetic universe which revolves around a few central fictions: a universe with its own laws and language and weather, unique and self-supporting, yet a powerful enlargement of our own familiar and disordered world. Like so many great artists of the twentieth century, Stevens began his work within inherited forms and gradually broke free to establish an independent world, in which the major conventions and traditions are drawn from his own artistic career.

18513

But unlike Ezra Pound's *Cantos* or William Carlos Williams' *Paterson* or James Joyce's *Finnegans Wake*, Stevens' final *mundo* is neither eccentric nor private. It is built upon the central reality of our age, the death of the gods and of the great coordinating mythologies, and in their place it offers the austere satisfactions of a "self" dependent on the pure poetry of the physical world, a "self" whose terrifying lack of belief is turned into a source of freedom. The final achievement of Wallace Stevens is a poetry of exclusions and denials which makes a sustaining fiction out of the search for irreducible reality.

The urgency and coherence of Stevens' later poetry have led to the general conviction that his entire career forms a single poem, larger in the whole than in the parts, of which the earlier works are peripheral aspects. There is some justification for this view. Stevens was slow to begin his major poetic career, and his earliest important poems—written when he was well into his thirties—are alive with suggestions of his later attitudes. As Marianne Moore once said, "the interacting veins of life between his early and late poems are an ever-continuing marvel." But it is one thing to trace the interactions and resemblances between different phases of Stevens' artistic life, and quite another to process the early verse into the final "poetic." Such an approach obscures the fine distinctions within the early career, and trivializes many of Stevens' greatest traditional poems. If Wallace Stevens had ceased writing in 1937, as he almost did in 1924, he would still be recognized as one of the greatest of modern poets: a poet whose long career from 1914 to 1937 was marked by constant interactions between his own sensibility and the conditions, both social and artistic, of his age.

My aim in this study is to evaluate and place in perspective the poems of 1914–37, both for their own sake and for the sake of the later verse, since the best reader of the last volumes is the reader instructed in the earlier poems. As I have suggested in a final chapter which surveys the last years of Stevens' career, his poetic progress after *Parts of a World* and *Notes toward a Supreme Fiction* (1942) differs in fundamental ways from the long process of experimentation and consolidation which shaped the earlier volumes. In this last phase of Stevens' art the sequence of composition becomes less important, as the structures of an achieved poetic world are explored again and again in subtle variations. With the earlier poetry, however, a chronological method is highly revealing, and I have chosen to follow the order of composition while ignoring for the most part the arrangement of the poems in *Harmonium* and *Ideas of Order*. This is not to say that those volumes are random selections: Stevens was always careful with the structure of his volumes, but he was neither an implacable enemy of chronology (like W. H. Auden, who arranged the poems in his 1945 *Collected Poetry* in alphabetical order) nor a believer in rigorous organization (like W. B. Yeats, who shaped *The Tower* along strictly thematic lines). He simply exercised fastidious taste in weeding out the weaker poems, and spread the more recent works throughout each volume on the basis of contrasts and similarities. When the earlier poems are read in the order of their composition or magazine publication, the stages in Stevens' development become clear and the poems within each stage virtually explain one another. Thus the poet of *Harmonium* emerges as a complex personality evolving through time, and the tensions which produced the poetry of the mid-1930's fall into place as motives in a developing "poetic." This chronological approach has its inherent dangers, and throughout the writing of the book I have been painfully conscious of Stevens' "forfeit scholar" (in "Three Academic Pieces"), with his "enlargings and pale arrondissements." No perspective on a poet's achievement can be as important in fact as it appears to be in critical discussion. Our imperfect experience of the poems is always greater and more diverse than our ability to describe them. I can only plead in defense of my particular method that it follows the natural contours of Stevens' poetic life, drawing its categories from his own writings wherever possible.

In the course of studying and teaching Wallace Stevens' poetry I have read most of the major criticism, but this book makes sparing use of it, since so many critical readings of the earlier poems are based on a retrospective view. I have tried, instead, to read the poems as contemporary documents, relating them to their immediate contexts in Stevens' poetic development. Specific debts to criticism and scholarship are acknowledged in the footnotes. My more general obligations to the many excellent studies of Stevens' poetry will be obvious to anyone familiar with the impressive criticism of the last decade.

For assistance in writing this study I am indebted to many friends, but most of all to Mrs. Holly Stevens, who generously allowed me to examine the manuscript materials in her possession, and whose careful edition of the *Letters* was the one indispensable source. Her ample selection of Stevens' most representative poems, *The Palm at the End of the Mind* (New York, 1971), did not appear until my work was completed, but I was pleased to find that its chronological arrangement, based on "manuscript evidence, correspondence, or date of publication," matches my own ordering of the poems in all but a few details. I am also deeply grateful to Professor Robert Buttel, of Temple University, both for his personal encouragement and for his study of the early poetry, *Wallace Stevens: The Making of 'Harmonium,'* which prints much of the early manuscript poetry and provides an essential background to my opening chapters. The staff of the Princeton University Library has been helpful as always, and I am especially indebted to the staff of the Harriet Monroe Modern Library at the University of Chicago, who made available to me their rich collection of correspondence and manuscripts.

To avoid needless detail and repetition, the publications of individual poems are identified by date only. Full bibliographical references are readily available in the standard *Wallace Stevens Checklist* (Denver, 1963), compiled by Samuel French

Morse, Jackson R. Bryer, and Joseph N. Riddel. In the text and footnotes the following abbreviations are used.

CP   *The Collected Poems of Wallace Stevens* (New York, 1954)

OP   *Opus Posthumous,* ed. Samuel French Morse (New York, 1957)

NA   *The Necessary Angel* (New York, 1951)

Letters   *Letters of Wallace Stevens,* ed. Holly Stevens (New York, 1966)

Buttel   Robert Buttel, *Wallace Stevens: The Making of 'Harmonium'* (Princeton, 1967)

Acknowledgments

Grateful acknowledgment is made to the publisher, Alfred A. Knopf, Inc., for use of quotations from the following copyrighted works of Wallace Stevens: *The Collected Poems of Wallace Stevens, Opus Posthumous, The Necessary Angel, Letters of Wallace Stevens, The Palm at the End of the Mind.* Quotations from *Collected Poems, Opus Posthumous, The Necessary Angel,* and the *Letters* are also reprinted by permission of Faber and Faber Ltd.

Permission to quote from writings of Wallace Stevens printed in this book and not included in the above volumes must be obtained from Holly Stevens, c/o Alfred A. Knopf, Inc., 201 East 50th Street, New York, N. Y. 10022.

Ezra Pound's "The Game of Chess" is reprinted by permission of New Directions Publishing Corporation from *Personae,* copyright 1926 by Ezra Pound, and by permission of Faber and Faber Ltd. from *Collected Shorter Poems.*

William Carlos Williams' "El Hombre" is reprinted by permission of New Directions Publishing Corporation and Laurence Pollinger Ltd. from *Collected Earlier Poems,* copyright 1938 by William Carlos Williams.

Table of Contents

PART I
The Poet of *Harmonium*

I N APRIL OF 1918 WILLIAM CARLOS WILLIAMS RECEIVED A LETTER
FROM WALLACE STEVENS WHICH STEVENS DESCRIBED, IN A
postscript, as "quarrelsomely full of my own ideas of discipline." Ostensibly a critique of Williams' latest volume of
verse, *Al Que Quiere!*, the letter is actually a somewhat self-
conscious justification for Stevens' reluctance to collect his
own poems.

> What strikes me most about the poems themselves [in
> *Al Que Quiere!*] is their casual character. . . . Person-
> ally I have a distaste for miscellany. It is one of the
> reasons I do not bother about a book myself.
> . . . My idea is that in order to carry a thing to the
> extreme [necessary] to convey it one has to stick to it;
> . . . Given a fixed point of view, realistic, imagistic or
> what you will, everything adjusts itself to that point of
> view; the process of adjustment is a world in flux, as it
> should be for a poet. But to fidget with points of view
> leads always to new beginnings and incessant new be-
> ginnings lead to sterility.

In short, "a book of poems is a damned serious affair." [1]
Williams published this letter as part of his long, rambling
"Prologue" to *Kora in Hell*, a group of "Improvisations"

The Notes are to be found at the end of Part I, on page 152.

3

written in 1917–18 and modeled after Rimbaud's *Illuminations*. In the context of the "Prologue," Stevens' remarks stand in revealing contrast to Williams' defense of spontaneity and the innocent eye. Although he clearly felt himself to be a part of the new movement in American poetry celebrated by Williams, Stevens looked to that movement for companionship and a sense of vitality, not for confirmation of his evolving poetic. His "ideas of discipline," which both intrigued and puzzled Williams, led Stevens to delay his first volume of verse until 1923, when he was forty-four years old and had been writing with great intensity and dedication for almost a decade. The resulting collection, *Harmonium* (augmented in 1931 by fourteen more poems of the 1918–24 period), culminated a "process of adjustment" so exhaustive and self-critical as to mask the "fidgets" and "new beginnings" that were an inevitable part of its creation. When he sat down to plan *Harmonium* Stevens carefully rejected his more "miscellaneous" efforts, balancing mood against mood and theme against theme in such a way as to obscure completely the chronological development of his art. The result is a finely orchestrated volume which seems to exist as a single personality, complex and even whimsically ambiguous though it may be. At one time Stevens considered calling the book *The Grand Poem: Preliminary Minutiae*, but he finally settled for *Harmonium*.[2]

It is my aim in this section to unravel the almost seamless fabric of *Harmonium* and trace the course of Stevens' poetic career from 1914 to 1924. This period of slightly more than ten years during which the poems of *Harmonium* were conceived and written is a remarkably self-contained stage in Stevens' artistic development. While a special student at Harvard (1897–1900) he wrote a good deal of poetry, most of which was published in the *Harvard Advocate*. But these juvenile verses, although often quite accomplished, follow models that he was later to reject, and have only a tangential relationship to the poems of *Harmonium*.[3] Of much greater importance are Stevens' sporadic experiments of the following years, many of which were collected in the "Little June Books" of 1908 and 1909—manuscript volumes prepared as gifts for his fiancée, Elsie Viola Moll.[4] Six poems from these "Little June Books" were published in 1914 in *The Trend*, and I have used them as the point of departure. They provide a neat summary of Stevens' poetic interests and changing values during the 1900–1913 period, and were obviously intended as a retrospective exhibit of where he had been and what he had to leave behind.

In so far as is possible I have examined the poems and plays of 1914–24 in the order of their composition or publication, grouping them according to common techniques and subjects (often these groupings are those indicated by Stevens himself in the major sequences of poems he prepared for the little magazines). I have paid particular attention to the poems which were excluded from *Harmonium*, since often these "new beginnings" and experiments in point-of-view are just as revealing as the more familiar poems that found a place in the collected works. Although it is obviously impossible to give detailed attention (or even passing notice) to every poem of this decade, I have tried to emphasize the poems which have received little critical comment. I hope this method will place the familiar anthology pieces—such as "Peter Quince," "Sunday Morning," and "Le Monocle de Mon Oncle"—in a new light.

The years of Stevens' work on *Harmonium* were bracketed on either side by long periods of relative silence during which his ideas and emotions underwent profound changes. His journal of 1898–1908 (which was briefly resumed in 1912) reveals a constant process of self-examination, and a steady maturing of taste and sensibility, but it was not until sometime around 1913 that these changes began to demand poetic expression. Just as William Carlos Williams felt "a great surge of interest in the arts generally" in the years immediately before the First World War, a breakthrough symbolized by the famous "Armory Show" of 1913, so Stevens found a sudden liberation in the new atmosphere of revolt and experiment.[5] Again, in the years from 1924 to 1932, Stevens wrote almost nothing, but during these years the new subjects and methods of *Ideas of Order* were taking form. Stevens certainly had this fallow period in mind when he wrote to Ronald Latimer in May 1937, but he could just as easily have been referring to the years before 1914:

> . . . a good many years ago, when I really was a poet in the sense that I was all imagination, and so on, I deliberately gave up writing poetry because, much as I loved it, there were too many other things I wanted not to make an effort to have them. I wanted to do everything that one wants to do at that age: live in a village in France, in a hut in Morocco, or in a piano box at Key West. But I didn't like the idea of being bedeviled all the time about money and I didn't for a moment like the idea of poverty, so I went to work like anybody else and kept at it for a good many years.[6]

There is no reason to doubt the substance of these remarks, even though they fit rather too neatly into the legend of the businessman-poet; but we do have reason to suspect that more complex factors played a part when Stevens "deliberately gave up writing poetry." Just as the manner of his undergraduate poems had to be broken before Stevens could find an authentic voice, so the styles and subjects of *Harmonium* had to be reformed before he could master the world of the later poems. As I shall attempt to demonstrate later, Stevens had by 1924 reached an aesthetic cul-de-sac, and the ensuing years of silence were dictated by a distaste for many kinds of "poverty," including a poverty of the imagination.

As a result of these intriguing gaps in Stevens' artistic career, commentary on *Harmonium* has tended to follow two opposed lines of argument. During the 1930's and early 1940's, before the direction of Stevens' later poetry had become entirely clear, most critics considered *Harmonium* to be his greatest achievement. This attitude is still shared by many readers who prefer the more familiar and "public" forms of *Harmonium* to the special idioms of the later verse. According to these readers, *Harmonium* is the essential work and the later poems are eccentric pendants to it. When told that Stevens' first title for his *Collected Poems* was *The Whole of Harmonium*, they immediately conclude that he considered *Harmonium* the anchor of all his thought.

From another and more sophisticated viewpoint, the poems of *Harmonium* may be seen as tentative statements of Stevens' persistent themes: "Preliminary Minutiae" for the "Grand Poem" of the later years. Critics of this persuasion tend to disregard the very real stages in Stevens' artistic development, and to gloss the early poems with quotations from *The Necessary Angel* and *Notes toward a Supreme Fiction*. Stevens himself provided them with a host of mottoes, as in these lines from "A Primitive Like an Orb":

> One poem proves another and the whole,
> For the clairvoyant men that need no proof:
> The lover, the believer and the poet. (CP 441)

Encouraged by the reflexive nature of the later works, such critics claim for the early Stevens a greater unity of idea and expression than he would have ever claimed for himself.

I have attempted to avoid both extremes of critical dogmatism. Without compromising my belief that Stevens' greatest achievements still lay before him in 1924, I have declined to approach the poems of *Harmonium* through the later poems and essays. The poet of *Harmonium*, as I use the term, is distinct from the dissatisfied man who, even as he prepared *Harmonium* for the press, could write to Harriet Monroe that "the reading of these outmoded and debilitated poems does make me wish rather desperately to keep on dabbling and to be as obscure as possible until I have perfected an authentic and fluent speech for myself." [7] The poet of *Harmonium* is almost a *persona*, an elegant figure made up of those qualities of Stevens' imagination which found their happiest expression in that volume, and the following pages may be read as his "biography."

I

Carnet de Voyage

Sometime in 1913–14, nearly fourteen years after his last undergraduate work had appeared in the *Harvard Advocate*, Wallace Stevens submitted a group of ten poems to a little magazine called *The Trend*. Eight of these poems were published in the September 1914 issue, under the title "Carnet de Voyage," while the remaining "Two Poems" were published in November (the entire *Trend* sequence is reprinted in Appendix B). One of the editors of *The Trend* was Pitts Sanborn, a good friend whom Stevens had first met at Harvard, and we can assume that Stevens broke his long silence partly as a favor to Sanborn; but publication in *The Trend* was also a sign of Stevens' quickening interest in the "new poetry" and in the development of his own art. A year before he had written to his wife:

> I have, in fact, been trying to get together a little collection of verses again; and although they are simple to read, when they're done, it's a deuce of a job (for me) to do them. Keep all this a great secret. There is something absurd about all this writing of verses; but the truth is, it elates and satisfies me to do it.[8]

We cannot say with certainty what was contained in this "little collection of verses," the first Stevens had put together since the manuscript "Little June Book" of 1909. He may have

been ordering and revising the poems which later appeared in
The Trend, but it seems more likely that he was struggling
with some of the experimental poems discussed in the next
chapter. In any event, by 1913 Stevens was well on the way to
modernizing his own poetic style, and although he felt com-
mitted to no particular movement or coterie he responded with
a fine intensity to the new spirit of freedom and self-confi-
dence that characterized the avant garde in American art and
letters. Like so many other American poets of the time he was
profoundly affected by the revolutionary achievements of
modern painting, which found native expression in the
"Armory Show" of 1913. Through his association with Walter
Arensberg, a friend from Harvard days, Stevens came into
contact with the people and events which, in retrospect, seem
to have set the tone of the New York literary scene during
those years when America was not yet engaged in a European
war. At Arensberg's apartment on West 67th Street the American painters who had already declared their liberation could
meet with poets such as Stevens and Williams and Alfred
Kreymborg, who were still searching for an artistic identity.
In view of this interest in experimentation which marked
Stevens' work during the years from 1913 to 1915, it is surprising to discover that almost all the *Trend* poems belong to
an earlier phase of his artistic development. One of them,
"Home Again," is found in the "Little June Book" of 1908;
five others, Poems III–VII of "Carnet de Voyage," appear in
the 1909 "Little June Book." Only the first poem of the series
("An odor from a star") and "From a Junk" seem at all con-
sonant with Stevens' work of 1914. Of course, it may be that
Stevens had no other materials in hand, and was forced to
plunder the earlier manuscript collections in order to satisfy
the request of his friend Sanborn. But this seems unlikely: he
was soon to begin work on the poems of "Phases," some of
which were published in *Poetry* magazine in November 1914,
and other new poems must have been available. Nor does it
seem likely that a fastidious and retiring poet would break a

silence of fourteen years by publishing against his better judgment. Although he confessed to his wife that he awaited the appearance of the *Trend* poems "as one awaits the reading of a will," [9] Stevens must have exposed these outmoded poems to public judgment for a good and sufficient reason: he wished to record where he had been, and establish a mark from which his later advances could be measured. The title "Carnet de Voyage" refers to the structure of the collection, an imaginary voyage to those exotic landscapes and seascapes that inspired so much of his verse during the post-Harvard years. But the poems are also a notebook of another journey, that of the apprentice poet, and they provide a record of his poetic interests and achievements during the years of relative isolation. Unimpressive by themselves, the *Trend* poems exhibit subjects and techniques which were later transformed into some of the most impressive characteristics of *Harmonium*.

The first thing to note about the *Trend* poems is their remarkable lack of distinction. Although the product of a mature mind, they often read like juvenilia; few great poets can have written such flimsy and derivative verse at the age of thirty and beyond. Like the 1909 *Poems* of William Carlos Williams, they are a shocking reminder of the distance a native American poet had to travel, in the years immediately before the First World War, if he wished to escape from the forms of academic romanticism and achieve a distinctive voice. Stevens' letters of the same period are much more alive, revealing the complex and grasping mind that was later to write some of the greatest poems of the century; but this promise is almost totally lacking in the *Trend* poems. Taken as a whole, they reveal that lack of a vital tradition which was the burden (and potential salvation) of American poetry in the years before the First World War.

Although the poems "From a Junk" and "Home Again" were published separately in the November issue of *The Trend*, they are clearly part of the "Carnet de Voyage" sequence, with "Home Again" as the conclusion to an exotic journey.[10] This final poem, the weakest in the collection, seems also to have been the earliest in composition, and it displays all the technical faults of Stevens' early verse, especially in its predictable rhymes and weak rhythms. One can only assume that it was salvaged because it provided such a neat "coda" to the entire sequence.

> Back within the valley,
> Down from the divide,
> No more flaming clouds about,
> O! the soft hillside,
> And my cottage light,
> And the starry night.

As early as 1909, shortly after this poem was written, Stevens was complaining about the "unpardonably 'expected'" rhymes of his early verse: "none of my rhymes are (most likely) true 'instruments of music.' The words to be rhymed should not only sound alike, but they should enrich and deepen and enlarge each other, like two harmonious notes." [11] Here we have a vivid example of the gap between Stevens' actual achievement at this time and his poetic theory, a theory which would later be translated into fact in some of the finest poems of *Harmonium*. It was evidently Stevens' intention in "Home Again" to express a theme very like that of Yeats' "Lake Isle of Innisfree"; in a letter to his fiancée written early in 1909 he spoke of "the cottage" as "the youthful ideal of all men," and clinched his point by quoting from Yeats' poem:

> 'Where morn is all aglimmer
> And noon a purple glow
> And evening, full of the linnet's wings.' [12]

But if the theme he aimed at was Yeatsian, the form—as Robert Buttel has pointed out—seems to owe much more to Bliss Carman's *Songs from Vagabondia*.[13] Stevens was reading Carman at this time, and in "Home Again" he is a prisoner of his current admiration.[14] At the age when Yeats had already fashioned his first "personal" style Stevens was still groping for distinctive forms.

But in spite of their technical weaknesses the *Trend* poems deserve attention, since they lead us into the first stage of Stevens' work on *Harmonium*. In them we see that penchant for the gaudy and the exotic, for expressing familiar themes through unfamiliar settings, which was to become a dominant strain in *Harmonium*. The direction of the imagination's voyage in "Carnet de Voyage" is vaguely Eastward, and most of the poems testify to Stevens' fascination with Oriental art and poetic *chinoiseries*. In Poem II the green of native corn and the blue of familiar lakes fade into a "far off" scene, where "the still bamboo / Grows green; the desert pool / Turns gaudy turquoise for the chanting caravan," and throughout the sequence there is a tension between the primary colors of everyday life and the more delicate shades of an imagined East. A manuscript poem of 1908, which Stevens retained but never published, gives this contrast its most direct expression:

> The house fronts flare
> In the blown rain;
> The ghostly street lamps
> Have a pallid glare.
>
> A bent figure beats
> With bitter droop,
> Along the waste
> Of vacant streets.
>
> Suppose some glimmering
> Recalled for him,
> An odorous room—
> A fan's fleet shimmering.
>
> Of silvery spangle—
> Two startled eyes—
> A still trembling hand,
> With its only bangle.[15]

Here "a fan's fleet shimmering" reminds us of the opening
lines to Poem IV in "Carnet de Voyage," where Stevens invokes "She that winked her sandal fan / Long ago in gray
Japan—." Obviously the world of Oriental art and ceremony
provided Stevens with images and colors that could stir his
imagination and freshen familiar themes. Many of his early
letters testify to this power, but none more powerfully than
the following, written to his wife on January 2, 1911:

> —Walked down Fifth Avenue to Madison Square and,
> after lunch, went into the American Art Galleries, where,
> among other things, they are showing some Chinese and
> Japanese jades and porcelains. The sole object of interest
> for me in such things is their beauty. Cucumber-green,
> camellia-leaf-green, apple-green etc. moonlight, blue, etc.
> ox-blood, chicken-blood, cherry, peach-blow etc. etc.
> Oh! and mirror-black: that is so black and with such
> a glaze that you can see yourself in it.—And now that
> I am home again, and writing, in semi-obscurity, lights
> lit, boats whistling, in the peculiar muteness and silence
> of fog—I wish, intensely, that I had some of those vivid
> colors here.[16]

The fascination which Chinese and Japanese art held for
Stevens' generation was part of a general enthusiasm which had
its origin in nineteenth-century France, and was intensified by
the enormous publicity devoted to Chinese culture at the time
of the Boxer Rising. Beginning in the mid-nineteenth century
as a kind of modish exoticism, akin to the *chinoiserie* of
eighteenth-century England, this curiosity in the East was
given an aesthetic sanction by the work of the Impressionist
painters.[17] The admiration accorded to Japanese and Chinese
art by the Impressionists, and especially by James McNeill
Whistler, seems closely related to Stevens' own interest. As
Ezra Pound later observed: "From Whistler and the Japanese,
or Chinese, the 'world,' that is to say, the fragment of the
English-speaking world that spreads itself into print, learned to
enjoy 'arrangements' of colours and masses." [18] In an extraor-

dinary letter written to his fiancée in March 1909 Stevens reveals the full range of his fascination:

> —Shall I send a picture or two to make a private exhibition for you? Well, here they are, and all from the Chinese, painted centuries ago:
>
>> "pale orange, green and crimson, and white, and gold, and brown;"
>
> and
>
>> "deep lapis-lazuli and orange, and opaque green, fawn-color, black, and gold;"
>
> and
>
>> "lapis blue and vermilion, white, and gold and green."
>
> I do not know if you feel as I do about a place so remote and unknown as China—the irreality of it. So much so, that the little realities of it seem wonderful and beyond belief.—I have just been reading about the Chinese feeling about landscape. Just as we have certain traditional subjects that our artists delight to portray (like "Washington Crossing the Delaware" or "Mother and Child" etc. etc!) so the Chinese have certain aspects of nature, of landscape, that have become traditional.—A list of those aspects would be as fascinating as those lists of "Pleasant Things" I used to send. Here is the list (upon my soul!)—
>
>> The Evening Bell from a Distant Temple
>> Sunset Glow over a Fishing Village
>> Fine Weather after Storm at a Lonely Mountain Town
>> Homeward-bound Boats off a Distant Shore
>> The Autumn Moon over Lake Tung-t'ing
>> Wild Geese on a Sandy Plain
>> Night Rain in Hsiao-Hsiang.
>
> This is one of the most curious things I ever saw, because it is so comprehensive. . . . And last of all in my

package of strange things from the East, a little poem
written centuries ago by Wang-an-shih:

> "It is midnight; all is silent in the house; the
> water-clock has stopped. But I am unable to
> sleep because of the beauty of the trembling
> shapes of the spring-flowers, thrown by the
> moon upon the blind."

I don't know of anything more beautiful than that any-
where, or more Chinese—[19]

Here we have the essence of Stevens' early interest in the
East: an attraction to its vast "irreality" tempered by a delight
in the "little realities" of color and landscape. But the poetry
in which he tried to express this complex response could not
carry the burden of his perceptions; it is vague and derivative,
a poetry of "mood" rather than idea, and we are forcefully
reminded that Stevens began his career under the influence
of the academic romanticism which characterized Harvard
poetry at the turn of the century.[20] The Eastern imagery of
"Carnet de Voyage" is hardly superior to that found in the
early poems of Arthur Davison Ficke, a friend from Stevens'
Harvard days who collected Japanese prints and tried to render
their qualities in his verse. In Ficke's adaptations, such as "The
Beloved: After the Japanese of Yôshi" (1907), the gap between
perception and poetic diction is painfully evident:

> Cold and silver and secret, she mounts from the purple
>   sea-floor.
> Slender and pale she moves through the tender rose of the
>   West.
> O Moon so long beloved, O trembling secret maiden,
> O bride who comest cold to the flush of thy bridal
>   doors! [21]

Much of Stevens' early career may be viewed as a self-
conscious attempt to replace this "group style" with a poetic
form which would adequately express his personal responses to

Eastern art. It was a long and difficult quest that culminated in the *haiku*-like stanzas of "Thirteen Ways of Looking at a Blackbird" (1917), where he appropriated the techniques of condensation and "super-position" which the Imagists had discovered in Japanese poetry and made them uniquely his own.

The Chinese landscapes which inspired Stevens' letter to his fiancée continued to haunt his imagination. On 14 May 1909 he copied the first two word-pictures into his journal: "Japanese color prints: Pale orange, green and crimson, and white, and gold and brown. / Deep lapis-lazuli and orange, and opaque green, fawn-color, black and gold." And finally the descriptions were set forth as a manuscript poem:

Colors

I

Pale orange, green and crimson, and
White, and gold and brown.

II

Lapis-lazuli and orange, and opaque green,
faun-color, black and gold.[22]

As Robert Buttel has argued, "Colors" resembles the color impressionism of Bliss Carman and the later "color symphonies" of John Gould Fletcher.[23] Like so many of his contemporaries who saw the world new-minted through the eyes of the Impressionists and Oriental print-makers, Stevens wished to incorporate their colors into his poetry; but his attempts in "Carnet de Voyage" serve only to illustrate the difficulty of translating effects from one medium to another. The colors of "Carnet de Voyage"—unlike those of Stevens' later verse—have neither symbolic nor imagistic value.

> And in the stream,
> Small fishes gleam,
> Blood-red and hue
> Of shadowy blue,
> And amber sheen,

> And water-green,
> And yellow flash,
> And diamond ash.

These lines from Poem III possess nothing but a weak incantatory power. The colors are named, not presented; nothing forces us to *see* the landscape as the poet must have seen it in his imagination. It is as if we were presented with the title of one of Whistler's nocturnes, but were denied the painting itself. The poet of "Carnet de Voyage" can describe the Impressionist palette, but he has not yet learned to use it. All the poems seem at one remove from the thing seen. Like the young Ezra Pound, Stevens had yet to recognize the difference between a poem which describes the effects of painting and one which re-creates those effects.

This difference is illustrated by "From a Junk," perhaps the most mature piece in the series. Alone among the *Trend* poems it conveys a compelling visual image, although once he has presented the image Stevens does not know how to exploit it. The title should of course not be "From a Junk" (a bit of *chinois* preciosity) but "The Moon," and the last four words are superfluous.

> A great fish plunges in the dark,
> Its fins of rutted silver; sides,
> Belabored with a foamy light;
> And back, brilliant with scaly salt.
> It glistens in the flapping wind,
> Burns there and glistens, wide and wide,
> Under the five-horned stars of night,
> In wind and wave . . . It is the moon.

This poem breaks away from the pastel colors and metronomic music of most of the other *Trend* poems to achieve effects not unlike those of T. E. Hulme's "Imagist" verses. Along with "An odor from a star" (the program piece of the collection and certainly one of the last to be composed), it has a music of its own which reminds one of some of the lesser poems in *Harmonium*. In "From a Junk" and "An odor from a star" the predictable rhymes and rhythms of the other *Trend* poems have given way to a more subtle musical statement, and Stevens is approximating one of the ideals set forth in the Imagist manifesto: composition "in sequence of the musical phrase, not in sequence of a metronome." [24]

"From a Junk" and "An odor from a star" inevitably bring the Imagist movement to mind, and remind us that in the years immediately before 1913–14 Stevens was moving independently toward the common ground of avant-garde poetry. As Pound said of T. S. Eliot, he "modernized himself *on his own*," [25] sensing the direction of the "new poetry" before it had fully declared itself in the little magazines. F. S. Flint's description of the circumstances that brought the first "Imagists" together in 1909 might be a description of the forces at work on Stevens' sensibility at that time.

> I think that what brought the real nucleus of this group together was a dissatisfaction with English poetry as it was then (and is still, alas!) being written. We proposed at various times to replace it by pure *vers libre;* by the Japanese *tanka* and *haikai*. . . . In all this Hulme was ringleader. He insisted too on absolutely accurate presentation and no verbiage; and he . . . used to spend hours each day in the search for the right phrase. . . . There was also a lot of talk and practice among us . . . of what we called the Image. We were very much influenced by modern French symbolist poetry.[26]

Like Flint and his companions, Stevens felt dissatisfied with the English and American poetic models then current, and he turned to other sources for sanction and inspiration: to the French symbolists, to the Impressionist painters, and to the arts of Japan and China. The *Trend* poems can be read as a "notebook" of these movements in Stevens' mind, illustrating both the conventions he rejected and the forms he hoped to perfect: and when read in this way they chart a more intriguing voyage than the Eastward journey which is their ostensible subject. In them the poet of *Harmonium* begins to emerge as a distinctive personality.

II

Experiment and Mastery

The progress of Stevens' poetic development during the years from 1914 to 1916 is complex and often baffling. Beginning with the "Primordia" sequence in early 1917, the pattern of his evolving interests becomes fairly clear; each viewpoint or technique is explored to its limits, and the published groups of poems ("Lettres d'un Soldat," "Pecksniffiana," "Sur Ma Guzzla Gracile," "Revue") display considerable unity in language and theme. In these later stages of his work on *Harmonium* Stevens was following the theory outlined in his well-known letter to William Carlos Williams, "that in order to carry a thing to the extreme [necessary] to convey it one has to stick to it." [27] But the earlier years were a time of "incessant new beginnings," and some of these new beginnings led to the sterility Stevens feared, as in the published and unpublished poems he ruthlessly excluded from *Harmonium*. In 1914 and 1915 the long-suppressed creativity of a major poet was suddenly released, and the ideas and images of fifteen years tumbled forth in such a profusion of forms that Stevens' poetic personality often appears on the verge of disintegration. The contrasts in quality and artistic direction are quite astounding: the familiar masterpieces such as "Sunday Morning" and "Peter Quince" jostle for place with poems which seem to be by a different author, and which often skirt the borders of mediocrity.

Typical of this complexity and unevenness are the poems

called "Phases," and it is with this sequence of "war poems" that Stevens' work on *Harmonium* properly begins. In September 1914 *Poetry: A Magazine of Verse* announced that a group of anonymous donors had offered a prize of one hundred dollars for the best war or peace poem "based on the present European situation." Stevens submitted a series of eleven poems, which arrived so late (the November "War Number" was already in proof) that Harriet Monroe, the editor, could find space for only four of them. Although Stevens did not win the prize (it went to "The Metal Checks" by Louise Driscoll, a decision which caused Ezra Pound to refer later to "the war-poem scandal"), Miss Monroe was fascinated by the poems; she carefully saved the unpublished sections in her "Jewel File" of favorite verses which never reached print, and wrote to Stevens that she "was heartbroken that we could not use more of your poem, especially the first section." [28]

It is only fitting that Stevens should have begun his public career with a series of "war poems," since the kinship of soldier and poet was to become one of the leading metaphors of his major verse. In the coda to *Notes toward a Supreme Fiction* (1942) the soldier and poet are companions-in-arms, each engaged in a war that depends upon the other: the poet, seeking to reconcile "mind / And sky," abstraction and change, finds his image in the soldier-hero and gives him a voice.

> Monsieur and comrade,
> The soldier is poor without the poet's lines,
>
> His petty syllabi, the sounds that stick
> Inevitably modulating, in the blood.
> And war for war, each has its gallant kind. (CP 407)

Such a relationship is dimly visible as early as "Phases," but Stevens is unable to prove the metaphor. In the later works war is the stuff of poetry because the soldier, like the poet, must confront the tragic interdependence of death and beauty, suffering and heroism. Yet in "Phases"—as in the early "Lettres d'un Soldat," where Stevens follows the journal of a young French painter at the front—war is ultimately interesting only because it sharpens the poet's eye, and provides him with an "occasion" for poetry. Unlike Ezra Pound's *Cathay*, which makes an oblique but profound comment on the world of 1914–15, "Phases" smells of the exercise-book. This is not to say that Stevens is "insincere": he clearly saw the subject as potentially more than an occasion for the display of his poetic range, and tried to process the realities of the distant conflict into his imagination, but without great success. One is reminded of a passage in a letter of 1909:

> There is a difference between the thought of motions long ago and the thought of sound long ago. I think of the siege of Rome, say, simply as motion, without sound —take an ancient siege. The trenches are dug, the guns are brought up, the regiments manouevre, the walls tumble. It is all visionary. The firing of the guns is merely a flash of color—a flick in the mind. The regiments are as quiet as leaves in the wind. The walls fall down mutely as all things happen in times far off.—But let sound enter—the hum of the men, the roar of the guns, the thunder of collapsing walls. The scene has its shock.[29]

The war of "Phases" is such an ancient conflict, without the sound of reality: "It is all visionary. . . . a flick in the mind." The danger which always threatens Stevens' poetry—that it will become merely hermetic, seizing upon general reality as an "occasion" rather than a subject—is evident throughout "Phases." Raphael and Claude Lorraine have a greater presence than Winkle and Hopkins, who know the "salty taste" of death. Although the four published sections of "Phases" appeared over Stevens' name, he had originally intended to use the pseudonym "Peter Parasol";[30] and the incongruity of a "war poem" by such a fictitious dandy is symptomatic of the many incongruities which make "Phases" both unsatisfactory and highly revealing.

Stevens worked hard on "Phases," trying to harmonize his current verse experiments with a vicarious experience of "the present European situation." The editing of the series—unlike Miss Monroe's later trimming of "Sunday Morning"—cannot easily be criticized, since Miss Monroe chose the strongest verses and Stevens himself experimented with various arrangements. The full sequence of eleven poems does, however, have a unified design, and we can see Stevens experimenting with the inner harmonies and repeated motifs that give integrity to so many of his longer poems (the full text of the sequence is printed in Appendix B). "Phases" opens with a retrospective vision of peacetime serenity, interrupted by the call to war: "A dead hand tapped the drum, / An old voice cried out, 'Come!' / We were obedient and dumb." But the roll of the drums is also a stirring serenade, setting the ambivalent tone of the series. This introduction is then followed by a panel of battlefield scenes, and these in turn give way to more generalized verses on the paradoxical nature of war which bracket Poem X, a final evocation of the peacetime landscape.

> Peace means long, delicious valleys,
> In the mode of Claude Lorraine;
> Rivers of jade,
> In serpentines,
> About the heavy grain;
> Leaning trees,
> Where the pilgrim hums
> Of the dear
> And distant door.
> Peace means these,
> And all things, as before.

In mood and tone the series of poems alternates between the simple patriotism of a war poster and the recognition of pointless waste, as Stevens tries to avoid the extremes of sentiment and sensationalism by balancing one against the other. Poems III and V, deliberate counterpoints, mark out the extremes:

> This was the salty taste of glory,
> That it was not
> Like Agamemnon's story.
> Only, an eyeball in the mud,
> And Hopkins,
> Flat and pale and gory!
>
> . . .
>
> Death's nobility again
> Beautified the simplest men.
> Fallen Winkle felt the pride
> Of Agamemnon
> When he died.
>
> What could London's
> Work and waste
> Give him—
> To·that salty, sacrificial taste?
>
> What could London's
> Sorrow bring—
> To that short, triumphant sting?

This contrapuntal design produces a dramatic suite of poems which acts out the paradox expressed in the epigraph from Pascal's *Pensées* (No. 298): "La justice sans force est contredite, parce qu'il y a toujours des méchants; la force sans la justice est accusée." The failure of "Phases" does not lie in its organization and "argument," which represent a great advance over Stevens' earlier work, but in the radical division between the hermetic world of the poet's imagination and the public world of his chosen subject.

But if "Phases" fails as a "war poem" or even a personal credo, it remains a rich and instructive museum of Stevens' verse experiments at the time when he was seeking to cast off

old forms and assimilate new techniques. Some of the poems
(e.g. Poems II and IX) merely carry forward the line of his
apprentice work, but others are engagements in the contemporary struggle between *vers libre* and the stricter stanzaic
and metrical forms. Stevens seems to be deliberately exploring
the limits of his own ability to handle various tensions between
rhythm and meter. His methods range from the freedom of
Poem I

> There was heaven,
> Full of Raphael's costumes;
> And earth,
> A thing of shadows,
> Stiff as stone,
> Where Time, in fitful turns,
> Resumes
> His own . . .

through variants of the rhymed quatrain to the almost manic
condensation of Poem VIII:

> What shall we say to the lovers of freedom,
> Forming their states for new eras to come?
> Say that the fighter is master of men.
>
> Shall we, then, say to the lovers of freedom
> That force, and not freedom, must always prevail?
> Say that the fighter is master of men.
>
> Or shall we say to the lovers of freedom
> That freedom will conquer and always prevail?
> Say that the fighter is master of men.
>
> Say, too, that freedom is master of masters,
> Forming their states for new eras to come.
> Say that the fighter is master of men.

Here the mesmeric repetitions in the first and third lines of
each tercet frame the central lines, which have their own
symmetry and virtually recapitulate the sense of the epigraph
from Pascal. The poem is interesting both as an experiment in

control and condensation, probably derived from English adaptations of the *villanelle*, and as a prefiguration of the tercet form which would become a major vehicle for Stevens' imagination (as in "Sea Surface Full of Clouds" and *Notes toward a Supreme Fiction*). In effect, the Stevens of "Phases" was rehearsing the central debate of early twentieth-century poetry, and declaring that his problems and aspirations were not very different from those of Pound, or Williams, or even W. B. Yeats. As phases in his own poetic development, the poems of this series point the way toward the experiments that were to follow.

Encouraged by the publication of "Phases II–V," Stevens gathered together another collection of experimental verses and sent them to Miss Monroe; but the subjects and forms were too eccentric for the editor of *Poetry*, who was still resisting the efforts of her London collaborator, Ezra Pound, to "modernize" the journal. On 27 January 1915 she wrote a rather testy letter of rejection:

> I don't know when any poems have "intrigued" me so much as these. They are recondite, erudite, provocatively obscure, with a kind of modern-gargoyle grin in them—Aubrey Beardsleyish in the making. They are weirder than your war series, and I don't like them, and I'll be blamed if I'll print them; but their author will surely catch me next time if he will only uncurl and uncoil a little—condescend to chase his mystically mirthful and mournful muse out of the nether darkness.[31]

Miss Monroe was not the only one to be frightened by the "modern-gargoyle grin" of Stevens' new verses. Carl Van Vechten remembered an evening in the winter of 1914–15 when Stevens read some of his poems to a group of friends and Mrs. Stevens commented: "I like Mr. Stevens' things when they are not affected; but he writes so much that is affected." [32]

There is no reason to quarrel with the judgments of Miss Monroe and Mrs. Stevens. Much of Stevens' minor verse of this period *was* affected and obscure to no purpose, as he tacitly acknowledged when he allowed many of the poems to die in manuscript and excluded others from *Harmonium*.[33] But affectation is a self-conscious defense against unconscious imitation, and in these verses Stevens was both cleansing his palette and trying out new forms. The experiments really flow in two directions: "weird" exercises in post-Impressionist abstraction, designed as antidotes to the trite subjects and vague outlines of Impressionist verse; and attempts at the new convention of the Imagist poem. Both directions led away from the language and themes of Stevens' apprentice poetry.

"Poetry is a sort of inspired mathematics," Ezra Pound declared in *The Spirit of Romance*, "which gives us equations, not for abstract figures, triangles, spheres, and the like, but equations for the human emotions." [34] In this definition Pound deliberately appropriated the language of science to emphasize the qualities of precision and "impersonality" which he wished to embody in a new poetic diction, and in some of his later verses he tried to go beyond Impressionist representation by dissolving the visual scene into an almost mathematical pattern of form and color. "Dogmatic Statement Concerning the Game of Chess: Theme for a Series of Pictures," which first appeared in *Poetry* for March 1915, is an extreme attempt to eliminate rhetorical formulas through a language of precise form.

> Red knights, brown bishops, bright queens,
> Striking the board, falling in strong 'L's of colour.
> Reaching and striking in angles,
>   holding lines in one colour.
> This board is alive with light;
>   these pieces are living in form,
> Their moves break and reform the pattern:
>   luminous green from the rooks,
> Clashing with 'X's of queens,
>   looped with the knight-leaps.

'Y' pawns, cleaving, embanking!
Whirl! Centripetal! Mate! King down in the vortex,
Clash, leaping of bands, straight strips of hard colour,
Blocked lights working in. Escapes. Renewal of contest.[35]

Compare with this the opening lines of Stevens' unpublished poem "Headache," which must have been written at almost the same time:

> The letters of the alphabet
> Are representative of parts of the head.
> Ears are *q*s
> *L*s are the edges of the teeth
> *M*s are the wrinkled skin between the eyes
> In frowns.
> The nostrils and the bridge of the nose
> Are *p*s or *b*s.
> The mouth is *o*.
> There are letters in the hair.
> The alphabet is a collection
> Of satirical design. . . .[36]

The aim here is to wash away all preconceived verbal formulas, all metaphors for the body that have degenerated into poetic cliché, and to reconstruct the noblest part of the human anatomy out of abstract signs which have the least possible human content. The intent of the poem is deliberately satirical, and the satire is directed both at man's romantic image of himself and the poetic conventions which embody that image. Having constructed his abstract design Stevens can do little with it, and the poem ends on a note of lame wit: "The maker of the alphabet / Had a headache." But in its radical rejection of all traditional metaphors "Headache" declares itself as a part of that general reaction against nineteenth-century poetic diction which lay at the heart of the "new poetry." Stevens was destroying part of himself in his search for a new voice.

Just as William Carlos Williams used the term "sonnet" as

shorthand for all stultifying poetic coventions, so Stevens employed the terms "rhetorician" and "rationalist" to stand for those habits of mind and language which screen us away from new perceptions of things as they are. An unpublished poem of *c.* 1914 begins in a confessional mood:

> I have lived so long with the rhetoricians
> That when I see a pine tree
> Broken by lightning
> Or hear a crapulous crow
> In dead boughs,
> In April
> These are too ready
> To despise me
> It is for this the good lord
> Gave the rooster his lustre
> And made sprats pink
> Who can doubt that Confucius
> Thought well of streets
> In the spring-time
> It is for this the rhetoricians
> Wear long black equali
> When they are abroad.[37]

In this elegant little poem, really a dress-rehearsal for Poem VI of "Six Significant Landscapes" (CP 75), Stevens associates "rhetoric" with the death of nature and the end of cyclical change. In that constant struggle between words and things which gives poetry its life, perceptions are constantly being distilled into a verbal formula which then takes on a life of its own. The "long black equali" of the rhetoricians, the robes of death, are protection from a world of constant change which demands constant adjustments between the old and the new. Like the colorless inhabitants in "Disillusionment of Ten O'Clock" (1915), who live in the world without imagination, the rhetoricians are not going to "dream of baboons and periwinkles," or catch "tigers / In red weather" (CP 66).

In one experimental "Exercise for Professor X" Stevens

mocks the rhetoricians by speculating on the true reality which lies outside of words.

> I see a camel in my mind.
> I do not say to myself in English,
> "There is a camel."
> I do not talk to myself.
> On the contrary, I watch
> And a camel passes in my mind.
> This might happen to a Persian.
> My mind and a Persian's
> Are as much alike, then,
> As moonlight on the Atlantic
> Is like moonlight on the Pacific.[38]

The delicate irony of this poem cuts two ways, producing a critique of both Professor X—who, in the tradition of Thomas Gradgrind, puts his faith in words rather than experience—and of the naïve poet who distrusts language as a vehicle. In fact, this little exercise points up a paradox which was to become a central concern of Stevens' art: the poet's double allegiance to things as they are in the silent language of the mind and things as they are in the public language of the poem. The poet talks to himself, but always with the intent of being overheard. He must be true to abstraction, to general nature, but also give it a local habitation and a particular name. "Moonlight on the Atlantic" and "moonlight on the Pacific" are alike, and yet totally different. In "An Exercise for Professor X," as in the other manuscript poems which group around it, Stevens was testing certain extreme aesthetic propositions in an attempt to discover his own place in the poetic tradition, which was at that moment undergoing one of its periodic spasms of self-examination.

Stevens' critique of the received idea of poetry extended to subject-matter as well as technique. Many of his "weird" and "modern-gargoyle" poems of 1914–15, such as "Dolls" or "Infernale," are a deliberate affront to the accepted notions of poetry's proper subject. Harriet Monroe was right in finding

a 'ninetyish, "Aubrey Beardsleyish" quality in them, for
Stevens (like Oscar Wilde or Ernest Dowson) flirted with the
decadent beauty of the gothic and the grotesque. His most
successful effort in this mode, saved for *Harmonium*, was "The
Worms at Heaven's Gate" (CP 49–50). Published in *Others*
for July 1916, this poem is a comic statement of that matter-
of-fact attitude toward death which occurs again and again in
Harmonium as the necessary counterpart to the sacramental
themes of "Peter Quince" and "Sunday Morning." In its own
grotesque fashion, "The Worms at Heaven's Gate" reminds
us that "The only emperor is the emperor of ice-cream."

> Out of the tomb, we bring Badroulbadour,
> Within our bellies, we her chariot.
> Here is an eye. And here are, one by one,
> The lashes of that eye and its white lid.
> Here is the cheek on which that lid declined,
> And, finger after finger, here, the hand,
> The genius of that cheek. Here are the lips,
> The bundle of the body and the feet.
>
>   . . .
>
> Out of the tomb we bring Badroulbadour. (CP 49–50)

Here Stevens, like Hamlet, displays his talent as a master of
the literal imagination. The Princess Badroulbadour is resur-
rected by a "convocation of politic worms," and the echo of
Shakespeare's Sonnet XXIX in the title reminds us of the grand
style which Stevens' irony both mocks and affirms.

Among Stevens' many experiments in new styles and new
subjects during the years from 1914 to 1916, the most interesting line of development involves his repeated attempts to
write the quintessential Imagist poem. The theories which T. E.
Hulme expounded to a small coterie in 1908–9 soon found a
wider audience, and by 1912 Imagism had taken on all the
attributes of a poetic "movement": in that year Pound printed
"The Complete Poetical Works of T. E. Hulme" as an appendix
to his volume *Ripostes*, and announced that *Les Imagistes*,

"the descendants of the forgotten school of 1909," had the future in their keeping. In January of the next year H. D. published three poems in *Poetry: A Magazine of Verse* over the signature "H. D., 'Imagiste,' " and these were to become models for the new movement: a good many of Stevens' experiments in 1914–15 would seem to derive from the color imagery and free musical structure of these verses. Two months later, in March 1913, *Poetry* published F. S. Flint's definition of "Imagisme" and Pound's "A Few Don'ts by an Imagiste" with this explanation from Miss Monroe: "In response to many requests for information regarding *Imagism* and the *Imagistes*, we publish this note by Mr. Flint, supplementing it with further exemplification by Mr. Pound. It will be seen from these that *Imagism* is not necessarily associated with Hellenic subjects [a reference to H. D.'s poems based on the Greek Anthology], or with *vers libre* as a prescribed form." Early the next year Pound's anthology *Des Imagistes* was published in New York, containing a liberal sampling of his own recent verse and poems by other writers (Joyce, H. D., Williams, F. S. Flint, Ford Madox Hueffer, and Amy Lowell among them) which would support the doctrine of the Image. Under the energetic guidance of Pound the pragmatic observations of Hulme and his followers were rapidly institutionalized.

Imagism was a "phase" through which the major poets of Stevens' generation passed at a crucial moment in their development, and it left a lasting mark on all of them. For some, such as H. D. and John Gould Fletcher, it was the watermark of their careers. Others, such as Pound and Eliot, saw it as merely one stage in their progress, an interval of condensation and clarification which was a necessary prelude to more ambitious efforts; but even in their careers it may be argued that the mosaic quality of Imagist structure had a permanent impact on their handling of the long poem. William Carlos Williams was probably the major poet most profoundly affected by Imagism, and his entire poetic life may be viewed as a working-out of the full implications of Imagist theory. Stevens' response to the new movement was ambivalent from the start, but of deep and lasting importance. Just as most men tend to measure all their passions against their first love, so Stevens returned again and again to the Imagist method as a means of cleansing his diction or re-establishing his contact with visual reality.

T. E. Hulme's "Lecture on Modern Poetry," first delivered in 1908–9 and again in 1914, is the best possible gloss on Stevens' experiments of 1914–16.[39] Although Stevens could not have read the essay (it was first published in 1938), parts of it chart his early decisions and revisions with almost uncanny accuracy. At one point Hulme observes that since modern poetry no long expresses epic subjects, "no longer deals with heroic action, it has become definitely and finally introspective and deals with expression and communication of *momentary phases in the poet's mind*." [40] These are the "Phases" which Stevens chose as title for his "war poem," and which he could never align with his "heroic" subject. In fact, the incessant attempts of Imagist poets to treat the great theme of their generation without violating their aesthetic reveal a good deal about the virtues and limitations of the form. Evidence that the form could be adequate is provided by the war sections of *Hugh Selwyn Mauberley*, and by the poem that Pound "Abbreviated from the Conversation of Mr. T. E. H." after Hulme had returned from the front:

> Over the flat slope of St Eloi
> A wide wall of sandbags.
> Night,
> In the silence desultory men
> Pottering over small fires, cleaning their mess-tins:
> To and fro, from the lines,
> Men walk as on Piccadilly,
> Making paths in the dark,
> Through scattered dead horses,
> Over a dead Belgian's belly.

The Germans have rockets. The English have no rockets.
Behind the lines, cannon, hidden, lying back miles.
Before the line, chaos:

My mind is a corridor. The minds about me are corridors.
Nothing suggests itself. There is nothing to do but keep on.[41]

What this poem possesses, and Stevens' "Phases" lack, is the authority of direct experience.

The burden of Hulme's "Lecture on Modern Poetry" is that the vital tendencies in early twentieth-century verse were related to the discoveries of Impressionist painting, and that free verse (not *vers libre* in a narrow sense, but musical form as opposed to regular meter) was the appropriate vehicle for these new effects.

> We still perceive the mystery of things, but we perceive it in entirely a different way—no longer directly in the form of action, but as an impression, for example Whistler's pictures. We can't escape from the spirit of our times. What has found expression in painting as Impressionism will soon find expression in poetry as free verse.

"We are no longer concerned that stanzas shall be shaped and polished like gems," Hulme declares, "but rather that some vague mood shall be communicated." And in order to express this mood, the poet constructs a "harmony" of images which creates its own musical verse-form.

> Say the poet is moved by a certain landscape, he selects from that certain images which, put into juxtaposition in separate lines, serve to suggest and to evoke the state he feels. To this piling-up and juxtaposition of distinct images in different lines, one can find a fanciful analogy in music. A great revolution in music when, for the melody that is one-dimensional music, was substituted harmony which moves in two. Two visual images form

what one may call a visual chord. They unite to suggest
an image which is different to both.[42]

These quotations are a fair summary of Stevens' "aesthetic"
at the time he was composing "Phases." Intent upon rendering
moods and impressions, phases of the poet's mind, he found
himself increasingly dissatisfied with the "vague" quality that
Hulme identified. The Symbolist love for the "suggestion" or
diffuse mood, and use of incantatory rhythms to reinforce these
effects, no longer seemed adequate; "Carnet de Voyage" was
the notebook of another self. In Hulme's lecture one senses
a deep tension between the earlier ideals of Symbolist diction
and rhythm, as outlined in Yeats' decisive essay "The Symbolism
of Poetry" (1900), and the theory of the organizing image,
which would promote precision and condensation. Under the
hands of Pound and others avant-garde poetry did indeed
move in a new direction, toward greater clarity and directness,
a movement not confined to the self-styled "Imagists" but
discernible in the work of Yeats and others who stood outside
any "school." The three cardinal "rules" of Imagism laid down
by F. S. Flint in the March 1913 issue of *Poetry*, and glossed
by Ezra Pound, indicate one direction in which Stevens was to
travel while working on *Harmonium*.

1. Direct treatment of the "thing," whether subjective or
   objective.
2. To use absolutely no word that did not contribute to
   the presentation.
3. As regarding rhythm: to compose in sequence of the
   musical phrase, not in sequence of a metronome.[43]

This is not to say that Stevens worked to any "theory," although he always claimed that there was a great deal of theory
in his poetry, but simply that the practice of the Imagists came
to his attention at a crucial moment and had a catalytic effect
on his art. A poet, like any dandy, cannot resist trying on the
latest fashions, and Stevens discovered that the fashion suited
the man. Many years later, in the collection of aphorisms which

he jotted down after the model of Valéry's *Tel Quel*, Stevens gave his final judgment on Imagism.

> Not all objects are equal. The vice of imagism was that it did not recognize this.
>
> · · ·
>
> The bare image and the image as a symbol are the contrast: the image without meaning and the image as meaning. When the image is used to suggest something else, it is secondary. Poetry as an imaginative thing consists of more than lies on the surface.[44]

Unlike William Carlos Williams, Stevens soon learned how to turn the "bare image" into the "image as symbol," thus avoiding the indiscriminate surface which was the chief vice of Imagism. Many of the poems of 1914–16, especially those published in the little magazine *Others*, are a record of how he assimilated Imagist practice and made it an essential part of his own poetic behavior.

Stevens' early exercises in the Imagist mode are often weakened by his penchant for fantastic settings and litanies of color. "The Silver Plough-Boy" (1914), which appeared in the first edition of *Harmonium* but was eliminated from the 1931 volume, is really a grotesque "nocturne" in silver and black: "A black figure dances in a black field. / It seizes a sheet, from the ground, from a bush, as if spread there by some washwoman for the night. / It wraps the sheet around its body, until the black figure is silver . . ." (OP 6). This attempt at word-painting, so reminiscent of the apprentice verse, is found in "To Madame Alda, Singing a Song, in a White Gown," a poem of 1914–15 which never reached print.

> So much sorrow comes to me out of your singing.
> A few large, round leaves of wan pink
> Float in a small space of air,
> Luminously.
> A white heron rises.

> From its long legs, drifting, close together,
> Drops of water slide
> And glisten.
> It drifts from sight.[45]

"To Madame Alda . . ." is a dilution of the Imagist formula, in the manner of Amy Lowell or John Gould Fletcher; the organizing image is there, but only vaguely related to the woman's singing. The result is a pleasing word-picture, but it is essentially an "image without meaning." The dramatic action implicit in even the shortest of the great Imagist poems (such as Pound's "Papyrus") is lacking here. Again and again in his poems of 1914–15 Stevens had difficulty in creating the "image as meaning," with the result that the poems often break down into weak editorial comment. In "Bowl" (OP 6–7), for example, the series of images is broken off with "Oxen . . . / I never tire / To think of this." This is the sort of anti-climax William Carlos Williams had in mind when he cut the last two lines from the manuscript version of "The Worms at Heaven's Gate," criticizing Stevens for "a weakening of the truth by a sentimental catch at the end." [46] According to Williams, the last two lines were "fully implied in the poem"; but it is precisely because many of his Imagist exercises did not fully imply the idea he had in mind that Stevens resorted to flat comment.

In contrast to these rather unsatisfactory experiments, "Tea" (1915) is a triumph of wit and compression.

> When the elephant's-ear in the park
> Shrivelled in frost,
> And the leaves on the paths
> Ran like rats,
> Your lamp-light fell
> On shining pillows,
> Of sea-shades and sky-shades,
> Like umbrellas in Java. (CP 112–13)

The dramatic contrast between the precise, colorless images of autumn and the exotic but unspecified colors of the "shining pillows" brings the climate of the day and the climate of the mind into significant alignment. Afternoon tea becomes an escape from the death of nature's colors, but all the "sea-shades and sky-shades" of imagined Java depend on a remembered impression of the begonia's colorful foliage before it "shrivelled in frost." The "umbrellas in Java" are a witty flourish, but they are not arbitrary because the exotic other-world has already been suggested by the colloquial "elephant's-ear." The perfection of "Tea" points forward to the best verses in the *Others* sequence of March 1916, a sequence which provides a neat cross-section of Stevens' changing interests and abilities.[47]

Of the seven poems gathered in *Others*, "Six Significant Landscapes" best reveals Stevens' ability to move freely within the Imagist formula, and to give the method a strong personal flavor. Having cut from the series two self-indulgent poems where the imagery exploits incongruity for its own sake,[48] he produced five delicate variations on the "anti-rational" theme of Poem VI: the conviction that changes in mood and weather and place demand changes in poetic behavior. Typical of these modulations on a dominant theme is Poem I:

> An old man sits
> In the shadow of a pine-tree
> In China.
> He sees larkspur,
> Blue and white,
> At the edge of the shadow,
> Move in the wind.
> His beard moves in the wind.
> The pine tree moves in the wind.
> Thus water flows
> Over weeds. (CP 73)

Here nothing is wasted: the mosaic of images, one superimposed upon the other in the mind of the reader, makes a complex statement on the paradox of permanence within change. Two of the lines ("His beard moves in the wind. / The pine tree moves in the wind.") might belong to the spare world of "Thirteen Ways of Looking at a Blackbird," so successful are they in making the bare natural images a vehicle for complex emotion. The poet of "Six Significant Landscapes" was no longer a student of Imagism, but a master: from this point forward the techniques were to be a permanent part of his poetic repertoire, a constant source of refreshment and clarification.

Certainly the most impressive poem in the *Others* sequence is "Domination of Black" (CP 8–9), which looks forward to "The Snow Man" (1921), its companion piece in *Harmonium*. "Domination of Black" seems to have sprung from the same vision of deprivation that prompted "Blanche McCarthy" (OP 10), but the highly regular meter and tight stanzaic form of that fugitive poem ultimately work against its theme. The refrain which opens each stanza of "Blanche McCarthy"—"Look in the terrible mirror of the sky"—is a grand beginning, but the monotonous structure leads to a final effect of depression rather than terror. In "Domination of Black," however, the musical structure and controlled repetitions (reminiscent of T. S. Eliot's "Rhapsody on a Windy Night," published the year before in *Blast*) provide a perfect form for the theme of perceived desolation. The colors of autumn find their correspondences in the flickering firelight, the darkness of "the heavy hemlocks" dominates in the dark corners of the room, and the desolate cry of the peacock is remembered because his tail is patterned with the colors of "the leaves themselves."

> At night, by the fire,
> The colors of the bushes
> And of the fallen leaves,
> Repeating themselves,
> Turned in the room,
> Like the leaves themselves
> Turning in the wind.

Yes: but the color of the heavy hemlocks
Came striding.
And I remembered the cry of the peacocks.

The darkness is in the cry of the peacocks, and as the poem
unfolds the images of motion, color, and sound are gathered
into an ominous mosaic which fulfills Ezra Pound's classic
definition of the Image: "that which presents an intellectual
and emotional complex in an instant of time." [49] The final stanza
gives the bare statement "I felt afraid" a precise and complex
resonance:

Out of the window,
I saw how the planets gathered
Like the leaves themselves
Turning in the wind.
I saw how the night came,
Came striding like the color of the heavy hemlocks
I felt afraid.
And I remembered the cry of the peacocks.

Many of the poems discussed so far in this chapter were
judged unworthy of *Harmonium*, and of those included some
may strike the reader as slight or merely experimental in spite
of their brilliant effects. Only in "Domination of Black" do we
hear the voice of a major poet, but we must remember that
Stevens had a taste for both major and minor tones.[50] He once
remarked that "All poetry is experimental poetry," and one of
his aims in structuring *Harmonium* was to preserve the best of
his minor experiments as well as his major poetic statements.
Indeed, the two classes of verse depend upon each other, and
Harmonium would be the poorer if it were simply a garland of
the major poems. Unlike the conventional poet who suppresses
his experiments, Stevens' imitated the modern painter who
makes public his rough sketches and trial designs as well as his
"finished" works. Poetry, like life, is an affair of manners and
fashions as well as morals, and Stevens was determined to
balance his witty experiments and minor exercises against the

great contemplative poems. As a self-conscious modern artist concerned with process as well as product, he wished to leave a record of where he had been. Years before, the young newspaperman just out of Harvard had observed in his journal that "Sonnets have their place . . . but they can also be found tremendously out of place: in real life where things are quick, unaccountable, responsive." [51] In the minor pieces of *Harmonium*, especially those cast in the freer verse forms, Stevens sought to preserve a sense of the inquisitive poet responding to the "quick, unaccountable" changes of life and poetry. The experimental verses saved for *Harmonium* provide an atmosphere or "environment" in which the more formal major poems take on added substance and range of implication.

∽

The poems we have been considering are satellites to Stevens' two great early works, "Peter Quince at the Clavier" and "Sunday Morning." First published in August 1915, "Peter Quince" (CP 89–92) is concerned with the same paradox which T. S. Eliot confronts in the fifth part of each of the *Four Quartets*: how can the form of beauty or art endure when it must be expressed in materials that are the wards of time.

> Words move, music moves
> Only in time; but that which is only living
> Can only die. Words, after speech, reach
> Into the silence. Only by the form, the pattern,
> Can words or music reach
> The stillness . . .[52]

The parable of Susanna and the elders, borrowed from the Apocrypha, is the fable about which the poem revolves. Susanna's piercing beauty is a kind of "music," and although it soon faded, leaving "only Death's ironic scraping," it lives again in the very form of Stevens' poem. As Joseph N. Riddel has argued, "Peter Quince" aspires toward the condition of music; "the four parts of the poem are stretched casually upon the three-part sonatina framework of exposition, development, and recapitulation with coda," [53] while the verse-forms change from section to section to harmonize with the mood of the argument. The unrhymed tercets of Part I, bound together by the quiet music of assonance and alliteration, are appropriate to the measured exposition of the basic simile between the "music of feeling" and "the strain / Waked in the elders by Susanna"; but in Part II, where Susanna's naked beauty is imaged directly, Stevens resorts to the sensuous rhythms of a more open form. With the noise of Susanna's discovery, the verse-form changes in Part III to the beat of regular couplets, and these give way in the "coda" to a flexible form which gradually modulates from rhymed couplets to a final tercet like those of the opening section. The entire musical development of the poem is so successful in its evocation of Susanna's beauty that the form acts out the fundamental theme of permanence within change.

The ironic contrast between the bumbling Peter Quince and the delicate music of the clavier is both a graceful gesture of self-deprecation and a foreshadowing of the clash between Susanna and the elders. But we must remember that Peter Quince and his fellow mechanics are the essential counterpart to the moonlit imagination of *Midsummer Night's Dream*, representing the lumpy reality without which imagination is mere moonshine. The dialectic of "Peter Quince at the Clavier" is one of contrasts, and without the lust of the elders or the literalness of Peter Quince the airy structures of sound and feeling could never be realized.

Part IV of "Peter Quince" opens with a startling reversal of our everyday assumption that earthly beauty is an evanescent reflection of the "ideal form" in the mind.

> Beauty is momentary in the mind—
> The fitful tracing of a portal;
> But in the flesh it is immortal.
> The body dies; the body's beauty lives.

Susanna's beauty is "immortal" because it is reincarnated in the music of feeling evoked by every beautiful woman, specifically by the one of "blue-shadowed silk" to whom the poem is addressed. Just as the green luxury of the earth is reborn cyclically after the "cowl of winter" has departed, so physical beauty endures *because* it dies: in the words of "Sunday Morning," "Death is the mother of beauty," and to think of a beauty that cannot die within nature's cycle is to dwell in sterile abstraction. Susanna's "music," like poetry, is a "constant sacrament," both because it is a mystery, a ritual, and because it celebrates the unchanging patterns of a changing world. With its emphasis on poetry as a possible alternative to the sacraments of religion, "Peter Quince" serves as a prelude to "Sunday Morning."

"Sunday Morning" is the grand summation of Stevens' education as a man and as a poet. As early as 1902 he had recorded in his journal: "An old argument with me is that the true religious force in the world is not the church but the world itself: the mysterious callings of Nature and our responses." [54] Like William James, whom he read and admired, Stevens believed that "The earth of things, long thrown into shadow by the glories of the upper ether, must resume its rights." [55] Years later he was to remark in an elegiac passage that "the great poems of heaven and hell have been written," but "the great poem of the earth remains to be written" (NA 142). "Sunday Morning" may be seen as a rehearsal for that "great poem of the earth."

The revolutionary aspect of "Sunday Morning" lies in its sharp break with the nineteenth-century tradition of poems on faith and doubt. Unlike the typical nineteenth-century poet who found himself, in Arnold's lines, "Wandering between two worlds, one dead, / The other powerless to be born," Stevens did not feel the tug of traditional faith. In his view, we live in "an age of disbelief," a space of time between the death of one great coordinating mythology and the birth of another; the poet's job is to record our lives and make them tolerable by supplying "the satisfactions of belief" (OP 206). For Stevens, the "death of God" is not a subject for debate but a premise from which to begin. It is this perception of what has now become our accepted lack of faith that makes "Sunday Morning" still the most "modern" of poems.

When Stevens sent the eight stanzas of "Sunday Morning" to Harriet Monroe in May 1915 she decided to print a "selection"; unaccountably, the poem must have struck her as no more unified than "Phases." Stevens acquiesced to this trimming process: "Provided your selection . . . is printed in the following order: I, VIII, IV, V, I see no objection to cutting down. The order is necessary to the idea." [56] In the event Miss Monroe decided to add another stanza, and VII was chosen: "No. 7 of *Sunday Morning* is, as you suggest, of a different tone," Stevens wrote in late June, "but it does not seem to me to be too detached to conclude with." [57] Stevens' willingness to alter his poem in this fashion, and his use of the terms "idea" and "tone," are highly significant. Although in its full eight-stanza structure "Sunday Morning" does possess a fine continuity of design, the poem is not a dialectical argument leading to some kind of resolution, and to read it as disguised philosophy is to distort its delicate balance of voices and attitudes. The original five-stanza form which appeared in *Poetry* for November 1915, and was not replaced until *Harmonium*, had a profound impact upon early readers of Stevens; even after the appearance of the full poem the earlier version was thought of for four decades as an Ur-"Sunday Morning" which embodied Stevens' early and fundamental order of perceptions.[58] Yvor Winters, for example, seems to have been permanently influenced by his reading of the earlier version. Although he quotes from the final form in his well-known essay "Wallace Stevens, or the Hedonist's Progress," [59] his view of the entire poem would imply a direct equation between the "hedonism" of stanza VII and Stevens' deepest convictions. It is fascinating to speculate on whether Winters' attitude toward "the greatest American poetic talent of the twentieth century" would have been substantially different if he had first encountered "Sunday Morning" and the early experimental verses in the full context of *Harmonium*.

The "idea" expressed by the sequence published in *Poetry* (I, VIII, IV, V, VII) depends upon the juxtaposition of what were to become the first and last stanzas. As Michel Benamou has pointed out, the first and last stanzas of the full poem (I and VIII) are symmetrically balanced, with the last corresponding "panel for panel" to the first, "but in reverse order." [60] When placed side-by-side they lose this framing effect, and become part of a four-stanza sequence (I, VIII, IV, V) which is a dialogue between the two halves of the woman's mind, or between her lingering doubts and the reassuring responses of the poem's "voice." This dialogue is then resolved in the "final" stanza VII, which takes on prophetic overtones and leaves the reader with a sense that some blood-fellowship not unlike that championed by D. H. Lawrence is Stevens' "solution" to the dilemmas posed in the preceding four stanzas. The truncated version of "Sunday Morning" may well, as Stevens said, follow a pattern "necessary to the idea," but the full-length poem is more than the expression of an "idea," and its powerful hold on our imagination is the direct result of its symmetrical structure and masterful blank verse.

The opening stanza is a double image of the intricate relationships between past and present. The sensuous satisfactions of the present moment, realized in the brilliant colors of a Matisse still-life ("Coffee and oranges in a sunny chair, / And the green freedom of a cockatoo") are turned into the lifeless trappings of some nightmarish ritual as the "old catastrophe" that Sunday morning celebrates draws the woman's mind into the dark past.

> The pungent oranges and bright, green wings
> Seem things in some procession of the dead,
> Winding across wide water, without sound.
> The day is like wide water, without sound,
> Stilled for the passing of her dreaming feet

> Over the seas, to silent Palestine,
> Dominion of the blood and sepulchre.

Stevens' view of the Christian mystery, like that of Yeats, emphasizes its violence and "odor of blood." The imagery of stanza I poses an urgent question: can we live in the spontaneous freedom of immediate sensation, or must we be perpetually drawn into the abstract "dominion" of the past?

Stanza II opens with an explicit statement of this question, "Why should she give her bounty to the dead?," and then elaborates upon the "comforts of the sun" in language of almost extravagant beauty.

> Passions of rain, or moods in falling snow;
> Grievings in loneliness, or unsubdued
> Elations when the forest blooms; gusty
> Emotions on wet roads on autumn night;
> All pleasures and all pains, remembering
> The bough of summer and the winter branch.
> These are the measures destined for her soul.

Stanzas II and III form a pair, since in them we hear only the meditative voice of the poem's maker. Stanza II fleshes out the cyclic permanence of ever-changing nature, the divinity of immediate sensation; stanza III, by contrast, takes the long view of man's passion for myth-making, and gives the poem depth and perspective by placing the woman's present-day dilemma in a historical context. The ancient myths uniting heaven and earth allowed for a commingling of the two: "Jove in the clouds had his inhuman birth," yet he could move among men "as a muttering king, / Magnificent, would move among his hinds." But man desired an even greater myth, and the shepherds discerned in a star the Christian king whose birth divided heaven from earth. Now that myth, like all myths, has lost its compelling force. At the end of stanza III the poem's voice returns to the question which began stanza II.

> Shall our blood fail? Or shall it come to be
> The blood of paradise? And shall the earth

> Seem all of paradise that we shall know? . . .
> Not this dividing and indifferent blue.

Stanzas IV and V are also complementary, forming a two-panel centerpiece for the poem. Each starts with a question by the woman, acknowledging the pleasures of earth but stating the old need for "some imperishable bliss."

> She says, "I am content when wakened birds,
> Before they fly, test the reality
> Of misty fields, by their sweet questionings;
> But when the birds are gone, and their warm fields
> Return no more, where, then, is paradise?"

To this question the poem's answer is unequivocal: "Death is the mother of beauty," not the easeful death of romantic reverie, but the inevitable change which gives nature her vitality and yields the eternal patterns of cyclic renewal. In words reminiscent of "Peter Quince" the poem reveals its deepest mystery.

> There is not any haunt of prophecy,
> Nor any old chimera of the grave,
> Neither the golden underground, nor isle
> Melodious, where spirits gat them home,
> Nor visionary south, nor cloudy palm
> Remote on heaven's hill, that has endured
> As April's green endures; or will endure
> Like her remembrance of awakened birds,
> Or her desire for June and evening, tipped
> By the consummation of the swallow's wings.

No ritual, no visionary myth, not even the imaginary world of visionary art (the echoes of *The Tempest* are unmistakable) can yield the satisfactions of nature's cyclic permanence.

Stanzas VI and VII, like II and III, make a contemplative pair. In parallel to stanza II, stanza VI begins with a question: "Is there no change of death in paradise?," and goes on to visualize a changeless perfection which seems dead and two-dimensional in comparison to "our perishing earth." "Alas, that they should wear our colors there": an other-worldly paradise can only be imaged in the colors of this world, where

> Death is the mother of beauty, mystical,
> Within whose burning bosom we devise
> Our earthly mothers waiting, sleeplessly.

After this reaffirmation of the primacy of earth the voice of the poem paints a speculative picture of a new myth, with the sun as a god naked among men.

> Supple and turbulent, a ring of men
> Shall chant in orgy on a summer morn
> Their boisterous devotion to the sun . . .
> Their chant shall be a chant of paradise,
> Out of their blood, returning to the sky;
> And in their chant shall enter, voice by voice,
> The windy lake wherein their lord delights,
> The trees, like serafin, and echoing hills,
> That choir among themselves long afterward.

This imagined world in which the myth lives on our pulse, and the vitality moves from earth to heaven rather than heaven to earth, gives full range to Stevens' speculative imagination. It is but one schema, one "scenario" for the future, but in a pluralistic universe anything is possible. If we take stanza VII as a metaphor for any myth which acknowledges the primacy of earth, then the "primitivistic" aspects of "Sunday Morning" which have troubled so many readers fall away. Stanza VII is not the conclusion of the poem, but the ultimate projection of its "idea": and in the last stave the poem returns to where it began, the ambiguous life of the present.

Yvor Winters, reading the last stanza through its predecessor, believed that "Sunday Morning" ends with a denial of the immortality of Jesus and a rosy vision of hedonistic bliss. If this were true, then the delicate mechanism of the entire poem would be useless. In fact, however, stanza VIII affirms the immortality of Jesus in the poem's special terms: by dissolving the Incarnation and transforming Jesus into one who lived and died, the poem restores him to "the heavenly fellowship / Of men that perish and of summer morn." The poem's first stanza ends with "silent Palestine," but the last stanza reverses the pattern and opens with a cry from across the wide waters of time:

> "The tomb in Palestine
> Is not the porch of spirits lingering.
> It is the grave of Jesus, where he lay."

The hold of the Christian myth is broken when it is placed in the perspective of natural change, and "Sunday Morning" ends with a series of modulations on the great theme of mutability and spontaneous freedom. "We live in an old chaos of the sun," in that space of time between the death of one co-ordinating faith and the birth of another: and although this is cause for elegiac regret, it is also cause for celebration. We are free because "unsponsored," and nature provides the final ambiguous image of our freedom in isolation.

> And, in the isolation of the sky,
> At evening, casual flocks of pigeons make
> Ambiguous undulations as they sink,
> Downward to darkness, on extended wings.

At its close "Sunday Morning" returns to the pictorial rendering of calmness and freedom with which it began. Stanza VIII gradually washes away the prophetic energy of the preceding stanza, and we are left simply with images for contemplation, the appropriate and inevitable conclusion to a great poem in the meditative tradition.

In many ways "Sunday Morning" bears an ambiguous relationship to Stevens' poetic life. In spite of its affinities with "Peter Quince," it stands alone among the poems of 1914–16, different from them in both language and mood. It is also an orphan in the larger context of *Harmonium*, and in the entire canon of Stevens' poetry. The mind which invented "Sunday

Morning" can be traced in the other poems, of course, and it is easy to place "Sunday Morning" in various lines of development. But when all this has been done the poem remains somewhat aloof, probably because it is the only truly great "traditional" poem that Stevens wrote. Wallace Stevens can be linked with a number of poetic traditions, but he was essentially an inventor, assimilating traditions and making them totally his own. The real tradition in Stevens' art is his own poetic progress, and as his career neared its close Stevens, like Yeats, built more and more upon himself. The typical process in Stevens' art is to invent or synthesize a highly personal form, as in "Le Monocle de Mon Oncle," and then play intricate variations on the form until it is exhausted. But "Sunday Morning" belongs not to a personal tradition but to the major line of meditative religious verse, and we learn to read it by reading traditional English poetry, not by reading Wallace Stevens. In his choice of the long blank-verse stanza Stevens was making a conscious gesture toward tradition, and his remarkable mastery of the form—remarkable since it went against the natural grain of his talent—gives "Sunday Morning" its special place as a poem which lives both within and without Stevens' poetic "mundo."

Years after the composition of "Sunday Morning" Stevens made this entry in his *Adagia*:

> The relation of art to life is of the first importance especially in a skeptical age since, in the absence of a belief in God, the mind turns to its own creations and examines them, not alone from the aesthetic point of view, but for what they reveal, for what they validate and invalidate, for the support that they give. (OP 159)

The entire course of Stevens' poetic life may be seen as an attempt to find satisfactions for "a skeptical age," and more and more these satisfactions are vested in the poet's "own creations," until in his later work the poem and the process that made it replace the objects of traditional meditation. The great virtue of "Sunday Morning," that which makes it central to our experience, is Stevens' refusal to use art or any special theory of the imagination as a substitute for lost certainty. "Sunday Morning" is about life in a world marked by "the absence of a belief in God," and the ample satisfactions of that world; but it offers no special view of "the relation of art to life" as a substitute mythology. By remaining skeptical and open the poem connects with the widest range of our personal and cultural experience, and avoids the hermetic quality which debilitates so many of Stevens' later works.

There is a curious and revealing pendant to "Sunday Morning" in the unfinished manuscript poem "For an Old Woman in a Wig," which was never published in Stevens' lifetime. Composed sometime in 1915–16, "For an Old Woman in a Wig" builds on the themes of "Sunday Morning," and was evidently to have been a three-part exploration of the role art must play in the world of "Sunday Morning." Judging from the erasures and revisions, Stevens obviously had great difficulty with his subject, and the poem was finally abandoned; but the problems it attempted to formulate were to become the persistent concerns of Stevens' art, and "For an Old Woman in a Wig" may be seen as a forerunner of some of the finest poems in his later career.

The most finished section of the poem, the opening of Part II, derives from stanza VI of "Sunday Morning."

> Is death in hell more death than death in heaven?
> And is there never in that noon a turning—
> One step descending one of all the seven
>
> Implacable buttresses of sunlight, burning
> In the great air? There must be spirits riven
> From out contentment by too conscious yearning.
>
> There must be spirits willing to be driven
> To that immeasurable blackness, or . .
> To those old landscapes, endlessly regiven,
> Whence hell, and heaven itself, were both begotten.[61]

Evidently Stevens' intent was to combine these perceptions from "Sunday Morning" with other emerging concerns of his art at that time: the relation of man to his physical and intellectual landscape, the function of the poetic imagination, the whole problem of "resemblance" and "remembrance" in poetry. But the most intriguing aspect of "For an Old Woman in a Wig" is not its pastiche of subjects, but its verse-form: Stevens chose to cast the poem in terza rima, as a tacit (though perhaps ironic) acknowledgment of its affinities with the *Divine Comedy* and Shelley's *ars poetica*, "Ode to the West Wind." The choice of terza rima seems almost perverse, in view of the paucity of English rhymes, but Stevens clearly desired both the authority of tradition and the taut structure provided by the tercets. Many have regretted that Stevens did not make greater efforts to develop the blank-verse form of "Sunday Morning," but it was not consistent with the various poetic fashions which interested him. Tercets such as those of "For an Old Woman in a Wig" were more congenial to the aims of Imagism, and in this poem one can see Stevens' efforts to combine the flowing diction of "Sunday Morning" with such Imagist lines as "Of crows that flap away beyond the creaking / Of wooden wagons in the mountain gutters" (p. 214). The amalgam was clearly a failure, and Stevens left the poem unfinished; but even in its present form "For an Old Woman in a Wig" is a prefiguration of things to come. In its tercet stanzas, which Stevens was to develop into his most flexible form, and in its attempts at a general grounding for poetic theory, "For an Old Woman in a Wig" reminds one of the poetry that followed *Harmonium*. Meanwhile, Stevens put aside his grand ambitions and returned to the long process of forging distinctive styles out of the poetic fashions of his time.

III

Theatrical Demonstrations

Wallace Stevens' brief and gingerly involvement with the experimental theatre is one of the most revealing episodes in his early career, since it brings into focus a persistent concern: how can the poet maintain his personal style, his individual integrity, and still be a part of his own time? The facts about Stevens' dramas are easily stated. In May 1916 Harriet Monroe, the editor of *Poetry*, informed Stevens that his play *Three Travelers Watch a Sunrise* had been awarded the Players' Producing Company prize for the best one-act play in verse. The donor and the staff of *Poetry* were the judges, and although they had some doubts about the play's "dramatic value" they were convinced by its intricate symbolism and "extraordinary poetic beauty." [62] Stevens was delighted by this recognition of his first attempt at drama, and he set out to revise *Three Travelers* along the lines suggested by the judges, hoping "to have the play a play and not merely a poem, if possible." [63] He knew that he had been successful in creating a "poetic atmosphere," [64] but he was eager to improve the mechanics of dialogue and staging. *Three Travelers* was published in *Poetry* for July 1916, and although it did not reach production that year Stevens was encouraged to continue his work in the drama. Laura Sherry, the director of the Wisconsin Players, was so intrigued by *Three Travelers* that she asked Stevens if he would supply her with another play. Stevens eventually sent

54

two, *Carlos among the Candles* and *Bowl, Cat and Broomstick*, and Mrs. Sherry was sufficiently impressed by them to include both plays in the program offered by the Wisconsin Players when they appeared at New York's Neighborhood Playhouse in October 1917. *Carlos among the Candles* was presented on Saturday evening, October 20, and *Bowl, Cat and Broomstick* was on the bill the following Tuesday. Both plays were failures, and were apparently never staged a second time: the sets were clumsy, not the "extremely delicate and extremely suggestive" [65] settings originally designed by Stevens' friends Bancel La Farge and Walter Pach, and the performances were botched, but Stevens knew that the fault did not lie entirely in production. He wrote later that the experience taught him "what poetry is, and is not, proper for the theatre," [66] but even before the productions by the Wisconsin Players he had begun to lose his enthusiasm for dramatic performance. He had tried to make *Three Travelers* "a play and not merely a poem," [67] but after the attempts to revise *Three Travelers* he frankly admitted that his intention in *Carlos among the Candles* was "not to produce a dramatic effect but to produce a poetic effect." [68] When *Three Travelers* was finally presented at the Provincetown Playhouse in 1920 Stevens did not see it or even bother to make inquiries: he remarked that "so much water has gone under the bridges since the thing was written that I have not the curiosity even to read it to see how it looks at this late day." And he added: "That's truth, not pose." [69] We may well believe him, since after the performances by the Wisconsin Players he had acknowledged that his interest in "a theatre without action or characters," [70] although perhaps legitimate, was not worth the pursuit.

Although *Three Travelers Watch a Sunrise* and *Carlos among the Candles* both appeared in *Poetry* magazine, Stevens never considered reprinting them, and he allowed *Bowl, Cat and Broomstick* to remain in typescript. Samuel French Morse included the two published plays in *Opus Posthumous*, but *Bowl, Cat and Broomstick* was not printed until 1969. [71] Strikingly different from the other two plays, it may impress the contemporary reader as better theatre, and it certainly reveals a great deal more about Stevens' artistic concerns. It raises anew the questions of why he decided to write for the theatre, why he did not succeed, and how the dramatic experiments are related to his early poetry.

The years 1915–16, when Stevens first began to interest himself in the writing of drama, were a time of excitement and innovation in the American theatre. The "new theatre" of Yeats, Gordon Craig, and others, with its emphasis on suggestion rather than statement, and on symbol rather than imitation, was already a world-wide force, and in the dynamic atmosphere of New York after the "Armory Show" the American theatre sought to adapt and develop the European innovations. Yeats' essay on "Certain Noble Plays of Japan" appeared in *The Drama* for November 1916, describing how his experience of the Japanese Noh plays had helped him to invent the "indirect and symbolic" form of *At the Hawk's Well.* The Provincetown Players moved to Greenwich Village in the autumn of 1916, and in November they staged the experimental play *Lima Beans* by Stevens' friend Alfred Kreymborg, in which the characters adopted the stylized movements of marionettes and the curtain festooned with vegetables played a leading role. It was the heyday of what Gordon Craig called the "unstage-like play," and at Kreymborg's skylight loft on East 14th Street (which doubled as a rehearsal hall), or at Walter Arensberg's studio on West 67th Street, Stevens would have discussed these new attempts to fuse post-Impressionist painting, the new staging, modern dance, and contemporary poetry into a fresh and radical form. Like William Carlos Williams, he must have felt in his restrained way that the writing of experimental drama was part of the contemporary experience. These were the years of Stevens' greatest involvement with current movements and fellow artists, of his participation in the group that supported the little magazine *Others*, and although he was never a man of movements and manifestos he must have been stirred by the exciting sense of a common purpose.

Yet however much he tried to be in the mode, Stevens remained forever himself. *Three Travelers Watch a Sunrise*, with its ritual movements and symbolic setting, may strike us now as a period piece, but its light-hearted *chinoiserie* and delicate verse are pure Stevens. Its theme, too, is drawn directly from Stevens' poetic world of that time, as he explained to Harriet Monroe.

> The play is simply intended to demonstrate that just as objects in nature offset us, as, for example
>
> > Dead trees do not resemble
> > Beaten drums,
>
> so, on the other hand, we affect objects in nature, by projecting our moods, emotions, etc.:
>
> > an old man from Pekin
> > Observes sunrise,
> > Through Pekin, reddening.[72]

The lines "Dead trees do not resemble / Beaten drums" are from a rejected section of "Eight Significant Landscapes" (published as "Six Significant Landscapes"), and they remind us that Stevens' plays were concerned with the same theme of man's relationship to his physical and intellectual climate that he was exploring in his poetry. The clash in *Three Travelers* between the realistic Pennsylvania landscape, with its drama of violence and death, and the elegant speculations of the three Chinese travelers, is a paradigm of the paradoxes in Stevens' own art.

In the same way, *Carlos among the Candles* was "intended to illustrate the theory that people are affected by what is around them." [73] The sole actor, "*an eccentric pedant of about forty*," is clearly a mask for Stevens the dandy, the future author of "Le Monocle de Mon Oncle." As he lights and extinguishes the ritual candles, commenting in mannered prose upon how the changing lights and shades affect the sensibility, he is both acting out one of Stevens' profoundest themes and parodying the preciosity of some of the early verse.

This combination of aesthetic speculation and witty self-parody is carried further in *Bowl, Cat and Broomstick*, which comes closest to exposing the paradoxes and complexities of Stevens' early verse. Perhaps this is why Stevens chose never to print it. The play is set in seventeenth-century France, in the age of poetic *préciosité*, yet the heroine turns out to be not a young poetess but an aging writer of Calvinist background: this contrast between appearance and actuality is clearly a comment on the contradictions of Stevens' own career. The play is replete with the themes and problems explored in the poems of *Harmonium*: the interdependence of tragedy and comedy; the disjuncture between a poet's personality and his work; the effect of people upon things and of things upon people; the sad recognition, as expressed in "Le Monocle de Mon Oncle," that love is "a book too mad to read / Before one merely reads to pass the time." Most of all, the play is concerned with the problem of poetic fashions and of "being one's self in one's day" (p. 29). Stevens obviously saw analogies between the "new poetry" of his day and the *préciosité* of seventeenth-century France, and when he mocks the poem by Claire Dupray which "consists of nothing more than the names of colors" (p. 31) he is performing a complicated act of criticism. The obvious target is "impressionist" poetry and the color symphonies of the minor Imagists, but the mannered verse of seventeenth-century France is also in view, while at its deepest reaches the witty passage mocks Stevens himself, who had once been inspired by Japanese prints to write this litany of colors (1909):

Colors

I

Pale orange, green and crimson, and
White, and gold and brown.

II

Lapis-lazuli and orange, and opaque green,
faun-color, black and gold.[74]

Walter Pach referred to *Bowl, Cat and Broomstick* as a "book review" (OP xxix), and one of the "books" under review is Stevens' juvenilia. Even the titles of Claire Dupray's poems are quintessential Stevens, and one—"Banal Sojourn"—became the title of a poem in *Harmonium*. As Bowl and Cat and Broomstick rehearse the current clichés of literary criticism Stevens is playing the elaborate game of laughing at both his contemporaries and his own Crispin-like *persona*.

Bowl, Cat and Broomstick may have failed as theatre in 1917, but its setting and characters show that Stevens had absorbed a great deal from contemporary experimental drama. The *commedia dell'arte* figures remind us of the early twentieth-century vogue for marionettes and masks, and of the stylized figures in symbolist drama; the opening stage direction, with its careful arrangement of colors and its golden curtain, suggests the expressive use of fabrics and lighting advocated by Gordon Craig. While *Three Travelers* and *Carlos among the Candles* now strike us as period pieces, bound to the modes of 1916–17, *Bowl, Cat and Broomstick* makes restrained use of those modernist techniques which were to have a lasting impact on the theatre. Laura Sherry thought that for all its awkwardnesses *Bowl, Cat and Broomstick* was "drama," not a book review, and she felt that if Stevens could "clear up the drama and strengthen & define the structural lines" of his plays he could join the ranks of those who had revolutionized the modern stage.[75] Mrs. Sherry may not have been a very perceptive critic, and her list of modern masters is not reassuring, bracketing as it does Synge and Shaw with Duhamel and Dunsany. But *Bowl, Cat and Broomstick* suggests that Stevens just might have produced, if he had persisted, that ideal of the avant-garde drama: a "theatre without action or characters" which can still command the audience. He soon recognized, of course, that he "had much less interest in dramatic poetry than in elegiac poetry," [76] and that to continue with the drama would be to work against the grain of his talent. But in *Bowl, Cat and Broomstick* he did manage to express his deepest concerns with characteristic wit, and to cast them in a dramatic convention which, although clearly "of his time," remains fresh and intriguing fifty years later. In its small way, *Bowl, Cat and Broomstick* is a model of "being one's self in one's day."

IV

Primordia

In March 1916 Stevens joined the New York branch of the Hartford Accident and Indemnity Co., and in early May he moved to Hartford.[77] His first months with the firm entailed a great deal of traveling, and his letters are studded with datelines from the South and Northwest—St. Paul, Atlanta, Miami (his first trip to Florida), Omaha, Houston. Out of this experience of new landscapes Stevens began to develop the acute sense of place and climate which would eventually inform his poetic theory and culminate in the imaginative realism of his later verse. But for the time being he was content simply to assimilate the new perceptions, developing his sense of the relations between landscape as primordial reality and landscape as a state of mind. In January 1917 the little magazine *Soil* published a series of landscape studies entitled "Primordia":[78] following Stevens' recent travels, the first five sections were based on experiences "In the Northwest," while the last four were "In the South." The coda to the series, "To the Roaring Wind," is a miniature invocation of the freshening wind which clarifies the landscape and is the wind of poetic inspiration. It later became the tailpiece to *Harmonium.*

> What syllable are you seeking,
> Vocalissimus,
> In the distances of sleep?
> Speak it.

The term "Primordia" means primitive sources, the rudiments of structure or process, and in this sequence Stevens is trying out different ways of rendering the fundamentals of the relation between landscape and feeling, scene and language. Sometimes the natural image is presented with only a slight overtone of "interpretation," as in the third poem of "In the Northwest":

> The blunt ice flows down the Mississippi,
> At night.
> In the morning, the clear river
> Is full of reflections,
> Beautiful alliterations of shadows and of things shadowed.

Here the word "alliterations" in the last line stretches the poem to another level of significance. At other times, as in the second poem of "In the South" (saved for *Harmonium* under the title "In the Carolinas"), Stevens adopts a more elaborate Imagist strategy.

> The lilacs wither in the Carolinas.
> Already the butterflies flutter above the cabins.
> Already the new-born children interpret love
> In the voices of mothers.
> Timeless mother,
> How is it that your aspic nipples
> For once vent honey?
>
> *The pine-tree sweetens my body*
> *The white iris beautifies me.* (CP 4-5)

In this complex structure the visual aspects of Spring modulate into "the voices of mothers," and these into the Timeless mother, Earth herself, who speaks in the summary couplet. This use of a separate couplet to expand the images, either through the introduction of a new visual perspective or a new voice, is a gambit Stevens may have learned from Pound's *Cathay*. In "Primordia" Stevens seems to be running system-

atically through his verse repertoire, seeking for methods best
suited to his new scenes.

Some of the techniques in "Primordia" are frankly experimental, such as the use of pure sounds to express a bizarre
mood ("La, la, la, la, la, la, la, la, / Dee, dum, diddle, dee,
dee, diddle, dee, da.") or the attempt to define a color through
an accumulation of primordial details.

> The child's hair is of the color of the hay in the haystack,
>   around which the four black horses stand.
> There is the same color in the bellies of frogs, in clays,
>   withered reeds, skins, wood, sunlight. (OP 8)

This is really an extension of Stevens' apprentice exercises in
color harmony, except the abstract names of colors have been
replaced by concrete details, an indication of the direction in
which his poetry was moving at this time.

The most interesting aspects of "Primordia" are the extreme
freedom of its verse-rhythms (the general reaction against *vers
libre* had not yet gathered force), and the many ways in which
it anticipates the triumphant form of "Thirteen Ways of Looking at a Blackbird." In Poem 1 of "In the Northwest" (OP 7)
the voice of the wind and the motion of the water are linked to
the bird's song and flight by complex resemblances, as in the
later series, while in Poem 5 the doubling of the image points
forward to the speculations on similitude and difference.

> The birch trees draw up whiteness from the ground.
> In the swamps, bushes draw up dark red,
> Or yellow.
> O, boatman,
> What are you drawing from the rain-pointed water?
> O, boatman,
> What are you drawing from the rain-pointed water?
> Are you two boatmen
> Different from each other? (OP 8–9)

Here the natural harmony between foliage and earth is contrasted with the solipsistic relation between the boatman and

his reflected image; or is it really two boatmen, identical but separate? The questions this little poem teasingly presents soon became part of the dialogue between perceptual theory and actual sensation in "Thirteen Ways of Looking at a Blackbird."

"Thirteen Ways" was published in *Others* for December 1917, along with four other poems,[79] and the clashes in style among the five works are dramatic evidence that Stevens was still experimenting with a variety of parallel and diverging poetic methods, searching for a repertoire of forms which would both express his habitual perceptions and serve as schemata, opening new windows to new landscapes. The most radical contrast is between "Thirteen Ways" and "Gray Room," an exercise in free rhythms that harks back to Stevens' earlier color harmonies and may owe an atmospheric debt to T. S. Eliot's "Portrait of a Lady," published two years before in *Others*.

> Although you sit in a room that is gray,
> Except for the silver
> Of the straw-paper,
> And pick
> At your pale white gown;
> Or lift one of the green beads
> Of your necklace,
> To let it fall;
> Or gaze at your green fan
> Printed with the red branches of a red willow;
> Or, with one finger,
> Move the leaf in the bowl—
> The leaf that has fallen from the branches of the forsythia
> Beside you . . .
> What is all this?
> I know how furiously your heart is beating.

Here Stevens is so intent on getting his color-composition right that the musical structure is neglected, and the rhythms fail to carry the poem. The "idea" of the poem is obvious, to sustain a complex relationship among feeling, music, and color; but

Stevens had long since discovered more precise ways of dealing with this relationship, and "Gray Room" seems a curious
anachronism when set beside the chiseled *haiku*-like stanzas of
"Thirteen Ways of Looking at a Blackbird."

Looking back on the series after ten years, Stevens said that
it was "not meant to be a collection of epigrams or of ideas, but
of sensations," [80] a clear indication that the poems of "Thirteen
Ways" carry on the experiment begun in "Primordia" of isolat-
ing and identifying the "sensations" prompted by different
landscapes. This does not mean that the group lacks a general
structure: it begins with a "neutral" scene of blackbird and
snowy mountains, a bare study in black-and-white, and returns at the end to the same desolation:

> It was evening all afternoon.
> It was snowing
> And it was going to snow.
> The blackbird sat
> In the cedar-limbs. (CP 95)

These are the bare sensations upon which the series em-
broiders, in stanzas which become more and more an interaction between mind and landscape as we move toward the center
panel (stanzas VI and VII), where the inner mood is dominant
and the setting is given a local habitation and a name: Haddam,
Connecticut. Read with this structure in mind, "Thirteen Ways
of Looking at a Blackbird" becomes a set of variations on an
epistemological theme. But the real virtue of the series does
not lie in its perceptual argument but in the absolute pitch of
its moods and sensations. It is not surprising that this group, of
all Stevens' poems, holds the most fascination for children: for
all its hidden sophistications, "Thirteen Ways of Looking at a
Blackbird" gives an overwhelming illusion of the innocent eye
spontaneously recording nature.

The success of the poem is the direct result of Stevens'
variations on the form of the Japanese *haiku*. As Earl Miner
has pointed out, the stanzas are *haiku*-like in "their short, con-

densed quality, the poetic weight placed upon a few natural images, and the interrelatedness of the elements in a natural scene." [81] The entire series recalls those Japanese prints in which a single setting is rendered from different viewpoints and at different seasons of the weather or mind, and the *haiku* is an ideal medium for such variations. The use of the *haiku* by Imagist poets really divides into two classes: the products of what Ezra Pound called "Amygism," impressionistic word-pictures in the manner of Amy Lowell's "Twenty-Four Hokku on a Modern Theme"; and more concentrated medallions such as Pound's "In a Station of the Metro," where the initial "impression" has been processed into significant form. Pound's famous account of how he composed "In a Station of the Metro" points up the essential differences:

> Imagisme is not symbolism. The symbolists dealt in "association," that is, in a sort of allusion, almost of allegory. They degraded the symbol to the status of a word. . . .
>
> On the other hand, Imagisme is not Impressionism, though one borrows, or could borrow, much from the Impressionist method of presentation. But this is only negative definition. If I am to give a psychological or philosophical definition "from the inside," I can only do so autobiographically. The precise statement of such a matter must be based on one's own experience. . . .
>
> Three years ago in Paris I got out of a "metro" train at La Concorde, and saw suddenly a beautiful face, and then another and another, and then a beautiful child's face, and then another beautiful woman, and I tried all that day to find words for what this had meant to me, and I could not find any words that seemed to me worthy, or as lovely as that sudden emotion. And that evening, as I went home along the Rue Raynouard, I was still trying, and I found, suddenly, the expression. I do not mean that I found words, but there came an equation . . . not in speech, but in little splotches of colour. It was just that—a "pattern," or hardly a pattern, if by

"pattern" you mean something with a "repeat" in it. But it was a word, the beginning, for me, of a language in colour. I do not mean that I was unfamiliar with the kindergarten stories about colours being like tones in music. I think that sort of thing is nonsense. If you try to make notes permanently correspond with particular colours, it is like tying narrow meanings to symbols. . . .

The "one image poem" is a form of super-position, that is to say it is one idea set on top of another. I found it useful in getting out of the impasse in which I had been left by my metro emotion. I wrote a thirty-line poem, and destroyed it because it was what we call work "of second intensity." Six months later I made a poem half that length; a year later I made the following *hokku*-like sentence:—

> "The apparition of these faces in the crowd:
> Petals, on a wet, black bough."

I dare say it is meaningless unless one has drifted into a certain vein of thought. In a poem of this sort one is trying to record the precise instant when a thing outward and objective transforms itself, or darts into a thing inward and subjective.[82]

The stanzas of "Thirteen Ways of Looking at a Blackbird" clearly belong to the "second generation" of Imagist poetry defined in Pound's autobiographical critique of "In a Station of the Metro." The deliberately vague "associations" of Symbolist verse have been phased away, along with its incantatory rhythms, and the "impressions" of form and color have been transformed into a precise verbal equation. Both Stevens and Pound were searching for ways to express the new impressions of the physical world delivered to them by the modern painters, who had provided fresh schemata for familiar scenes, but they were unwilling to settle for a diffuse surface which would simply blur the impression or sensation. In the technique of "super-position," the juxtaposition of precise images, they found one way of recording a complex perception in condensed

form. Poem XII of "Thirteen Ways of Looking at a Blackbird"
has all the qualities of this form:

> The river is moving.
> The blackbird must be flying. (CP 94)

Stevens once complained to a friend that a translation of Poem
XII missed the essential point, which is "the compulsion fre-
quently back of the things that we do." [83] The blackbird is
compelled by the cycles of natural change, just as we are; but
that metaphoric extension of the scene reaches beyond the
words, and is implied by the interaction of the two super-im-
posed visual images. Many of the stanzas in "Thirteen Ways of
Looking at a Blackbird" may be read as covert explications of
this theory. "At the sight of blackbirds / Flying in a green
light," we are told in Poem X, "Even the bawds of euphony
/ Would cry out sharply"; the natural object defies sentimental harmonies. Similarly, in Poem III the blackbird is described as "a small part of the pantomime," and the entire
group of poems may be interpreted as a "pantomime" where
the dramatic interaction between the visual images is just as
important as the words which render those images. As the
poet muses in Poem V:

> I do not know which to prefer,
> The beauty of inflections
> Or the beauty of innuendoes,
> The blackbird whistling
> Or just after. (CP 93)

Just as the pleasure of song lingers after the notes have faded,
so the thematic innuendoes of Stevens' little poems spread out
in ever-widening circles, giving "Thirteen Ways of Looking at
a Blackbird" an importance which belies its playful and
epigrammatic appearance.

Years later, brooding upon the usual charge that his verses
were decorative treatments of imagined landscapes, Stevens
was on the point of categorically denying it when he "re-

membered that when *Harmonium* was in the making there was a time when I liked the idea of images and images alone, or images and the music of verse together. I then believed in *pure poetry*, as it was called." [84] It would be difficult to pinpoint a particular "time" in the making of *Harmonium* when this tendency was dominant, since a self-indulgent passion for pure color and pure sound was a permanent strain in Stevens' poetic personality. We can say, however, that his work on "Primordia" and "Thirteen Ways of Looking at a Blackbird" was an antidote to this tendency, a reaching out toward tangible and familiar reality. One interesting aspect of these poems is that Stevens chose to express his sensations and immediate impressions through forms which, although flexible, have recognizable traditions behind them. In the same year when D. H. Lawrence was calling for a "Poetry of the Present" which would ignore all prescribed forms in expressing the flamelike moments of spontaneous perception, Stevens was making constant experimental adjustments between traditional form and individual emotion. Like T. S. Eliot, he believed that good free verse is simply one more form, and that "the essential thing in form is to be free in whatever form is used." [85] Stevens' early career may be seen, in terms drawn from E. H. Gombrich's *Art and Illusion,* as an intricate series of accommodations between "making" and "matching"; between a sense of the world as perpetually renewed and a realization of how dependent we are on inherited ways of seeing and saying. Stevens knew that his adoption of the *haiku* form would bring with it a special way of seeing, just as his personal sensations of nature would subtly alter that form. It is this constant adjustment between form and freedom which makes the Stevens of *Harmonium* such a fascinating poet.

Borrowing a phrase from Mallarmé's "Letter to Verlaine," we might say that Stevens' lifelong aim was an "orphic explication of the earth," [86] and that the poems of his "Primordia" phase expose the necessary foundations of such an enterprise: the actual contours and climates of the physical world. If "I am what is around me," as Stevens proposed in a witty little poem called "Theory" (CP 86),[87] then it becomes terribly important to see those surroundings with exactitude. Once Stevens' vision of the earth had been refreshed by his travels and the poems that grew out of them he could proceed to "explication." Terms such as "theory," "explanation," and "anecdote" begin to creep into his titles. "Earthy Anecdote," later to become the program piece of *Harmonium*, was published in mid-1918 with a fanciful illustration by Walter Pach which provoked Stevens to comment: "Walter Pach's illustration [a composition of swirling forms] is just the opposite of my idea. I intended something quite concrete: actual animals, not original chaos." [88] The poem itself supports Stevens' point:

> Every time the bucks went clattering
> Over Oklahoma
> A firecat bristled in the way.
>
> Wherever they went,
> They went clattering,
> Until they swerved
> In a swift, circular line
> To the right,
> Because of the firecat.
>
> Or until they swerved
> In a swift, circular line
> To the left,
> Because of the firecat.
>
> The bucks clattered.
> The firecat went leaping,
> To the right, to the left,
> And
> Bristled in the way.
>
> Later, the firecat closed his bright eyes
> And slept. (CP 3)

It is easy to see why the illustrator, used to a different poetic mode, turned these verses into a symbolic and suggestive design. But, as Stevens remarked, "there's no symbolism in the "Earthy Anecdote." There's a good deal of theory about it, however; but explanations spoil things." [89] At the risk of spoiling what was obviously one of Stevens' favorite poems, we might observe that the firecat organizes the "chaos" of the clattering animals, driving them into an ordered pattern that is mirrored in the verse structure. The poem is therefore an "anecdote" which, like its companion piece "Life Is Motion" (CP 83),[90] exemplifies the theory that beauty in poetry and life is a matter of patterned motion: "How can we know the dancer from the dance?" The theory is not presented symbolically, as Stevens might have done in an earlier phase, but through concrete images which are themselves primordia. The "firecat" is not Blake's tiger, but an actual animal, and whatever theories we build upon his actions cannot obscure his direct presence.

$\sim$

If landscape supplies the primordia of man's visual life, war is the catalyst of his deepest emotions; and it is not surprising that in the summer of 1917, shortly after America's entrance into the First World War, Stevens once again turned his hand to a series of "war poems." In part they must have been his private reaction to the new wave of emotional involvement that swept the country; in part they were a reaction against the artificiality of such experiments as *Bowl, Cat and Broomstick* and *Carlos among the Candles*. On 1 September 1917 Stevens sent Harriet Monroe a sequence of at least thirteen poems based upon the *Lettres d'un soldat* of Eugène Emmanuel Lemercier, a young French painter who "disappeared" on the Western Front in April 1915. He also enclosed "the book on which the poems are based." [91] Early the next year, in March 1918, Stevens was in Chicago and went over the sequence of "war poems" with Miss Monroe. By then his enthusiasm for some of the poems, and perhaps for their subject, had diminished; Stevens and Miss Monroe "weeded out the bad ones," and in

May 1918 nine of the poems appeared in *Poetry*.[92] Later Stevens was even more selective, including only three of the published poems in the second edition of *Harmonium* along with another saved from the manuscript.[93] A reconstruction of the entire "Lettres d'un Soldat" series as it existed in the summer of 1917 is printed in Appendix B.

Lemercier's letters from the Western Front, written to his mother in 1914–15, were first published in the *Revue de Paris* in August 1915, and the next year they were gathered into a little book which had run through nineteen editions by 1918. An American translation appeared in 1917, almost coincident with the April declaration of war. It is easy to understand the appeal of the letters: sensitive and compassionate, tinged with a youthful romanticism, they avoid the disillusionment of the later war memoirs and preserve the grand hopes of the years 1914–15. More important for Stevens, they are a record of war as seen through the painter's eye, and Lemercier is much more concerned with the interactions between men and landscape than he is with the actual carnage. This "painterly" quality jibed perfectly with Stevens' current poetic interests, enabling him to enlarge the emotional range of his art without abandoning the impulses that we find in "Primordia" and "Thirteen Ways of Looking at a Blackbird." The sequence of "war poems" follows the course of Lemercier's brief career, and quotations from his highly charged prose are used as epigraphs which supply much of the imagery and substance for the individual poems. Stevens obviously cherished the "poetic" prose of Lemercier's letters: in writing to Harriet Monroe he requested that if a "translation of the citations" were used it be placed "away from my text, somewhere in the back of the magazine." As he once told René Taupin, "La légèreté, la grâce, le son et la couleur du français ont eu sur moi une influence indéniable et une influence précieuse," [94] and this remark applies just as much to the citations from Lemercier's letters as to the French tags of the later poetry.

The general epigraph to the poems, taken from André

Chevrillon's preface to the French edition of *Lettres*, sets the tone for the entire series: "To fight with his brothers, at his own place, in his own rank, with open eyes, without hope of glory or of gain, and simply because such is the law: this is the commandment of the god to the warrior Arjuna, who had doubted whether he were right in turning from the absolute to take part in the human nightmare of war. . . . Plainly, it is for Arjuna to bend his bow among the other Kshettryas!" Stevens was attracted to the image of the youth as virile poet, and the tension between contemplation and action which marked Lemercier's brief life provides the energy for much of his finest verse. It is a tension which runs like a leitmotif through the "Lettres d'un Soldat" series, as Stevens chooses those citations from Lemercier's letters where his own sensibility chimes with that of the young soldier. As we trace the progress of the series we can observe Stevens ransacking his poetic repertoire for old and new forms to express the ever-changing relations between landscape and mind, action and contemplation.

"We are embarked on the adventure, without any dominant sensation except perhaps a sufficiently calm acceptance of fatality." Poem I, "Common Soldier," elaborates on this feeling in measured unrhymed tercets of regular rhythm, a moderate form appropriate to the mood. Here, as in "For an Old Woman in a Wig," Stevens is exploring a stanza which was to become his most personal form. Then, in Poem II, the consolation that Lemercier derives from the majesty of the constellations and sparkling Venus is cast in more flexible tercets, the distinctive invention of "Lettres," where the stanzas narrow to a summary two-foot line:

> The multiform beauty, sinking in night wind,
> Quick to be gone, yet never
> Quite going?

> She will leap back from the swift constellations,
> As they enter the place of their western
> Seclusion.

In Poems III and IV Stevens extracts the essential idea from each citation and illustrates it. "Violence" is presented in the fantastic imagery of "Anecdotal Revery," whose loose form harks back to the earlier experiments in *vers libre* but lacks their diffuse quality. The dramatic action of the "anecdote," culminating in a stage direction—"(The blind men strike him down with their sticks.)"—serves as a counterbalance to the easy rhythms. The citation to Poem IV, by contrast, presents an abstract change of heart and demands the epigrammatic form:

> And so France feels. A menace that impends,
> Too long, is like a bayonet that bends.

Here Stevens is, in effect, making an editorial comment, extending the soldier's personal feeling into a national mood.

The epigraph to Poem V, where Lemercier observes the field-mice with painterly precision ("They were as pretty as a Japanese print, with the inside of their ears rosy as a shell"), gives Stevens a perfect opportunity to express his own sense of life redeemed by "resemblances." Art enables us to see nature as a composition: here in "Lettres d'un Soldat" the sensibility of the soldier and that of the poet have become as one.

Comme Dieu Dispense de Graces

> Here I keep thinking of the Primitives—
> The sensitive and conscientious schemes
> Of mountain pallors ebbing into air;
>
> And I remember sharp Japonica—
> The driving rain, the willows in the rain,
> The birds that wait out rain in willow leaves.
>
> Although life seems a goblin mummery,
> These images return and are increased,
> As for a child in an oblivion:
>
> Even by mice—these scamper and are still;
> They cock small ears, more glistening and pale
> Than fragile volutes in a rose sea-shell.

In the next few poems Stevens performs a series of divagations on the emotions of the soldier. "The Surprises of the Superhuman" (Poem VI) questions in witty couplets Lemercier's "confidence in eternal justice," while Poem VII turns his description of a landscape tranformed by moonlight into a somewhat different "Lunar Paraphrase." Seizing upon Lemercier's phrase "le pathétique des calvaires," Stevens declares that "The moon is the mother of pathos and pity" and builds an overwhelmingly "pathetic" portrait of late autumn where even the moon seems infected by the season, "depending" upon the branches through which she shines. The "earlier season of quiet" exists only as a "golden illusion," and the details of the soldier's landscape—although still present in bare outline—have been completely expropriated into Stevens' world.

Poem VIII continues this process of imaginative displacement. Cast in the same blank verse as "Lunar Paraphrase," but more regular and majestic in the manner of "Sunday Morning," this fourteen-line stanza responds to the soldier's passionate devotion to his mother by celebrating "another mother whom I love," not France but the "mightier mother" of us all, a figure compounded of Virgin and Muse who commands all things. Reminiscent in its theme of Robert Graves' "To Juan at the Winter Solstice," this magnificent stanza holds the promise of "voluble hymns" to come. But its tone is immediately counterpointed by the next poem in the series (IX), "Negation," where the image of the great Potter from the *Rubáiyát of Omar Khayyám* is given "theoretical" treatment. The soldier's belief that "we must confide ourselves to an impersonal justice, independent of any human factor, and to a useful and harmonious destiny, in spite of the horrors of its form," is given a gay and almost comic treatment:

> Hi! The creator too is blind,
> Struggling toward his harmonious whole,
> Rejecting intermediate parts,
> Horrors and falsities and wrongs;
> Incapable master of all force,

> Too vague idealist, overwhelmed
> By an afflatus that persists.
> For this, then, we endure brief lives,
> The evanescent symmetries
> From that meticulous potter's thumb.

The light tone of "Negation" is carried over into the next poem, where the "drunkenness, quarrels, cries, songs, and shouts" of the soldier's bivouac are rendered as a dance tune, with an experimental use of "pure sounds" already tried in "Primordia" and an echo of the soldier's exclamation "Voilà la vie!"

The feverish gaiety of Poem X suddenly gives way to the stark motto of Poem XI, "The death of the soldier is close to natural things," and out of this ultimate reality Stevens constructs the finest poem in the series, published in the revised version of *Harmonium* as "The Death of a Soldier." The diminishing tercets already tried out in Poem II are ideally matched to the subject, and each end-stopped stanza is like a tombstone. The great theme of war and death finds its absolute expression in the landscape, where stillness and movement make a single harmony.

> Death is absolute and without memorial,
> As in a season of autumn,
> When the wind stops,
>
> When the wind stops and, over the heavens,
> The clouds go, nevertheless,
> In their direction.

The alternate title would be, of course, "Primordia."

After this triumphant matching of subject and image the series trails off: the cancellations and renumberings are signs that Stevens had exhausted his material. In Poem XII the citation is first interpreted in a quatrain which, as Samuel French Morse has observed, suggests "the obliquity of poems to come":[95]

In a theatre, full of tragedy,
The stage becomes an atmosphere
Of seeping roses—banal machine
In an appointed repertoire . . .

This false-start was abandoned in favor of regular rhymed stanzas with refrain, based on the soldier's experience of the cranes returning during a storm, but this promising donnée never found adequate form. The final poem in "Lettres d'un Soldat," headed by a quotation from one of the soldier's last letters, elaborates upon the macabre image of the pickaxe "tormenting" the dead in their graves, but the ellipses and the weak ending ("You know the phrase.") testify to Stevens' waning interest in his subject.

"Lettres d'un Soldat," like "Phases," could not satisfy Stevens' fastidious taste, partly because of the uneven quality of the poems and partly (we may guess) because the general design of the series depended too much on the content of the citations and the interaction between the citations and individual poems. In a sense, the quotations from Lemercier's *Lettres* provided the "plot" that was needed to sustain the mosaic techniques of Imagism over an extended time-span: they are like the chunks of legend and history processed into William Carlos Williams' *Paterson*. But Stevens could not be content with such a mechanical frame, especially since it would soon lose its topical significance. What "Lettres d'un Soldat" do exhibit, in contrast to "Phases," is a remarkable growth in the range and sophistication of Stevens' poetic world. The meditative strength of "Sunday Morning" and the clear vision of "Thirteen Ways of Looking at a Blackbird" are fitfully present, combined with a vigor in technical experiment which, unlike the many retrospective exercises of "Phases," holds a promise of greater things to come.

V

Pierrot and Pecksniff

The poems of 1918 which appeared between "Lettres d'un Soldat" (May) and "Le Monocle de Mon Oncle" (December) can be re-ordered to form a rough paradigm of Stevens' new poetic impulses.[96] "Earthy Anecdote" and two others depend upon the familiar theme of man's relation to the non-symbolic landscape. "Anecdote of Men by the Thousand" (CP 51–52) states the theme directly, in language reminiscent of *Three Travelers Watch a Sunrise*:

> There are men whose words
> Are as natural sounds
> Of their places
> As the cackle of toucans
> In the place of toucans.
>
> . . .
>
> The dress of a woman of Lhassa,
> In its place,
> Is an invisible element of that place
> Made visible.

We are where we live, and what we wear. Any attempt to build ingenious metaphors upon this primordial truth may end in failure, as the structure of "Metaphors of a Magnifico" (CP 19) testifies. The elaborate speculations with which this poem opens simply will not declare themselves as "meaning," and they fade away into the concrete details of a particular scene:

> The boots of the men clump
> On the boards of the bridge.
> The first white wall of the village
> Rises through fruit-trees.
> Of what was it I was thinking?
>
> So the meaning escapes.
>
> The first white wall of the village . . .
> The fruit-trees. . . .

But Stevens was obviously tiring of these "theoretical" poems which exclude so much in their attempt to define the ground-bass of poetry. As he remarked in a late essay,

> What the eye beholds may be the text of life. It is, nevertheless, a text that we do not write. The eye does not beget in resemblance. It sees. But the mind begets in resemblance as the painter begets in representation . . . (NA 76)

Obviously Stevens had never left metaphor and symbol behind, even in his most rigorous attempts at recording "the text of life," but now he gave freer rein to his natural desire to embroider and gloss that text. His native wit and love of extravagance, his taste for the fanciful and grotesque, his gift for impersonation and role-playing, began to reassert themselves. "Anecdote of Canna" (CP 55), with its contrast between vision and actuality, and "Depression Before Spring" (CP 63), with its surreal images and expressive nonsense-sounds, are signs of a new boisterousness.[97] So is "The Apostrophe to Vincentine" (CP 52–53), where the lean nude figure standing "nameless" between "Monotonous earth and dark blue sky" is gradually invested by the imagination with name and color and feeling, until the poet can exclaim: "Monotonous earth I saw become / Illimitable spheres of you." Here the relationship in "Anecdote of Men by the Thousand" (which stands in *Harmonium* as companion piece) has been neatly inverted, and the physical world takes on the tinge and form of thought.

Even more revealing is the arabesque Stevens describes around an image borrowed from William Carlos Williams. "Nuances of a Theme by Williams" (CP 18) opens with the text of Williams' "El Hombre," a condensed Imagist poem which epitomizes the poet's determination to confront immediate sensations without the benefit of any "humanizing" symbols, to reject all reflected light:

> It's a strange courage
> you give me ancient star:
>
> Shine alone in the sunrise
> toward which you lend no part! [98]

But Stevens cannot resist interpreting the taut couplets, in supple verses that pile metaphor upon metaphor. The resulting contrast between text and interpretation is both a graceful tribute to Stevens' fellow poet and friend, at the time of their closest collaboration, and a covert announcement that Stevens was no longer content to be a connoisseur of naked perceptions.

> I
>
> Shine alone, shine nakedly, shine like bronze,
> that reflects neither my face nor any inner part
> of my being, shine like fire, that mirrors nothing.
>
> II
>
> Lend no part to any humanity that suffuses
> you in its own light.
> Be not chimera of morning,
> Half-man, half-star.
> Be not an intelligence,
> Like a widow's bird
> Or an old horse.

The second part of Stevens' poem is, in effect, a spelling out of the theme-without-words which hovers between the two couplets of Williams' "El Hombre" and is suggested by the title.

The method adumbrated in "Nuances of a Theme by Williams" is carried much farther in "Architecture for the Adoration of Beauty" (OP 16–18), Stevens' most sustained poetic effort since "Sunday Morning" and "For an Old Woman in a Wig." The seven irregular stanzas are bound together by a single gathering metaphor, the construction of a "building of light" which is in its design the archetype of the grand poem: a castle "De pensée" whose genius is the chaste "demoiselle" of pure imagination. Both in its use of a single governing "resemblance," on which all the subsidiary metaphors depend, and in the central images of "sun" and "moon" and "palm," the poem points forward to the design of the long poems which crown Stevens' career. Every detail of the "chastel de chasteté"—its "closes / Overlooking whole seasons," its "portals, east and west, / Abhorring green-blue north and blue-green south," the speech and dress of its inhabitants —is a detail of Stevens' developing poetic. Like Henry James' "house of fiction," the castle of "Architecture for the Adoration of Beauty" embodies a full theory of the poem's life. The stones are hewed from "sun" and "moon," the building unites reality with imagination, and although its dizzy towers "tuft the commonplace" they are rooted in the physical world: "Only the lusty and the plenteous / Shall walk / The bronze-filled plazas / And the nut-shell esplanades."

In "Lettres d'un Soldat," the "narrative" of Lemercier's letters had provided a rather mechanical solution to the architectural demands of a long poem; in "Architecture" Stevens found another and more congenial solution, the use of a single metaphoric design to hold together the "mosaic" of individual lyrics. Throughout "Architecture" he never ceases "to deploy the structure" of his controlling Image, so that the entire poem, in retrospect, takes on the quality of Ezra Pound's famous

definition: "an emotional and intellectual complex appre-
hended in an instant of time." As an extended working-out of
one design "Architecture" is a real tour de force, containing
effects new to Stevens' art; but it is easy to see why he excluded the poem from the second edition of *Harmonium*. The
local details of description often belong to "interior decoration" rather than architecture, the color-symbolism is pastel
rather than primary, and the language is sometimes mannered
to no purpose. The alliterative verse of stanza VI, one of Stevens' first attempts at the coruscated style of "Le Monocle de
Mon Oncle" and "The Comedian as the Letter C," seems
unrelated to its subject:

> And, finally, set guardians in the grounds,
> Gray, gruesome grumblers.
> For no one proud, nor stiff,
> No solemn one, nor pale,
> No chafferer, may come
> To sully the begonias, nor vex
> With holy or sublime ado
> The kremlin of kermess.

Such verse can be highly effective in a poem spoken by a
persona, where irony and self-mockery have free play, but in
the direct address of "Architecture" it is a mannerist distrac-
tion.

Although the language of "Architecture" may be viewed as
a dress-rehearsal for "Le Monocle de Mon Oncle," [99] this great
poem abrupts into Stevens' poetic world with such energy and
polished perfection that its origins must remain partly in
mystery. Like "Sunday Morning," it towers over the poems
which precede and follow it; but unlike "Sunday Morning"
it does not fit easily into the tradition of English poetry. Its
wry flavor and pawky language are quintessential Stevens, and
we may say that "Le Monocle" contains more of the poet of
Harmonium than any other poem in the volume. Its iambic
pentameter lines are more individual than those of "Sunday

Morning," allowing for much greater metrical variation, and the quirky progress of the poem's argument is marked by occasional rhymes or clusters of alliteration. Whereas "Sunday Morning" had the symmetrical design of a poetic triptych, "Le Monocle" proceeds by a series of oblique meditations. Each verse-panel is a self-contained statement, and the entire poem is a kind of "interior monologue." The language of "Le Monocle," unlike that of "Sunday Morning," constantly skirts the edges of self-indulgent mannerism. Only the firm stanzaic structure and the dominance of a central *persona* keep the poem from degenerating into the excesses of the alternate stanzas entitled "The Naked Eye of the Aunt" (OP 19), where the effects are grotesque (*"Oh, hideous, horrible, horrendous hocks!"* . . . *"Oh, lissomeness turned lagging ligaments!"*).

"Le Monocle" is a poem about language and love, a hymn to the "faith of forty" sung by a poet who is entering his fortieth year. The title, a copybook phrase from the French schoolroom, sets the witty and slightly pedantic tone of the poem. The collision of words, the transformation of "monocle" into "mon oncle" by a slight realignment, tells us that the play of language will be as much the subject as the play of personality. The title also introduces us to the *persona* of the piece, a middle-aged conflation of Pierrot and the poetic dandy, whose fastidious point-of-view will be the source of both pathos and irony. In his early journal Stevens had remarked that "there is a perfect rout of characters in every man—and every man is like an actor's trunk, full of strange creatures, new & old." [100] Among the characters in his "actor's trunk" was Pierrot, one role he assumed while courting his wife.[101] Stevens was familiar with the Pierrot figure from the French tradition, as well as from the English adaptations of Dowson and others; and he also was aware of the ironic treatments of Pierrot the lover. In 1914 his friend Walter Arensberg had published a version of the "Complaint of Lord Pierrot," from Jules Laforgue, and Stevens of course knew Laforgue in the original.[102] Like Eliot, Stevens had been exposed to Laforgue at a formative stage in his life, but unlike Eliot he put the Laforguian techniques to a more witty and less introspective use. The dandy-Pierrot of "Le Monocle" is a less anxious and less pensive version of J. Alfred Prufrock, a mock-hero who accepts the ironies of his position and makes them tolerable through the solace of language.

The opening stanza of "Le Monocle," like that of "Sunday Morning," establishes the dramatic setting of the poem and fixes its contrasting tones. The tones, of course, are of primary importance. In Stevens' infrequent and often evasive responses to criticism of his poems he always insisted that the "basis of criticism is the work, not the hidden intention of the writer," [103] so we should be careful in using the glosses that he occasionally provided: but one post-facto comment on "Le Monocle" seems worthy of record. "Your analysis of this poem is much too close," Stevens wrote to L. W. Payne, Jr. in 1928. "I am sure that I never had in mind the many abstractions that appear in your analysis. I had in mind simply a man fairly well along in life, looking back and talking in a more or less personal way about life." [104] The life of "Le Monocle" is in its language, and a scrupulous paraphrase will tell the reader far less about this poem than about "Sunday Morning." Paraphrase is certainly not a heresy, it is the basic method of the critic, and any poem which cannot be paraphrased is probably negligible; but in the case of "Le Monocle" we must proceed with special care. As Stevens himself remarked, there is "excitement" and even "provocation" in the sounds of words:[105] "Le Monocle" is not only about love and language, it is an exciting and provoking experience in its own right, almost a surrogate for the sexual passion that it treats in elegiac fashion.

The mock-invocation which opens stanza I is addressed to no single deity, but to a complex blending of Muse and love-goddess and actual woman.

> "Mother of heaven, regina of the clouds,
> O sceptre of the sun, crown of the moon,

There is not nothing, no, no, never nothing,
Like the clashed edges of two words that kill."

"And so I mocked her in magnificent measure." The speaker, in the manner of poets, has protected himself from the realities of a quarrel in middle age by resorting to an elaborate irony, contrasting the aging woman with her younger "ideal" self through an address to her as Muse or goddess. But the irony, in the characteristic motion of the poem, turns back upon himself. As in Eliot's "The Love Song of J. Alfred Prufrock," where each venture into imagined action is qualified by ironic self-recognition, so in "Le Monocle" the consolations of poetic "high talk" are constantly undercut by a rueful recognition of things as they are.

Or was it that I mocked myself alone?
I wish that I might be a thinking stone.
The sea of spuming thought foists up again
The radiant bubble that she was. And then
A deep up-pouring from some saltier well
Within me, bursts its watery syllable.

The vision of the youthful Muse-woman tossed up by the "sea of spuming thought" reminds us of Botticelli's Venus, "born of the crystalline sea of thought and its eternity," but the dubious word "foists" suggests that this ideal is a trick of the imagination. The "saltier well" of reality bursts the illusion, which after all was only a "watery syllable," a vision created by language.

Stanza II begins as if it were describing a work of art, a painting or mosaic, but the "golden floor" dissolves into the sunlit landscape of spring, and the splendid "red bird" becomes a part of the choir welcoming the season. But in the "choirs of wind and wet and wing" there is a hint of the coming autumn, when the "torrent" of song will be drowned in the actual torrent of wind and wet. How can the speaker rejoice with spring when his actual state is that of the poet in Shakespeare's Sonnet LXXIII?

> That time of year thou mayst in me behold
> When yellow leaves, or none, or few, do hang
> Upon those boughs which shake against the cold,
> Bare ruin'd choirs where late the sweet birds sang.

The "much-crumpled" life of middle age cannot be smoothed, but the "much-crumpled" metaphors of the stanza's opening can be "uncrumpled," interpreted, in direct verses which belie the woman's desire to live in the "anecdotal bliss" of "starry" fictions.

> I am a man of fortune greeting heirs;
> For it has come that thus I greet the spring.
> These choirs of welcome choir for me farewell.
> No spring can follow past meridian.
> Yet you persist with anecdotal bliss
> To make believe a starry *connaissance*.

The third stanza gives a witty and elegant point to the dramatic irony. Refusing to "play the flat historic scale" of philosophic speculation, the speaker conjures up an image of delicate eighteenth-century beauty in the braids of "Utamaro's beauties" and the "mountaineous coiffures of Bath," only to bemoan their evanescence with the mock-tragic exclamation: "Alas! Have all the barbers lived in vain / That not one curl in nature has survived?" This treatment of the mutability theme is deliberately frivolous, the language "tittivating," but in the last two lines the poem makes one of its characteristic shifts from light to sombre tones as the reality of the present intrudes upon the play of imagination. The actual image of the woman, rising like a middle-aged Venus from the waters of sleep, makes a pitiless comment on the dandy's witty conceits:

> Why, without pity on these studious ghosts,
> Do you come dripping in your hair from sleep?

The stage is now set for a series of meditations on the pathetic theme that love "is a book too mad to read / Before one merely reads to pass the time." No other-worldly myth of some lost Eden is necessary, since the "luscious and impeccable fruit of life / Falls, it appears, of its own weight to earth." The speaker of the poem who, like Laforgue's Hamlet, can read in the book of himself, strikes the pose of Hamlet in the graveyard and takes the apple as his object of contemplation. The complex plays on the word "round," which combines the meaning of song ("this great hymn") with a suggestion of the apple-skull and a pun on "around," are reflected in the circularity of the rhythms and rhyme.

> An apple serves as well as any skull
> To be the book in which to read a round,
> And is as excellent, in that it is composed
> Of what, like skulls, comes rotting back to ground. (IV)

This witty evocation of cyclic mutability is carried into stanza V, where the "furious star" (Venus) of youthful love dwindles to the "firefly's quick, electric stroke," which "Ticks tediously the time of one more year." If "The measure of the intensity of love / Is measure, also, of the verve of earth," then what are the consolations of middle age?

Stanza VI is partly an answer to this question, and it opens with regular lines entirely free of the dandy's usual wit and word-play.

> If men at forty will be painting lakes
> The ephemeral blues must merge for them in one,
> The basic slate, the universal hue.
> There is a substance in us that prevails.

This "substance," to be explicated later in the poem, is in direct contrast to the "quirky turns" of youthful love, which demand a different language of changing moods and nuances.

> But in our amours amorists discern
> Such fluctuations that their scrivening
> Is breathless to attend each quirky turn.

The aging amorist must leave youthful love and its fluctuating language behind him ("It is a theme for Hyacinth alone"), content to be an introspective exile, "lecturing."

In stanzas VII and VIII the "dull scholar" of forty lectures on the "curriculum" of love, its course and theory. In pictorial terms reminiscent of stanza VI of "Sunday Morning" he presents a visionary background of angels descending from heaven against a realistic foreground of rough centurions who "guffaw and beat / Their shrilling tankards on the table-boards." It is a parable which amounts to this: "The honey of heaven may or may not come, / But that of earth both comes and goes at once." The stanza trails off into speculation on what might be if the muleteers actually brought "A damsel heightened by eternal bloom," but such speculation is essentially fruitless, since the "trouble with the idea of heaven is that it is merely an idea of the earth." [106] We are bound to the earth, and love is part of its cyclic progress, an "ancient aspect touching a new mind": "It comes, it blooms, it bears its fruit and dies." The closing lines of stanza VIII elaborate on this trope in imagery of grotesque self-mockery, the dandy and his lover transformed into two "golden gourds" shriveled by the autumn of the year.

Stanza IX returns to the question of language, which has never been far away. "The faith of forty, ward of Cupido" (in this context the god of lust and desire, as opposed to Hyacinth) demands its own language.

> Most venerable heart, the lustiest conceit
> Is not too lusty for your broadening.
> . . . Where shall I find
> Bravura adequate to this great hymn?

The romantic language of the "fops of fancy" (X), of which we have had ample example in earlier stanzas, will not serve. The "substance that prevails" at forty needs a lustier music, since the delicately-fruited tree of youthful love is no longer an adequate image. Only the phallic tree which outlasts the fancies of youth can be "adequate to this great hymn."

> It stands gigantic, with a certain tip
> To which all birds come sometime in their time.
> But when they go that tip still tips the tree.

In their monosyllabic language and heavy stresses, these final lines of stanza X declare that we have reached the "basic slate" of love's multi-colored illusions.

But the simplicity of devotion to this "first, foremost law" (XI) of sexual reality is also an illusion. We are not mechanical puppets of desire who "squeak, like dolls, the wished-for words," [107] and it is our fate always to blend sentiment with reality, heroics with the everyday. Stanza XI rounds to its conclusion with a comic-pathetic scene that sums up the actualities of aging love.

> . . . Anguishing hour!
> Last night, we sat beside a pool of pink,
> Clippered with lilies scudding the bright chromes,
> Keen to the point of starlight, while a frog
> Boomed from his very belly odious chords.

The tension between the delicate, slightly synthetic colors and the primeval call of the frog embodies the full paradox of the romantic realist.

In so far as "Le Monocle" has a paraphrasable argument, Stanza XI is its climax: but, as in "Sunday Morning," Stevens prefers to close with a more complex verse-panel which holds all the poem's diverse impulses in easy counterbalance.

> A blue pigeon it is, that circles the blue sky,
> On sidelong wing, around and round and round.
> A white pigeon it is, that flutters to the ground,
> Grown tired of flight. Like a dark rabbi, I
> Observed, when young, the nature of mankind,
> In lordly study. Every day, I found
> Man proved a gobbet in my mincing world.

> Like a rose rabbi, later, I pursued,
> And still pursue, the origin and course
> Of love, but until now I never knew
> That fluttering things have so distinct a shade.

The flight of the pigeon describes the progress of the speaker in the poem, from the confidence of early love to the uncertain "fluttering" of middle age. But was the pigeon ever blue, or did it simply take on the imaginative coloration of the sky it mastered? The poem leaves us with the question, open and insistent, as the final stanza turns to another form of summary. The "dark rabbi" and "rose rabbi" represent two stages in youthful pretension to wisdom: in the first, as in the first phase of the poet's voyage described in "The Comedian as the Letter C," man is "the intelligence of his soil, / The sovereign ghost." The "mincing world" of the young poet, with its overtones of both arrogance and pretension, is one where the mysteries are easily digested "gobbets." Later, in a more philosophic stage, the "rose rabbi" seeks to divine the "origin and course / Of love." [108] But for the dandy-Pierrot of "Le Monocle" these heroic quests are no longer relevant, and he must resign himself to discovering the exact shade of "fluttering things," a process of discovery which is the poem.

"Le Monocle de Mon Oncle" is such an extravagant success because it treats a great theme of ordinary human experience in a form and language which are unique without being eccentric. The ironic focus provided by the *persona*-speaker, and the intricately balanced formal stanzas, serve as checks on the natural excesses of Stevens' poetic diction. The comic alliterations and oblique word-plays are in the service of the poem's dramatic form; the most "precious" lines belong to the characterization of love's illusions, and are constantly controlled by the ironic self-awareness of the *persona*. The problem of what Stevens would do with his new exuberance of language when it was put to the service of lesser themes, and

in non-dramatic lyrics, remained to be confronted in the poems
of "Pecksniffiana."

∽

Several years later, while writing "The Comedian as the
Letter C," Stevens remarked to Harriet Monroe that "prolonged attention to a single subject has the same result that
prolonged attention to a senora has according to the author-
ities. All manner of favors drop from it." [109] Among the
"favors" which dropped from Stevens' concentrated work on
"Le Monocle de Mon Oncle" we may count the poems
collected together in mid-1919 under the self-deprecating title
"Pecksniffiana." [110] Readers of Dickens' *Martin Chuzzlewit*
will remember the pompous and oracular Mr. Pecksniff, Archi-
tect, who "had never designed or built anything," but whose
pupils were asked to draw cathedrals from every possible angle
and to construct castles out of the air. Mr. Pecksniff was devoted to "exercises," being convinced that drawing a "lamp-
post is calculated to refine the mind" and designing an "orna-
mental turnpike has a remarkable effect on the imagination."
He was "in the frequent habit of using any word that occurred
to him as having a good sound, and sounding a sentence well,
without much care for its meaning." [111] By entitling his group
of poems after Dickens' comic master of inflated rhetoric,
false-elegance, and sterile aesthetic exercises, Stevens was obviously acknowledging the inherent dangers of his current poetic
method. The poems rejected from "Pecksniffiana," such as
"The Indigo Glass in the Grass" (OP 22) or "Piano Practice
at the Academy of the Holy Angels" (OP 21–23) might have
been written by a sophisticated modern version of Mr. Pecksniff with a taste for the excesses of avant-garde verse.
Although some of the poems in "Pecksniffiana" are among
Stevens' finest, we may regret that almost the entire series
found its way into *Harmonium*. Scattered through the volume,

the poems from "Pecksniffiana" almost tip the delicate balance of major against minor tones, and were partly responsible for Stevens' early reputation as a "decorative" poet.

Most of the "Pecksniffiana" poems are light exercises in poetic theory. Typical of these is "The Paltry Nude Starts on a Spring Voyage" (CP 5-6), where Stevens performs an elaborate variation on the theme and iconography of Botticelli's "Birth of Venus" already used in "Le Monocle." [112] On the surface the poem speaks of differences between the "paltry" goddess of spring, who must be content with a "first-found weed" instead of Botticelli's sea-shell, and the "goldener nude" of summer whom she envies. But on another level it speaks of the "archaic" poem of bare observation, which longs for the pomp of rich language instead of its "meagre play." The opening lines of the second movement—"She too is discontent / And would have purple stuff upon her arms"—links the disquiet of the "paltry nude" with that of the poet longing for richer expression as well as warmer days.

Another poem about poetry is the famous anthology piece, "Anecdote of the Jar" (CP 76), where an artificial form inserted into the "slovenly wilderness" acts as a catalyst and tames the disorder of nature. The colorless jar, "gray and bare," is a sterile and almost menacing object, but like the line that Lily Briscoe draws at the end of *To the Lighthouse* it becomes the focus of order. In "Anecdote of the Jar," as in so many poems from "Pecksniffiana," nature and its cycles have become the source of ennui; the poet longs for an infusion of new orders and new colors, no matter how artificial or "decorative."

The endless "droning of the surf" in "Fabliau of Florida" (CP 23), the monotony of late summer in "Banal Sojourn" (CP 62-63), the "perpetual undulation" of thought and sensation in "The Place of the Solitaires" (CP 60), the "long motions" of "The Curtains in the House of the Metaphysician" (CP 62)—all these point to a malady of the quotidian which needs refreshment, whether through the gaiety of almost surreal imagery, as in "Ploughing on Sunday" (CP 20), or through the conceit of the singer who pulls his cloak over his head in "Of the Surface of Things" (CP 57), knowing that the moon of imagination "is in the folds of the cloak." Like "The Weeping Burgher" (CP 61), who would wish to return to this world of "sorry verities" as a ghostly "belle design / Of foppish line," the poet of "Pecksniffiana" is searching for ideas of order that will relieve the boredom of everyday sensations, mediating between the artificial demands of language and the urgent claims of a physical world. "Homunculus et la Belle Étoile" (CP 25–27), the most impressive poem in the entire sequence, may be taken as an exemplum of the dilemma Stevens found himself in after writing "Le Monocle de Mon Oncle."

The "homunculus" of the title is the shrunken man without imagination, a mere cipher; more explicitly, he is "the artificial man that Paracelsus, the alchemist, boasted he could make from chemicals." [113] The setting of the poem is the Bay of Biscayne, off Miami (the poem was written in Miami), the farthest reach of Stevens' actual experience. The distant reflection of "la belle étoile" marks the border between two kinds of reality, and the poem details in discrete quatrains the comfort such a point of order may offer to "drunkards, poets, widows, / And ladies soon to be married." Only the philosophers and scholars should be wary, since the point of light may destroy their Platonic reflections. What if "la belle étoile" should reflect the actuality of their mistress, not the abstract "idea" of her beauty:

> It might well be that their mistress
> Is no gaunt fugitive phantom.
> She might, after all, be a wanton,
> Abundantly beautiful, eager,
>
> Fecund,
> From whose being by starlight, on sea-coast,
> The innermost good of their seeking
> Might come in the simplest of speech.

> It is a good light, then, for those
> That know the ultimate Plato,
> Tranquillizing with this jewel
> The torments of confusion. (CP 26–27)

The composing power of the imagination is the "ultimate Plato," bringing similarity out of diversity, the single image out of the flux of experience. In his late essay "Imagination as Value" (1948) Stevens remarks that the job of the imagination is to produce images of order out of the diversity of the world. "The primitivism disappears. The Platonic resolution of diversity appears" (NA 151).[114] In "Homunculus et la Belle Étoile" Stevens recorded the division which had developed in his own poetry between the rendering of local sensations and the construction of universal "resemblances." Poetry is the "ultimate Plato" because it brings order out of diversity, but it can only operate on the impressions of one time and one place. At the completion of *Ideas of Order*, Stevens could look back upon "Homunculus et la Belle Étoile" as "an early poem of order." [115]

When "Pecksniffiana" appeared in late 1919 Hart Crane wrote to his friend Gorham Munson that Stevens "is a man whose work makes most of the rest of us quail. His technical subtleties alone provide a great amount of interest. Note the novel rhyme and rhythm effects." [116] The series is indeed a virtuoso performance, the product of an accomplished craftsman, but it lacks a sense of purpose. Retrospective exercises stand side-by-side with prefigurations of the later poetry, and the general tone is one of bored accomplishment. Evidently Stevens felt that he had reached a dead-end, since only six poems were published in the next two years, all but two written in the manner of "Pecksniffiana." [117] With both friends and critics labeling his verse as "precious," [118] and dissatisfied in his own right, Stevens devoted most of his energies to his growing business responsibilities. The months of late 1919–early 1920 yielded but a few minor verses, and in May 1920 he wrote to his wife that "I have not had a poem in my head for a month, poor Yorick." [119] It was not until 1921 that Stevens published his first major poems after the "Pecksniffiana" sequence, "Cortège for Rosenbloom" and "The Man Whose Pharynx Was Bad."

VI

Fictive Things

When "Cortège for Rosenbloom" (CP 79–81) appeared in March 1921, those who were closely following Stevens' poetic career must have been struck by the abrupt departure from the tone and verse-forms of "Pecksniffiana." "Cortège" is a "poetic" word, part of the high talk we use to disguise the facts of death; by contrast, "Rosenbloom" suggests the ordinary man who belongs to the world of natural things (rose-in-bloom). The clash of attitudes in the title is then explored in the poem, whose heavy rhythms and repeated monosyllabic rhymes convey a feeling of gloom and deadness.

> Now, the wry Rosenbloom is dead
> And his finical carriers tread,
> On a hundred legs, the tread
> Of the dead.
> Rosenbloom is dead.

At first the carriers are described as insects, bearing a dead morsel to its natural end; but the "tread of the carriers does not halt / On the hill, but turns / Up the sky."

> It is the infants of misanthropes
> And the infants of nothingness
> That tread
> The wooden ascents
> Of the ascending of the dead.

As Richard Ellmann has observed, the "mourners are infants because their concepts of man are undeveloped and founded on a dislike of man's real nature; hence they love their extra-human illusions." [120] "Cortège for Rosenbloom" trails off into the mournful accents of a world without the "prose" of ordinary life.

> To a jangle of doom
> And a jumble of words
> Of the intense poem
> Of the strictest prose
> Of Rosenbloom.

In its insistence that poetry must confront the "prose" of life, "Cortège for Rosenbloom" marks one of the extremes in the last phase of the poet of *Harmonium*. Stevens' poetic development in the years 1921–22 may be seen as a constant oscillation between "sun" and "moon," between the demands of reality and of the "fictive" imagination which must be reconciled in the grand poem. As he said in a later comment on "Cortège for Rosenbloom":

> From time immemorial the philosophers and other scene painters have daubed the sky with dazzle paint. But it all comes down to the proverbial six feet of earth in the end. . . . Why not fill the sky with scaffolds and stairs, and go about like genuine realists? [121]

The heavy tread which opens "Cortège for Rosenbloom" is the ground-bass of *Harmonium*.

The title Stevens gave to his long series of poems published in *Poetry* for October 1921 is partly ironic. "Sur Ma Guzzla Gracile" suggests elegant variations upon the sort of antique musical instrument which attracted Stevens the connoisseur,[122] but the first poems in the series are anything but tuneful.[123] It must have been these verses which, in their investigations of dreary reality, gave some readers the impression that Stevens had produced "hideous ghosts" of his former self.[124] The "disbeliever" of "Palace of the Babies" (CP 77), unlike the dreaming children, walks in the moonlight but is untouched by it.

> The walker in the moonlight walked alone,
> And in his heart his disbelief lay cold.
> His broad-brimmed hat came close upon his eyes.

We are reminded of the "rationalists" of "Six Significant Landscapes," who are blind to new "resemblances" and new orders. A complementary annihilation is dramatized in "From the Misery of Don Joost," where the death of the senses is memorialized. In diminishing tercets reminiscent of "The Death of a Soldier," the "dying animal" faces the end of his "combat with the sun":

> The senses and feeling, the very sound
> And sight, and all there was of the storm,
> Knows nothing more. (CP 47)

Similar themes are dramatized in "The Doctor of Geneva" (CP 24), where "lacustrine man," conditioned by the Calvinist rationality of his lakeside home, is unsettled by the "ruinous waste" of the limitless Pacific; and in "Gubbinal" (CP 85), where a stubborn refusal to transform the gobbets of sensation leads to the flat refrain: "The world is ugly, / And the people are sad." Another poem of ennui and voiceless nature is "The Man Whose Pharynx Was Bad," originally published in this form:

> The time of year has grown indifferent.
> Mildew of summer and the deepening snow
> Are both alike in the routine I know.
> I am too dumbly in my being pent.
>
> The wind attendant on the solstices
> Blows on the shutters of the metropoles,
> Stirring no poet in his sleep, and tolls
> The grand ideas of the villages.

The malady of the quotidian . . .
Perhaps, if summer ever came to rest
And lengthened, deepened, comforted, caressed
Through days like oceans in obsidian

Horizons full of night's midsummer blaze;
Perhaps, if winter once could penetrate
Through all its purples to the final slate,
Persisting bleakly in an icy haze;

One might in turn become less diffident—
Out of such mildew plucking neater mould
And spouting new orations of the cold.
One might. One might. But time will not relent.[125]

Stevens withheld the poem from the first edition of *Harmonium*, and when it was published in the second edition (1931) the two seasonal stanzas had been condensed into one quatrain on the "basic slate, the universal hue":

The malady of the quotidian. . . .
Perhaps, if winter once could penetrate
Through all its purples to the final slate,
Persisting bleakly in an icy haze

The deliberate rhetoric, and the stanza form borrowed from "In Memoriam," make this poem Stevens' most successful evocation of the "malady of the quotidian." The only salvation from such ennui, as the revised third stanza suggests, is a vision of winter in its "final slate," a perception of nothingness that can yield "new orations of the cold": and "The Snow Man" (CP 9–10) is just such an oration.

The single complex sentence of "The Snow Man," cast in the flexible unrhymed tercets which had become Stevens' favorite meditative form, embodies Stevens' ultimate vision of unadorned reality.

One must have a mind of winter
To regard the frost and the boughs
Of the pine-trees crusted with snow;

And have been cold a long time
To behold the junipers shagged with ice,
The spruces rough in the distant glitter

Of the January sun; and not to think
Of any misery in the sound of the wind,
In the sound of a few leaves,

Which is the sound of the land
Full of the same wind
That is blowing in the same bare place

For the listener, who listens in the snow,
And, nothing himself, beholds
Nothing that is not there and the nothing that is.

The simplicity of the diction, the controlled variations on the tetrameter line, and the transfixing effect of the final Alexandrine—all contribute to the overpowering impression of undeflected emotion. "The Snow Man" is not a poem of negation, as has often been claimed, but an affirmation of primary reality. The imagery of the first two stanzas, which reminds one of "Thirteen Ways of Looking at a Blackbird," cries out for "interpretation," for the exercise of the pathetic fallacy, but in this poem Stevens resists all humanizing symbolism. The poet is not *like* the snow man, he has *become* the man of snow, the man of one place and one climate, who, having become nothing himself, can see "Nothing that is not there and the nothing that is." Rather than being a critique of the man without imagination, "The Snow Man" lays bare that irreducible reality upon which the poet builds his fictive structures, just as the lusher seasons build upon the frozen outlines of winter. And in the second half of "Sur Ma Guzzla Gracile" Stevens turns to his developing theme of the transforming imagination.

"Tea at the Palaz of Hoon" (CP 65) poses the figure of Hoon, whose own personality infuses the world, against the remembered figure of the snow man, who has become part of the world around him. Speaking in words that foreshadow one aspect of "The Idea of Order at Key West," Hoon claims the universe for Bishop Berkeley and the percipient mind:

> I was the world in which I walked, and what I saw
> Or heard or felt came not but from myself;
> And there I found myself more truly and more strange.

At this late stage in the making of *Harmonium* Stevens' poetic fluctuated between the extremes of these two poems, seeking for ways to harmonize them; and the later poems of "Sur Ma Guzzla Gracile" dramatize various accommodations. Some are colorful escapes from the "malady of the quotidian" ("Hibiscus on the Sleeping Shores" would be a good example), poems which embody a theory rather than illustrate it; but others are preliminary "poems of order" which talk about themselves. Along with "Stars at Tallapoosa" (CP 71–72)[126] and "The Bird with the Coppery, Keen Claws" (CP 82), they reflect Stevens' growing interest in a theory of poetry which might also be a theory of life.

In "On the Manner of Addressing Clouds" (CP 55–56), Stevens explores the implications of the poet's role as an "interpreter" (the term is used in the first line of the companion poem, "Of Heaven Considered as a Tomb"). The title is formal and somewhat pompous, like a sub-heading from a handbook of rhetoric, and the entire poem treats the poet's desire to gorge himself on language with gentle irony. The opening line is an address to the clouds in language not unlike that of the "fops of fancy" in "Le Monocle," a poetic diction soon to be given free play in "The Comedian as the Letter C."

> Gloomy grammarians in golden gowns,
> Meekly you keep the mortal rendezvous,
> Eliciting the still sustaining pomps
> Of speech which are like music so profound
> They seem an exaltation without sound.

The sunlit clouds, drifting to their death, are "grammarians" because they provide the forms for such "sustaining pomps /

Of speech" as the opening lines. The resemblance between their "mortal rendezvous" and our own is the stuff of poetry's cloudy language. Even the most abstract philosophers of death must use the metaphors, the "pomps of speech," derived from the natural world.

> Funest philosophers and ponderers,
> Their evocations are the speech of clouds.

As R. P. Blackmur pointed out in his early essay on *Harmonium*, each word in this witty aside is a *mot juste*.[127] "Funest" means "mournful" or "fatal," stemming from the Latin *funus*, "funeral"; but hidden in "Funest" is the fun of language, the play of poetry. Similarly, "evocations" combines its usual poetic meaning with the more traditional meaning "to call up the dead"; and it may also contain overtones of the word's definition as a grammatical term, "a reduction of the third person to the first," a making personal of the impersonal. The gist of the aside is that "Funest philosophers and ponderers" use the "speech of clouds" both because its subject is mutability and because they can only express themselves through figures drawn from the external world.

Since the speech of the clouds' "processionals" (fusing the meaning of "hymn, song" with their movement through the sky) has become part of our manner of addressing them, it is present in every casual evocation of their "tread / Across the stale, mysterious seasons."

> So speech of your processionals returns
> In the casual evocations of your tread
> Across the stale, mysterious seasons. These
> Are the music of meet resignation; these
> The responsive, still sustaining pomps for you
> To magnify, if in that drifting waste
> You are to be accompanied by more
> Than mute bare splendors of the sun and moon.

The "pomps" of language are "responsive" because they answer, or respond to, the mute procession of the clouds, hu-

manizing the heavens and giving voice to what would other-
wise be "the mute bare splendors of the sun and moon."
Throughout the poem the language has religious overtones:
"exaltation," "evocations," "processionals," "mysterious,"
"magnify" (in the sense of "celebrate" as well as reinforce), all
contribute to the feeling of a hymn or anthem. If poetry is to
supply the satisfactions of a lost religion, it must do so
through its transfigurations of nature. The language of "On
the Manner of Addressing Clouds" is full of wit and playful-
ness, but at the same time it expresses the exalted theme of
a reciprocal relationship between speech and nature, each in-
tensifying and "magnifying" the other.

"On the Manner of Addressing Clouds" depends upon a
traditional view of the poet's relation to natural objects, but in
other poems of the same time Stevens takes a more radical approach. In "Stars at Tallapoosa" (CP 71–72) the imagination
is presented as an abstracting, idealizing force, a kind of inspired mathematics, which seeks to trace the pure naked forms
behind the lush irregularities of nature. The "straight and
swift" lines between the distant stars find their likeness in the
ordering mind of the "secretive hunter," the poet.

> Wading the sea-lines, moist and ever-mingling,
> Mounting the earth-lines, long and lax, lethargic.
> These lines are swift and fall without diverging.

The same desire for an image of "pure intellect" occurs in
"The Bird with the Coppery, Keen Claws" (CP 82), where
the imagination visualizes a "parakeet of parakeets," a "perfect cock," poised motionless above the forest with the "rudiments of tropics" around him. The end-stopped triplets of the
poem emphasize the static, ideal quality of the image, but its
lacquered colors and acute details are drawn from observation
of the real-life bird. The "parakeet of parakeets" is not a
ghostly paradigm, but a heroic replica of the actual bird. The
"ultimate Plato" can only create simulacra of natural things.

The tentative "poems of order" scattered through *Har-*

monium are often processed by critics into some master view of Stevens' thought or imagery based upon the poems of his final years. Such a method always leads to distortion, the individual poems being warped to fit an ideal design. The poet of *Harmonium* had no master theory of the imagination, but rather a number of provisional theories which matched his changing moods and the tempers of his environment. General patterns can be easily traced, but the poems must be allowed to speak for themselves as moments of order in the flux of experience. When this is done, they reveal themselves not as "Preliminary Minutiae" to the grand poem of the future, but as important and charming statements in their own right.

◇

In the December 1921 issue of *Poetry: A Magazine of Verse*, the Poetry Society of South Carolina announced that a prize of $250 would be awarded annually to the best original poem submitted for competition, with special consideration given to "sustained poems of length." Stevens rose immediately to the challenge. As he told Harriet Monroe, "what's the use of offering prizes if people don't make an effort to capture them." [128] Obviously Stevens felt that he had at last achieved the metrical repertoire and sense of structure necessary for a "sustained poem," and that such a performance was necessary to focus his forthcoming volume of poems. He must also have had in mind the example of all those other poets, both traditional and modern, who had extended and defined their art through the building of a long poem. At the same time as Eliot was constructing the *Waste Land*, and for many of the same reasons, Stevens plunged into the composition of a "grand pronunciamento" which was to be the center of his poetic activity until the design of *Harmonium* was completed in October–November 1922. The deadline for the Blindman Prize of the Poetry Society of South Carolina was near at hand, but Stevens managed to complete a preliminary version of "The Comedian

as the Letter C" in time for the competition. "From the
Journal of Crispin" (which has not survived) did not win the
award, although the judge, Amy Lowell, "hesitated a long
time" before relegating the poem to Honorable Mention.[129]
It is easy to see why a first version of "The Comedian," in
spite of its appeal as an epic journey to the Carolinas, would
have been found unsuitable for the Poetry Society of South
Carolina. More "obscure" than anything Stevens had yet
attempted, its ironic and mannered surface must have baffled
even so adept a follower of the avant garde as Miss Lowell.

Stevens must have found the writing of "The Comedian
as the Letter C" a liberating experience. As he remarked many
years later about "An Ordinary Evening in New Haven," a
long poem "acquires an impetus of its own." [130] The impetus
of the highly personal subject under review, and the narrative
drive of the expanding poem, acted as a spur to his creativity.
The result of this prolonged attention to a single subject, as
he told Harriet Monroe, was that all manner of favors dropped
from it,[131] and among these favors were the many shorter
poems which Stevens produced in the last months before the
completion of *Harmonium*. Sometime in 1921–22 he organized
the notes he had kept on possible subjects or titles for poems,
a process which in itself reveals the catalytic effect of his
work on the long poem. Some of these "Schemata" or "Memo-
rias Antiguas," as Stevens called them, are titles for poems
which were destroyed or never written, such as "Bandits in
Plum Thickets" or "The Man Who Could Not Sell Even
Nectarines." Others are headings for the journal of Crispin:
"A Nice Shady Home," "On Being One's Own Native," "The
Man Who Wanted to Think of One Thing Only," "The
Error of Crispin Approaching the Carolinas," "The Idea of a
Colony," "The World without Imagination," "Book of Moon-
light." A few of the notes are *données* for unwritten poems
("Holly, kingfishers, grapes and cosmos," "Twenty quail fly-
ing in moonlight") or lines around which actual poems or-
ganized themselves ("Poetry is the supreme fiction").[132]

Pawky, gay, suggestive, the "Schemata" testify to the energy and variety which infused Stevens' poetry at this time.

The shorter poems of 1921–22 fall naturally into two groups, which we may label—borrowing the titles from Stevens— "Revue" and "The Book of Moonlight," with "To the One of Fictive Music" standing as coda to the entire phase. In the spring of 1922 Stevens sent a number of poems to Gilbert Seldes, an editor at *The Dial*, suggesting that they be published under the title "Mostly Moonlight." Seldes returned several of the poems, including two that Stevens referred to as "moonlight poems," and as a result Stevens suggested that the title be changed from "Mostly Moonlight" to *Revue*.[133] The new title, a finicky use of the French word which had lately been imported to describe an episodic musical review of current fashions, implies that the poems are a light and witty "re-seeing" of Stevens' recent subjects, and this is true of all but one of the verses published in *The Dial*. The "moonlight poems," on the other hand, represent a slightly new angle of vision, and have a distinctive style. By stretching the headings "Revue" and "The Book of Moonlight" to include all of Stevens' shorter pieces of this period we gain a clearer view of his poetic development.[134]

The poems of "The Book of Moonlight" stem from the dialectic between sun and moon, between realism and fancy, dramatized in "The Comedian as the Letter C." In "Anecdote of the Prince of Peacocks" (CP 57–58), the dialectic sharpens into an aggressive confrontation:

> In the moonlight
> I met Berserk,
> In the moonlight
> On the bushy plain.
> Oh, sharp he was
> As the sleepless!
>
> And, "Why are you red
> In this milky blue?"
> I said.

"Why sun-colored,
As if awake
In the midst of sleep?"

"You that wander,"
So he said,
"On the bushy plain,
Forget so soon.
But I set my traps
In the midst of dreams."

I knew from this
That the blue ground
Was full of blocks
And blocking steel.
I knew the dread
Of the bushy plain,
And the beauty
Of the moonlight
Falling there,
Falling
As sleep falls
In the innocent air.

Here Stevens' developing "color code," in which red is the color of sun-drenched reality and blue the color of moonlit imagination, is made explicit. The "Prince of Peacocks" is the master of lush imagery and gaudy language, while "Berserk" represents the destructive energy of stripped reality. If we compare this poem with a manuscript poem of the same title (which may date from as early as 1915, although 1918–19 seems more likely), the progress in Stevens' style and symbolic patterns is immediately evident.

In the land of the peacocks, the prince thereof,
Grown weary of romantics, walked alone,
In the first of evening, pondering.

"The deuce!" he cried.

And by him, in the bushes, he espied
A white philosopher.
The white one sighed—

He seemed to seek replies,
From nothingness, to all his sights.

"My sighs are pulses in a dreamer's death!"
Exclaimed the white one, smothering his lips.

The prince's *frisson* reached his fingers' tips.[135]

As Robert Buttel comments, the original encounter between
the gaudy peacock and the "white philosopher" is described
with "mannered, arch, and febrile irony." [136] In the completely
recast version, however, the white peacock has been transformed into an elemental force, and the sentimental *frisson*
of the "Prince of Peacocks" has become a gripping dread of
the "traps" set to catch him. On the surface, the poem would
appear to identify Berserk as an enemy of the poet; but in
the complex interplay of nuances which marks the final poems
of *Harmonium* it is best to avoid such simplistic interpretations. Although Berserk does not represent the "reality" which,
in Stevens' later phases, is the "necessary angel" of earth, he
may symbolize the energy necessary for masculine and realistic
verse. Without reading the patterns of the later Stevens into
the poem, we can discern from the imagery and rhythms that
the "Prince of Peacocks" is the archetypal poet in his "romantic" phase, unable to cope with the energies of reality and
seeking an escape in the illusions of moonlight.

The same themes are rehearsed in "The Virgin Carrying a
Lantern" (CP 71), a comic variation on the imagery of
Shakespeare's "Book of Moonlight," *Midsummer Night's
Dream*. The poem is so closely tied to its source that one may
posit a re-reading of the play as the impulse behind all of
Stevens' "moonlight poems."

There are no bears among the roses,
Only a negress who supposes
Things false and wrong

About the lantern of the beauty
Who walks there, as a farewell duty,
Walks long and long.

The pity that her pious egress
Should fill the vigil of a negress
With heat so strong!

In *Midsummer Night's Dream* (III.i) Peter Quince, contriving the play of Pyramus and Thisby, says that someone "must come in with a bush of thorns and a lantern . . . to present the person of Moonshine." And at the beginning of Act V, shortly before the play is presented, Theseus makes his great speech on the "The lunatic, the lover, and the poet," describing the joys and dangers of the imagination.

And as imagination bodies forth
The forms of things unknown, the poet's pen
Turns them to shapes, and gives to airy nothing
A local habitation and a name.
Such tricks hath strong imagination
That, if it would but apprehend some joy,
It comprehends some bringer of that joy;
Or in the night, imagining some fear,
How easy is a bush suppos'd a bear?

In Stevens' adaptation, the comic mistakes of Shakespeare's sub-plot have been merged with his great theme of "moonshine" and transfiguring poetry. The lantern of the virgin, a stock symbol of peace and tranquillity, has been turned by the negress's heated imagination into something quite different, and the imagined scene shows the dangers of "moonshine." Whatever distorted view of the lantern the negress has taken does indeed show "How easy is a bush suppos'd a bear." The rollicking triplets of this delightful poem embody in miniature the world of *A Midsummer Night's Dream*, the virgin and the negress depending upon each other as Shakespeare's "high" and "low" plots interact with each other. The imagination can both transfigure and falsify, and Stevens' "moonlight poems" reveal the tension between the ennobling and pejorative overtones of the word "fiction."

The exaltations and betrayals of moonlight are given their finest expression in "The Ordinary Women" (CP 11–12). When placed side-by-side, the first and last stanzas tell the story:

> Then from their poverty they rose,
> From dry catarrhs, and to guitars
> They flitted
> Through the palace walls.
>
>   . . .
>
> Then from their poverty they rose,
> From dry guitars, and to catarrhs
> They flitted
> Through the palace walls.

The "dry catarrhs" of ordinary life yield to the "dry guitars" of the sterile fancy. But between these extremes, the poem acts out the allures and dangers of the imagination. The ordinary women fling "monotony" and ennui behind, only to find that the stage illuminated by imagination is something of a sham:

> The lacquered loges huddled there
> Mumbled zay-zay and a-zay, a-zay.
> The moonlight
> Fubbed the girandoles.

These famous lines have become almost a symbol of the difficulties and "mandarin qualities" of *Harmonium*. Yet in the context of the poem they are precise and simple: the moonlight cheats (i.e. imitates) the light of the candles, fobbing itself off as the interior illumination. For a moment the theatre of mere artistry becomes the theatre of the imagination.

The central stanzas of the poem epitomize its meaning:

And the cold dresses that they wore,
In the vapid haze of the window-bays,
Were tranquil
As they leaned and looked

From the window-sills at the alphabets,
At beta b and gamma g,
To study
The canting curlicues

Of heaven and of the heavenly script.
And there they read of marriage-bed.
Ti-lill-o!
And they read right long.

In the theatre of moonlight the ordinary women look at the abstract hieroglyphs of life, at the "beta b" and "gamma g" which follow "alpha," and there they read of "marriage-bed," life's living text. At the mid-point of the poem the ordinary women are balanced between reality and imagination, but as the poem unwinds the initial situation is reversed: the last half of "The Ordinary Women" is a mirror-image of the first half, and in the last stanza the ordinary women leave the poverty of the "dry guitars" (as they had fled the poverty of the "dry catarrhs" in the first stanza), dancing through the palace of art to the music of bare reality ("catarrhs"). In its mirror structure and ambivalent imagery, "The Ordinary Women" sings the paradox of the imagination.

Most of Stevens' shorter poems of 1922–23 may be classified under the heading "Revue," since they re-animate and define the various concerns of his earlier work. "New England Verses" (CP 104–106), for example, summarizes in its witty couplets the themes of the last years of *Harmonium*.[137]

I
The Whole World Including the Speaker
Why nag at the ideas of Hercules, Don Don?
Widen your sense. All things in the sun are sun.

II

The Whole World Excluding the Speaker
I found between moon-rising and moon-setting
The world was round. But not from my begetting.

. . .

XV

Scène Flétrie
The purple dress in autumn and the belfry breath
Hinted autumnal farewells of academic death.

XVI

Scène Fleurie
A perfect fruit in perfect atmosphere.
Nature as Pinakothek. Whist! Chanticleer. . . .

These aphoristic couplets, which look forward to the more flexible stanzas of "The Man with the Blue Guitar," are themselves grouped in pairs; and each pair epitomizes a paradox in the final world of *Harmonium*. The whole world including Don Don is all himself, just as "all things in the sun are sun"; but the whole world excluding him is totally independent. The withered autumn landscape is an academic subject, but the "perfect fruit in perfect atmosphere" of flowered spring is a theme for Chanticleer alone. The fact that Stevens could condense his complex ideas into these counterbalanced couplets shows that the making of *Harmonium* was a process of definition as well as a process of amplification.

Other poems of "Revue" recapitulate and revivify familiar themes. "Sonatina to Hans Christian" (CP 109–110), for example, takes the familiar fable of the ugly duckling and turns it into a series of questions:

What of the dove,
Or thrush, or any singing mysteries?
What of the trees
And intonations of the trees?

What of the night
That lights and dims the stars?
Do you know, Hans Christian,
Now that you see the night?

Who is the mother of our keenest perceptions? The poem provides no answer (although "To the One of Fictive Music" can be taken as answer), but it poses the essential question of Stevens' early poetry. Throughout the poems of "Revue" Stevens muses on the question of whether our sense of "resemblances" comes from nature or from art, from energetic reality or from the artifices of the imagination. In eccentric and alliterative language often borrowed from "The Comedian as the Letter C," the verses of "Revue" perform various turns in Stevens' aesthetic. "Floral Decorations for Bananas" (CP 53–54) speaks of the need for harmonizing substance with decoration, content with form; "The Revolutionists Stop for Orangeade" (CP 102–103), based on Stevens' experience of Havana and his passion for orangeade, provides a counterbalance by insisting that a frivolous artifice is the necessary coloring of poetry: "There is no pith in music / Except in something false." "In the Clear Season of Grapes" (CP 110–111) elaborates on another theme: the integrations of nature, the natural harmony in the "conjunctions of mountains and sea and our lands," mean more than the composed colors of a still-life or an arranged "show" of fruit. They partake of the salty life of the sea's reality. In similar fashion, "Two at Norfolk" (CP 111–112) celebrates the harmony of natural (as against intellectual) things: one skeleton in the cemetery belonged to an alien from imagination ("For him the moon was always in Scandinavia"), another belonged to one who preferred the music of Bach to his son's music, but the daughter and son "never meet in the air so full of summer / And touch each other, even touching closely, / Without an escape in the lapses of their kisses." The final injunction to the faithful caretakers, "Make a bed and leave the iris in it," contains the central symbol. Iris, the goddess of the rainbow, was identified by the ancients with natural phenomena; she had no cult of her own, being simply thought of as the personification of the rainbow which touches both earth and sky. As the fathers were divided by thought, so the children are united by feeling. In its stately quatrains and solemn diction, this poem recapitulates one of the gathering themes of *Harmonium*.

Typical of the way in which the "Revue" poems capture and extend an earlier subject is the movement of "The Emperor of Ice-Cream" (CP 64). This famous anthology-piece takes up the idea and imagery of "Cortège for Rosenbloom," but the matter of the earlier poem has been given a more buoyant form. Instead of the funereal rhythms and rhymes of "Cortège for Rosenbloom," we are presented with an alliterative structure which exalts the here-and-now. The sounds are those of the letter C, the sounds of Crispin ("In kitchen cups concupiscent curds"), and the "color of horn" which linked Rosenbloom with the gates of horn has been transmuted into the comic-grotesque image, "If her horny feet protrude, they come / To show how cold she is, and dumb." The matched couplets which end the two stanzas of "The Emperor of Ice-Cream" are a witty extension of "Cortège for Rosenbloom": the twin associations of ice-cream, intense pleasure (life) and intense cold (death), are balanced out:

> Let be be finale of seem.
> The only emperor is the emperor of ice-cream.
>
> . . .
>
> Let the lamp affix its beam.
> The only emperor is the emperor of ice-cream.

Other poems of the "Revue" sequence sustain and vary the harmonies of Stevens' early poetry. The spirit of Florida in "O Florida, Venereal Soil" sums up the ambivalences of Stevens' early encounters with a tropical landscape. Florida is a "Virgin of boorish births," both chaste and fecund; like traditional representations of the constellation Virgo, she carries a leafy quince in her hand (compare Robert Graves' "To Juan at the Winter Solstice," where the figure is identified with the White Goddess). Lascivious and tormenting when she might be a "scholar of darkness," the spirit of Florida embodies Stevens' complex response to the stimulus of a more sensuous climate. The title sums up the ambivalence: derived from the astrological concept of being born "under Venus," the term "venereal" has come to mean the infection of desire. In a like manner, the bizarre poem "Frogs Eat Butterflies. Snakes Eat Frogs. Hogs Eat Snakes. Men Eat Hogs" (CP 78) acts out the cyclic theme of its title. The ordinary man of the central stanza, who like the anti-hero of "The Comedian as the Letter C" erected his cabin and tended his field, "Knew not the quirks of imagery." Yet all around him the rivers "went nosing like swine" to the sea, and the entire "rattapallax" of nature's cyclic life (an onomatopoeic coinage from the French *rataplan*, the rat-a-tat of a drum) could only be expressed in the richest metaphor.

Perhaps the best-known of all Stevens' early poems is "Bantams in Pine-Woods" (CP 75–76), which is usually taken as an encounter between pompous pretension and realistic confidence, or between the individual and his cosmic surroundings.

> Chieftain Iffucan of Azcan in caftan
> Of tan with henna hackles, halt!
>
> Damned universal cock, as if the sun
> Was blackamoor to bear your blazing tail.
>
> Fat! Fat! Fat! Fat! I am the personal.
> Your world is you. I am my world.
>
> You ten-foot poet among inchlings. Fat!
> Begone! An inchling bristles in these pines,
>
> Bristles, and points their Appalachian tangs,
> And fears not portly Azcan nor his hoos.

The conventional interpretations are clearly relevant, but when taken in the context of a "Revue" of Stevens' recent work "Bantams in Pine-Woods" is seen to be a debate between the "high" and "low" styles in poetry, between encrusted poetic diction and the personal idiom, between Vachel Lindsay and H. D. The exotic can overwhelm with its pretense to "reality" (". . . as if the sun / Was blackamoor to bear your blazing tail."), but the mocking language of the inchling emphasizes his skill at "pointing" (defining, adding precise detail). In "Bantams in Pine-Woods" Stevens both exercises and mocks his penchant for "high talk."

In "A High-Toned Old Christian Woman" (CP 59) the "Book of Moonlight" begins to blend with the "Revue" of familiar themes. The offhand address is a new effect in Stevens' poetry ("Poetry is the supreme fiction, madame."), but the sustained architectural imagery harks back to the poems of 1918–19, especially "Architecture for the Adoration of Beauty" (OP 16–18). The "moral law" of the old Christian woman can be converted by poetic imaginings into the cathedral of "haunted heaven," the groin-vaults of which are like the palms of Palm Sunday; but the same process can seize upon the "opposing law" of the senses and convert it into a "peristyle / And from the peristyle project a masque / Beyond the planets."

> Thus, our bawdiness,
> Unpurged by epitaph, indulged at last,
> Is equally converted into palms,
> Squiggling like saxophones. And palm for palm,
> Madame, we are where we began.

The stuff of life can just as easily be converted into the "palm" of tropic pleasure as the "palm" of frozen morality; and as the poem rounds toward a conclusion the poet conjures up a subversive vision of religious flaggelants "in the planetary scene" disaffecting from the moral law to indulge in "jovial hullabaloo among the spheres." The entire poem is formed in a conversational, cynical style, and the crackling alliterations of the last two lines are almost an insult to the high-toned old Christian woman.

> This will make widows wince. But fictive things
> Wink as they will. Wink most when widows wince.

"A High-Toned Old Christian Woman" leads directly into the splendid invocation which is the secret conclusion to *Harmonium*: "To the One of Fictive Music" (CP 87–88).

> Sister and mother and diviner love,
> And of the sisterhood of the living dead
> Most near, most clear, and of the clearest bloom,
> And of the fragrant mothers the most dear
> And queen, and of diviner love the day
> And flame and summer and sweet fire, no thread
> Of cloudy silver sprinkles in your gown
> Its venom of renown, and on your head
> No crown is simpler than the simple hair.
>
> Now, of the music summoned by the birth
> That separates us from the wind and sea,
> Yet leaves us in them, until earth becomes,
> By being so much of the things we are,
> Gross effigy and simulacrum, none
> Gives motion to perfection more serene
> Than yours, out of our imperfections wrought,
> Most rare, or ever of more kindred air
> In the laborious weaving that you wear.
>
> For so retentive of themselves are men
> That music is intensest which proclaims
> The near, the clear, and vaunts the clearest bloom,
> And of all vigils musing the obscure,
> That apprehends the most which sees and names,
> As in your name, an image that is sure,
> Among the arrant spices of the sun,
> O bough and bush and scented vine, in whom
> We give ourselves our likest issuance.

Yet not too like, yet not so like to be
Too near, too clear, saving a little to endow
Our feigning with the strange unlike, whence springs
The difference that heavenly pity brings.
For this, musician, in your girdle fixed
Bear other perfumes. On your pale head wear
A band entwining, set with fatal stones.
Unreal, give back to us what once you gave:
The imagination that we spurned and crave.

The word "fictive" in the title, already used pejoratively in Part IV of "The Comedian as the Letter C" as "counterfeit" or "masquerade" (CP 39), is given a wicked twist in "A High-Toned Old Christian Woman": here it is exploited in both the sense of "fictional" and of "feigning," the supreme enlargement and the supreme evasion. The title has the form of an invocation, an address to the deity, and the phrase "fictive music" may recall the term *musica ficta* which was used by medieval theorists to describe accidentals that lie outside a harmonic system. The muse-goddess addressed in "To the One of Fictive Music" reigns over a universe of natural harmonies and artificial "accidentals," and the gist of the poem is that poetry must tremble between semblance and resemblance. "Yet not too like, yet not so like to be / Too near, too clear . . ."; the opening of the last stanza echoes Yeats' "To the Rose Upon the Rood of Time," where the Rose of Intellectual Beauty and pure contemplation must not overwhelm the world of common things.

Come near, come near, come near—Ah, leave me still
A little space for the rose-breath to fill!
Lest I no more hear common things that crave . . .[138]

Both Stevens and Yeats wish to exalt the world of common things, the one through artifice, the other through symbolism.

"To the One of Fictive Music" opens with an invocation to the naked imagination, pure and simple, a figure compounded of Muse and Virgin and earthly woman who is mistress of the music celebrated in the second stanza. The orchestrated stanzas, derived from the music of "Sunday Morning" but much more fluent, actually break down into Stevens' favorite tercets, and the pyramiding of three-part and nine-part units adds to the "sacramental" tone of the poem. The music of stanza two is that of organic nature to which we belong, a music "That separates us from the wind and sea, / Yet leaves us in them": but with the image of the earth as "Gross effigy and simulacrum" of ourselves, and the startling adjective "laborious" in the last line, the stanza turns the poem away from an organic theory of art toward a celebration of the power that names and feigns. In stanza three the "naming" of immediate reality is exalted: ". . . of all vigils musing the obscure, / That apprehends the most which sees and names, / As in your name, an image that is sure." But the last stanza draws back from this vaunting of "the clearest bloom," reminding us of Stevens' remark to Harriet Monroe, while he was preparing *Harmonium* for the press, that he wished "to be as obscure as possible" until he had "perfected an authentic and fluent speech." [139] The final icon of "To the One of Fictive Music" is strangely bloodless: "pale," "fatal," "Unreal." Living as we do in a time between mythologies, we must woo the ancient muse of earth's embracing rhythms through a "fictive" image of herself. By all the feints of language and thought exemplified in *Harmonium*, the poet must nurse back to life "The imagination that we spurned and crave."

VII

Valet and Saint

During the summer of 1922 Stevens re-wrote and expanded
"From the Journal of Crispin," altering the title to "The
Comedian as the Letter C." This change in title, like Joyce's
decision to replace "Stephen Hero" with "A Portrait of the
Artist as a Young Man," reflects a distancing of the autobiographical subject-matter and a deliberate attempt to gen-
eralize upon the type of the artist. The personal "Crispin" has
been subsumed in the cipher C, and the hero has become the
universal figure of the artist-comedian. In its final form "The
Comedian as the Letter C" belongs to a familiar literary genre,
the voyage of discovery which becomes an "introspective"
voyage of self-discovery, but its deeper affinities are with the
confessional fictions produced by the Romantic impulse to
explore and define the self. Like Wordsworth's *Prelude*, "The
Comedian" traces the "Growth of a Poet's Mind," but Stevens'
models came from the end rather than the beginning of the
introspective tradition. The poem is closer to Joyce's *Portrait
of the Artist* than to the *Prelude* or Rousseau's *Confessions*
because it is both a "grand pronunciamento" (CP 43) in the
Romantic manner and a "disguised pronunciamento" (CP
45) which employs the ironic obliquities and masks of the
modern artist. Crispin is the ordinary man, "an every-day man
who lives a life without the slightest adventure except that
he lives it in a poetic atmosphere as we all do," [140] yet his

voyage describes the archetypal progress of the poet in the modern world. Stevens called "The Comedian" an "anti-mythological" poem, and this is certainly true: the movement is from romance to realism, and the sustaining myths and fables which have glorified the artist through the ages are deliberately excluded. The hero is Candide or Crispinus, not Orpheus or Prometheus, and "The Comedian" is remarkable among English long poems for its paucity of reinforcing allusions to myth and literature. The fable is bare, without the usual rich setting in legend and tradition; but the language is lush and highly individual, producing the contrast which Stevens desired between the "every-day plainness of the central figure and the plush, so to speak, of his stage." [141] If the actor in the drama is an anti-hero, language itself is the true hero; and although the mannered language of Crispin (sharpened in counterpoint by the plain language describing his life) is subjected to constant irony, it survives as the only "myth" of the poem. There is clearly some truth in Helen Vendler's contention that the poem "speaks one language in its narrative plot, another in the success or failure of its rhetoric," [142] but throughout most of the poem the successes or failures of the language are part of the characterization, part of the fable, like the language of Stephen Dedalus' poem in *A Portrait of the Artist*. When "The Comedian as the Letter C" is read as if it were a modern novel, with a complex *persona*-hero qualified by the author's ironic point-of-view, the apparent disparities between rhetoric and narrative plot fall away.

"The Comedian as the Letter C" is unique among Stevens' longer poems in its use of a picaresque narrative, complete with incident and scenic detail, to provide the general unity of design. Like most twentieth-century poets who were the heirs of Imagism, Stevens had to guard against the danger that a long poem would be merely a rough mosaic of shorter pieces. He wrote in "natural" units of fifteen lines or less, and only gradually learned how to orchestrate a series of these short poems. While constructing "An Ordinary Evening in

New Haven" in 1949 he told a friend that, like most long poems, it was "merely a collection of short ones." [143] This does not mean that the longer poems of the last volumes lack a general harmony, but only that they are held together by master images and *leitmotifs* which serve the "conversational" progress of the argument (a progress reminiscent of Coleridge's "conversation" poems). "The Comedian as the Letter C," however, has the unity of a picaresque novella; the central design is the *persona* in action, and the development of his character is our chief interest. Although most of Stevens' poems are impervious to a critical attack through "sources" and "influences," the origins of the Crispin-figure tell us a great deal about the method of "The Comedian."

Borrowed from the dramatis personae of the seventeenth- and eighteenth-century French theatre, Crispin had his distant origin—like Pierrot—in the stock figures of the *commedia dell' arte*. As Guy Davenport discovered, the description of Crispin in the *Nouveau Larousse Illustré* is a perfect image of Stevens' hero,[144] and the fuller history of the character given in Larousse's *Grand Dictionnaire Universel* contains so many details used in the poem that Stevens may well have pillaged it. Crispin is "a mocking valet, timid, boasting, knavish, with a smattering of Latin and philosophy, always ready to flatter or trick his masters, dressed like them (a little hat and black clothes, a white ruff, soft boots, a buff leather belt and a long rapier), a jack of all trades." A burlesque figure, he has a touch of the poet about him, a way with words. Numerous details of his appearance and stage history are woven into "The Comedian." His famous moustaches are transmuted into the "waves that were mustachios" (CP 27); his role as valet in Le Sage's *Crispin rival de son maître* (1707) recurs throughout the poem; his late seventeenth-century roles in *Crispin musicien* and *Crispin précepteur* suggest "musician of pears" and "Preceptor to the sea" in the poem's opening lines. But Stevens' Crispin is not just the anti-hero of French burlesque; he is also that figure's distant relative, the poet Crispinus who challenged Horace to see which of them could write faster, and more specifically Ben Jonson's reincarnation of Horace's archetypal bad poet in the Crispinus of *The Poetaster*.[145] The absurd words of which Crispinus is literally purged in Jonson's play—words such as "obstrupefact" and "quaking custard"— would fit easily into the high style of "The Comedian."

Crispin as amalgam of comic valet and bad poet is the basic *persona* of the poem, but lurking within that ironic type are potentialities for both the commonplace and the transcendent. Saint Crispin, the patron saint of shoemakers, labored at a humble trade although he was of noble birth, and Stevens wishes his readers to recall this other Crispin. "Crispin-valet, Crispin-saint!" is his address to the tattered hero in "Anecdote of the Abnormal" (OP 24). Just as Crispin's decline from youthful romanticism has pathetic and even tragic overtones, so the comic language has from time to time the oversound of heavenly harmonies.

The hypothesis that "The Comedian as the Letter C" was begun as a poetic autobiography, and then recast into a more general exploration of fictive language, is supported by Stevens' often-repeated comments on the "real meaning" of the title. Unlike some of his mock-explanations, the following comment from a letter to Hi Simons has the ring of sincerity:

> . . . It is true that the letter C is a cypher for Crispin, but using the cypher was meant to suggest something that nobody seems to have grasped. I can state it, perhaps, by changing the title to this: THE COMEDIAN AS THE SOUNDS OF THE LETTER C. You know the old story about St. Francis wearing bells around his ankles so that, as he went about his business, the crickets and so on would get out of his way and not be tramped on. Now, as Crispin moves through the poem, the sounds of the letter C accompany him, as the sounds of the crickets, etc. must have accompanied St. Francis. I don't mean to say that there is an incessant din, but you ought not to be able to read very far in the poem without recognizing what I mean. The sounds of the letter C include all related or

derivative sounds. For instance, X, *TS* and Z. To illustrate: In

"Bubbling felicity in Cantilene"

the soft C with the change to the hard C, once you
notice it, ought to make that line a little different from
what it was before. Sometimes the sounds squeak all over
the place, as, for example, in the line

"Exchequering from piebald fiscs unkeyed"

The word exchequering is about as full of the sounds of
C as any word that I can think of. You have to think of
this incidentally as you read the poem; you cannot think
of it directly. To think of it directly would be like listen-
ing to Till Eulenspiegel exclusively for the personal
passages. You have to read the poem and hear all this
whistling and mocking and stressing and, in a minor way,
orchestrating, going on in the background, or, to say
it as a lawyer might say it, "in, on or about the
words." . . .

The natural effect of the variety of sounds of the letter
C is a comic effect. I should like to know whether your
ear agrees.[146]

The letter C, that "merest minuscule" (CP 29), is just as important a character in the poem as Crispin, journeying through
a world of sound as Crispin journeys through a world of
incidents and landscapes; and the attentive ear can sense the
fluctuations of his voyage without reference to the plot, although in an ideal reading the fable and the music would move
together. This emphasis on "The Comedian" as a poem about
language serves as a pertinent reminder that ambiguity, the
essential quality of poetic language, was Stevens' persistent
concern. In 1931 R. P. Blackmur wrote to him on this subject:
"I hadn't thought anyone, beyond a mere personal friend of
mine, and vaguely myself, had ever considered ambiguity as
the *explicit* virtue of poetry." [147] Blackmur then went on to
recommend and discuss William Empson's *Seven Types of
Ambiguity*, published the previous year. Obviously Stevens

had spoken of abiguity as the "*explicit* virtue of poetry" during their correspondence, and Blackmur rightly interpreted the word as meaning not "uncertainty" or "equivocation," but the precise control of alternative implications as discussed by Empson. Since the methods of verbal analysis developed by I. A. Richards, Empson, and their followers were necessary responses to the new poetic effects and new views of the poetic tradition delivered by contemporary writers, it is not surprising that Stevens had formulated his own notions of poetry's essential "ambiguity" long before Empson's study was begun.

∽

"The Comedian as the Letter C" unfolds a pattern of intellectual development which is radically "ambiguous" and susceptible to interpretation on many levels. It is a disguised autobiography, following the path of Stevens' own development as a poet and speculating on his future; therefore it contains covert references to many of his early works and enthusiasms. But as in any good autobiography the personal details have been rearranged and clarified to produce a portrait of *the* artist, a model of the necessary stages which any modern poet must pass through. On another and more general level, the poem may be read as a cultural history of the last two hundred years, Romanticism and its aftercourses. And at its deepest reaches the poem speaks of archetypal motions in the human mind and in the collective mind of society: as Stevens wrote to Hi Simons, "I suppose that the way of all mind is from romanticism to realism, to fatalism and then to indifferentism, unless the cycle re-commences and the thing goes from indifferentism back to romanticism all over again. . . . At the moment, the world in general is passing from the fatalism stage to an indifferent stage: a stage in which the primary sense is a sense of helplessness. But, as the world is a good deal more vigorous than most of the individuals in it, what the world looks forward to is a new romanticism, a new belief." [148]

The letter in which this comment occurs was written in response to Hi Simons' fine essay on " 'The Comedian as the Letter C': Its Sense and Significance," published in the Winter 1940 issue of the *Southern Review*. Stevens had gone carefully through both the poem and the essay, and his praise of Simons' interpretation was unstinting: "What you have said is correct, not only in the main but in particular, and not only correct but keen, with here and there a phrase that I envy: for example, 'the crude splendors of the contemporary.' " [149] Stevens' admiration for this reading of the poem was so complete, and so much in contrast to his usual dislike of explanations, that we must give the essay considerable weight. At the beginning of his explication Simons outlines the poem as "doctrinal" allegory:

> . . . The hero's development may be summarized as a passage from (1) juvenile romantic subjectivism, through (2) a realism almost without positive content, consisting merely in recognizing the stark realities of life, (3) an exotic realism, in which he sought reality in radical sensuousness, (4) a kind of grandiose objectivism, in which he speculated upon starting a sort of local-color movement in poetry, but which he presently saw as romantic, and finally, through (5) a disciplined realism that resulted in his accepting his environment on its own terms, so to speak, and (6) marrying and begetting children, to (7) an "indulgent fatalis[m]" and skepticism. The protagonist's marriage was actual but also symbolic of complete adjustment to society. From the point of view of the poem, this homemaking was an enriching experience, for which the hero was grateful; nevertheless, he was conscious that his eventual "return to social nature" was something of a capitulation to society.[150]

This is a faithful paraphrase of the poem's development, a model for the various lines of argument. It is upon this frame that we must stretch any interpretation of "The Comedian as the Letter C," and it should not be surprising that the more grandiose readings have become less interesting with time. The philosophical and political aspects traced in Simons' essay now seem out of date, while the fable of changing subjects and styles continues to grip us. As a dramatization of Crispin's— and Stevens'—evolving poetic "The Comedian" remains fresh and relevant, a fitting culmination to the growth of *Harmonium*. The poem is an idealized record of Stevens' poetic progress during the years 1914 to 1922, a *carnet de voyage*, and as such it claims our detailed attention.

I. *The World without Imagination* (CP 27–30). The poem opens with a note from Crispin's journal, which is immediately interpreted and mocked in the narrator's ironic high style.

> Nota: man is the intelligence of his soil,
> The sovereign ghost. As such, the Socrates
> Of snails, musician of pears, principium
> And lex. Sed quaeritur: is this same wig
> Of things, this nincompated pedagogue,
> Preceptor to the sea?

An ordinary man of "simple salad-beds," with a "barber's eye," Crispin embarks on his poetic voyage convinced that nature is but a spume that plays upon a ghostly paradigm of things, that the visible world can be transformed into a "mythology of self." The poetic diction used to describe this romantic illusion (perhaps the illusion of a whole "century of wind") is the style of the "fops of fancy," a deliberate parody of Stevens' own penchant for alliteration and the eccentric *mot juste*. It is Stevens' natural passion for sound and color freed from the restraints normally provided by form and dramatic context, the sort of language a poetic Robinson Crusoe might invent if thrown up on a deserted island with nothing but the twelve volumes of the *Oxford English Dictionary*. In "The Comedian" it is both the language of Crispin and the language which mocks Crispin, a subtle exercise in self-mockery on Stevens' part. The method is very much like that of Ezra Pound's *Hugh Selwyn Mauberley*, where Mauberley is both author and subject in many parts of the poem. In the opening lines of "The Comedian" many of the details of the traditional Crispin-figurĕ (his smattering of philosophy and Latin, his wig and mustachios, his impersonations of musician and teacher) are embedded in the language, so that the words on the page actually become Crispin.

Once at sea, Crispin pursues his "mythology of self" by trying to project his own personality into the inscrutable ocean. Seeking a romantic image of self in the mirror of the sea, Crispin beholds the actual valet and thane, "A skinny sailor peering in the sea-glass." His identity is "washed away by magnitude," annihilated in the mysterious sounds of the sea which he cannot interpret: "Polyphony beyond his baton's thrust."

The second movement of Part I opens with a question whose syntax is deliberately knotty and ambiguous.

> Could Crispin stem verboseness in the sea,
> The old age of a watery realist,
> Triton, dissolved in shifting diaphanes
> Of blue and green?

Is the "verboseness" Crispin's, or the sea's? The answer is that they are mirror-images of each other, products of a "wordy, watery age."

> A wordy, watery age
> That whispered to the sun's compassion, made
> A convocation, nightly, of the sea-stars,
> And on the clopping foot-ways of the moon
> Lay grovelling. Triton incomplicate with that
> Which made him Triton, nothing left of him,
> Except in faint, memorial gesturings,
> That were like arms and shoulders in the waves,
> Here, something in the rise and fall of wind

That seemed hallucinating horn, and here,
A sunken voice, both of remembering
And of forgetfulness, in alternate strain.

The once-powerful mythologies represented by Triton have
dwindled away, leaving only faint "memorial gesturings," intimations of a past order. The sea has become metaphor for
a "wordy, watery" poetic diction that dissolves all into "shift-
ing diaphanes," and can only whisper to the compassion of
the realistic sun while grovelling "on the clopping foot-ways
of the moon." Crispin is both victim and practitioner of a
watered-down romanticism, and at this point in the poem we
can begin to flesh out the disguised autobiography. Crispin
first appeared on the French stage in Scarron's *L'Ecolier de
Salamanque*, hence his "cloak / Of China, cap of Spain": but
if the cap of Spain belongs properly to Crispin, the cloak of
China is the mantle of exotic Oriental subjects that Stevens
wore in some of his earliest verse. Like Crispin, Stevens began
as a "watery" romanticist, product of a "century of wind,"
wearing the hand-me-down trappings of a greater age; and
the opening section of "The Comedian" is disguised self-
criticism. We are confronted with almost a secret level to the
poem, since most of Stevens' earliest work was unknown in
1922 and the organization of *Harmonium* along thematic lines
obscured the chronology of his more recent poetic development. The autobiographical pattern in "The Comedian" is
made up of essentially private material out of which Stevens
built his type of the modern artist, and it must be of secondary
importance in any full reading of the poem. But it is of the
highest importance in a tracing of Stevens' introspective voyage of poetic discovery, since it gives us a unique model for
the world of *Harmonium*.

The "ancient Crispin" annulled in the salty tempest of
mysterious experience, a Peter Parasol without true imagination, becomes an "introspective voyager" and sets out on his
"jaunt" to Carolina via Yucatan and Havana.

> The salt hung on his spirit like a frost,
> The dead brine melted in him like a dew
> Of winter, until nothing of himself
> Remained, except some starker, barer self
> In a starker, barer world, in which the sun
> Was not the sun because it never shone
> With bland complaisance on pale parasols,
> Beetled, in chapels, on the chaste bouquets.

In this bare world, far from the parasols and pastel colors of his early verse, Crispin faces "the veritable ding an sich" of a visible speech "noway resembling his," the voice of reality. "The last distortion of romance / Forsook the insatiable egotist."

> The imagination, here, could not evade,
> In poems of plums, the strict austerity
> Of one vast, subjugating, final tone.

At the end of Part I all of Crispin's poetic "ruses" are shattered, and he is face-to-face with the universal slate of reality. The trauma, reminiscent of Stevens' first attempt in "Phases" to deal with a reality other than that delivered by stale convention, leaves the valet-artist helpless.

II. *Concerning the Thunderstorms of Yucatan* (CP 30–33). The scene now shifts from the "strict austerity" which closed Part I, a tone like that in "Domination of Black," to luxurious Yucatan, where "the Maya sonneteers" are still evading the bright reality around them through the use of stale poetic conventions ("As if raspberry tanagers in palms, / High up in orange air, were barbarous"). But Crispin, "fresh from discoveries of tidal skies," can find no comfort in the commonplace, just as Stevens found most of the "local color" work of his American contemporaries irrelevant. Penetrated by the "savage color" of the tropics, the poet who had once spoken of autumn with "decorous melancholy" and written "his couplet yearly to the spring" finds that his enlarged apprehension

has made him "intricate . . . and difficult and strange." Like
the Stevens of 1914–15, who experimented in the bizarre and
grotesque and wrote aesthetic "fables," Crispin moves toward
"an aesthetic tough, diverse, untamed, / Incredible to prudes,
the mint of dirt, / Green barbarism turned paradigm." This
new poetry of "elemental potencies and pangs," an "indigenous" art, reminds us of the Stevens of "Primordia," and
especially of his first successful poems on the South.

> The fabulous and its intrinsic verse
> Came like two spirits parleying, adorned
> In radiance from the Atlantic coign,
> For Crispin and his quill to catechize.

The new reality absorbed into Crispin's poetry is so lush, so
full of primary colors and living forms, that it almost over-
whelms itself: "That earth was like a jostling festival / Of
seeds grown fat, too juicily opulent, / Expanding in the
gold's maternal warmth." The joy of this new contact with
primordial things was such that Crispin, like Stevens, experimented with pure sound and rhythm, a momentary *jeu d'esprit*
which the poet dismisses in a sly aside.

> The affectionate emigrant found
> A new reality in parrot-squawks.
> Yet let that trifle pass.

But these attempts at an indigenous poetry failed, because
they too became evasions of reality. Stevens dismisses them
affectionately but without regret: "So much for that. . . .
let that trifle pass."

A tropic thunderstorm containing the "note of Vulcan," the
quintessential force that Crispin has been imitating at a safe
remove, drives the valet-poet into the cathedral, where this
"connoisseur of elemental fate" kneels with the rest and broods
upon the storm's proclamation:

> The storm was one
> Of many proclamations of the kind,

> Proclaiming something harsher than he learned
> From hearing signboards whimper in cold nights
> Or seeing the midsummer artifice
> Of heat upon his pane.

Here, as at several other points in the poem, the mask of the *persona* drops away and we hear the elegiac voice of Stevens himself. The more delicate intimations of elemental things, expressed here in the language of "Sunday Morning," cannot satisfy a valet who seeks to own "the note of Vulcan." Crispin feels the power of the "polar" north, and departs for the Carolinas.

III. *Approaching Carolina* (CP 33–36). Crispin's progress from Yucatan to Carolina is a figure of the "sweating changes" which his creator went through during the last stage in the growth of *Harmonium*. Crispin is a "fagot" (in the double sense of sacrificial victim and impostor) in the "lunar fire" of imagination, which itself both purifies and deceives. He voyages toward an imagined North which will satisfy his new austerity, a world of stripped reality like that of "The Snow Man," and in his mind even the change of seasons is informed by winter's gauntness.

> The spring came there in clinking pannicles
> Of half-dissolving frost, the summer came,
> If ever, whisked and wet, not ripening,
> Before the winter's vacancy returned.
> The myrtle, if the myrtle ever bloomed,
> Was like a glacial pink upon the air.
> The green palmettoes in crepuscular ice
> Clipped frigidly blue-black meridians,
> Morose chiaroscuro, gauntly drawn.

This torturous progress toward the North, like Stevens' poetic progress as he neared the completion of *Harmonium*, is a matter of false-starts and self-denials. (Havana is never mentioned, perhaps to underline the difficulty of the voyage; but it seems more likely that Havana is a vestige from a suppressed section in "From the Journal of Crispin.) The self-denials of Crispin are like Stevens' austere rejections of the many poems that remained in manuscript or on the pages of the little magazines.

> How many poems he denied himself
> In his observant progress, lesser things
> Than the relentless contact he desired;
> How many sea-masks he ignored . . .
> And what descants, he sent to banishment!

At times the "Arctic moonlight" gave to Crispin "the blissful liaison, / Between himself and his environment, / Which was, and is, chief motive, first delight, / For him, and not for him alone." But at other times it seemed a perverse illusion, "Wrong as a divagation to Peking" (perhaps a covert allusion to Stevens' divagation in *Three Travelers Watch a Sunrise*). For Crispin the aspiring realist, that "niggling nightingale," moonlight was "an evasion, or, if not, / A minor meeting, facile, delicate."

Out of these "sweating changes" between the poles of his temperament Crispin evolved a master metaphor which can be applied to the final form of *Harmonium*.

> Thus he conceived his voyaging to be
> An up and down between two elements,
> A fluctuating between sun and moon,
> A sally into gold and crimson forms,
> As on this voyage, out of goblinry,
> And then retirement like a turning back
> And sinking down to the indulgences
> That in the moonlight have their habitude.

The poet of *Harmonium* fluctuates between sun and moon, and his poems when taken together describe a cycle of constant change which encompasses sun and moon, North and South, the real and the imagined, thereby giving to change the form of permanence. But such final resolutions were beyond the horizon of the valet-poet, and Crispin tossed

> Between a Carolina of old time,
> A little juvenile, an ancient whim,
> And the visible, circumspect presentment drawn
> From what he saw across his vessel's prow.

As Crispin approaches Carolina, a poet-hero now stripped to essentials, the "moonlight fiction" of his juvenile imagination disappears. It is springtime, a time "abhorrent to the nihilist / Or searcher for the fecund minimum": the illusion of a land in which fecund change can be transformed by the boreal imagination is shattered. As Crispin's ship moves up-river he inhales the actual smells of the steaming land, and all these "arrant stinks" help him to "round his rude aesthetic out." It is the final "curriculum for the marvelous sophomore."

> He gripped more closely the essential prose
> As being, in a world so falsified,
> The one integrity for him, the one
> Discovery still possible to make,
> To which all poems were incident, unless
> That prose should wear a poem's guise at last.

A poetry of life's prose is the final but unachieved ideal.

IV. *The Idea of a Colony* (CP 36–40). Part IV opens with another plain entry from Crispin's journal, a reversal of the notation which began the poem. "Nota: his soil is man's intelligence." This plain talk in the language of the ordinary man closes the book of moonlight, and announces a new direction for "The Comedian as the Letter C."

> That's better. That's worth crossing seas to find.
> Crispin in one laconic phrase laid bare
> His cloudy drift and planned a colony.

Exit the mental moonlight, exit lex,
Rex and principium, exit the whole
Shebang. Exeunt omnes.

At this point in the poem the allegory of Stevens' poetic
career ends, and is replaced by speculation on the future which
takes a "doctrinal" form. Like Pound's *Hugh Selwyn Mauberley*, "The Comedian" divides into two complementary sections, each with a different dramatic context. Just as the first
half of *Mauberley* gives the fictional history of a *persona* based
obliquely on the actual experiences of Pound in London, so
the first half of "The Comedian" is a disguised history of how
Crispin-Stevens wrote *Harmonium*, cast in mock-heroic and
ironic forms which reveal the roles that a modern poet must
play. The second half of *Mauberley*, on the other hand, dramatizes an imaginary career for Mauberley quite different from
that of his creator, one which stands in ironic contrast to the
actual achievement of E. P. "The Comedian as the Letter C"
does not follow the exact strategy of *Mauberley* in its second
half, but there is a separation of the poet from his *persona*.
The Crispin who settles down to marriage and children is
completing a cycle of personal and artistic development that
Stevens had not yet completed, and although the last three
parts of "The Comedian" do foreshadow some aspects of
Stevens' later life, the designs must be taken as theoretical or
speculative. Beginning with "The *Idea* of a Colony," Crispin
and the poem move into the realm of social possibilities, and
the hero's investigation of life as poetry re-enacts many of
the "fluctuations" earlier disclosed in his poetic progress.

Briefly, Part IV fleshes out an ideal colony where "his soil
is man's intelligence." "To make a new intelligence prevail,"
Crispin rejects the "appointed power" of fiction and makes his
"first central hymns, the celebrants / Of rankest trivia, tests
of the strength / Of his aesthetic, his philosophy," deliberately
anti-poetic. Upon the dogmatic premise that "The natives of
the rain are rainy men," he projects an ideal colony where

> The man in Georgia waking among pines
> Should be pine-spokesman. The responsive man,
> Planting his pristine cores in Florida,
> Should prick thereof, not on the psaltery,
> But on the banjo's categorical gut,
> Tuck, tuck, while the flamingoes flapped his bays.

Each product of the soil should have its own intelligence, its own celebration: "The melon should have apposite ritual, / Performed in verd apparel, and the peach, / When its black branches came to bud, belle day, / Should have an incantation." The preciosity of these ideals, which are actually burlesques of certain tendencies in Stevens' early poetic, should alert us that Crispin has once more swung unconsciously toward stale romance. The ritual of the peach and incantation of the melon bring us back to where the first half of the poem began.

> These bland excursions into time to come,
> Related in romance to backward flights,
> However prodigal, however proud,
> Contained in their afflatus the reproach
> That first drove Crispin to his wandering.

Having sunk once more into "fictive flourishes," Crispin must become a less ambitious realist.

V. *A Nice Shady Home* (CP 40–43). As the title indicates, a chastened Crispin subsides into the pleasures of the commonplace, the easy rhythms of the text of life that no longer seem, as in "The Man Whose Pharynx Was Bad" (CP 96), the "malady of the quotidian." He turns to "salad beds" again, and like Candide tends his own garden, but with the added satisfactions of a wife and nature's pleasures. Poetry is no longer needed, since "the words of things entangle and confuse." To contemplate a plum is to be a realist of nature's text: "The plum survives its poems." "Fugal requiems" and "a tragedian's testament" hold no appeal for Crispin, and as the poem approaches his quotidian contentment through a series of rhetorical questions the diction falls into simplicity.

> What is one man among so many men?
> What are so many men in such a world?
> Can one man think one thing and think it long?
> Can one man be one thing and be it long?
> The very man despising honest quilts
> Lies quilted to his poll in his despite.
> For realists, what is is what should be.

Unlike the quotidian of "The Man Whose Pharynx Was Bad" (CP 96) or "Last Looks at the Lilacs" (CP 48–49), which "saps" our energy and delight, the quotidian Crispin embraces is a part of nature's cycles. Part V ends with a lusty passage that expresses Crispin's acceptance of the world as fact, with only a final grace-note of haunting regret.

> But the quotidian composed as his,
> Of breakfast ribands, fruits laid in their leaves,
> The tomtit and the cassia and the rose,
> Although the rose was not the noble thorn
> Of crinoline spread, but of a pining sweet,
> Composed of evenings like cracked shutters flung
> Upon the rumpling bottomness, and nights
> In which those frail custodians watched,
> Indifferent to the tepid summer cold,
> While he poured out upon the lips of her
> That lay beside him, the quotidian
> Like this, saps like the sun, true fortuner.
> For all it takes it gives a humped return
> Exchequering from piebald fiscs unkeyed.

For Crispin the quotidian "saps like the sun," returning in ample measure the strength it draws out, and only the ex-quisitely mannered final line—Stevens' favorite example of the letter "c" as an actor in the poem—reminds us through its music of the fictive world Crispin has lost.

VI. *And Daughters with Curls* (CP 43–46). Crispin's four lively daughters, whom Frank Kermode has identified with the four seasons,[151] take the place of poems, "Leaving no room upon his cloudy knee, / Prophetic joint, for its diviner young." Having returned to social nature, Crispin must be content— and is content—to see his "buffo" life continue in them, "four more personae." Helen Vendler is certainly right when she detects a "sexual flinching" in Stevens' description of the "ostentatious lustiness" of the second daughter, and "revulsion" in his picture of the baby ("All din and gobble, blasphemously pink").[152] The language of Part VI seems to draw away from its "doctrine," as Stevens exhibits an unconscious revulsion at the fate he has given to Crispin. It is as if he were assenting to a theory of life in the "design" of Part VI, but rejecting that theory in the "form." Here alone does the poem appear to speak "one language in its narrative plot, another in the success or failure of its rhetoric."

At the conclusion of "The Comedian as the Letter C," Crispin concocts "doctrine from the rout" of action and language.

> The world, a turnip once so readily plucked,
> Sacked up and carried overseas, daubed out
> Of its ancient purple, pruned to the fertile main,
> And sown again by the stiffest realist,
> Came reproduced in purple, family font,
> The same insoluble lump. The fatalist
> Stepped in and dropped the chuckling down his craw,
> Without grace or grumble.

Crispin's homey anecdote, "Invented for its pith, not doctrinal / In form though in design," can be interpreted in two different ways. If Crispin is a heroic realist, as he sees himself to be, then the anecdote must be scored in "those portentous

accents, syllables, / And sounds of music coming to accord /
Upon his lap, like their inherent sphere," the music of his
daughters and the seasons they represent. But if he is only a
valet, "if the music sticks, if the anecdote / Is false, if Crispin
is a profitless / Philosopher, beginning with green brag, / Concluding fadedly," then what does it matter, since as in all
comedies the "relation comes, benignly, to its end?" "The
Comedian as the Letter C" ends with a choice between heroism
and mock-heroism, between the fable and its telling, and the
final detached line—"So may the relation of each man be
clipped"—wryly combines the cutting-short of the tale with
the original image of the comic barber.

The second half of "The Comedian" is less successful than
the first, partly because it lacks the thrust of autobiography,
but also because the ironic interplay between language and
subject becomes less functional. The poem is too long ·for
such a mannered and exacting style, and by 1938 Stevens was
thinking of eliminating it from a projected volume of collected
verse, since it had "gathered a good deal of dust." [153] No other
major poem is so much the property of *Harmonium*, where
it acts as center and summation, and so little an organic part
of "The Whole of Harmonium." A continuing respect for the
integrity of *Harmonium* must have been Stevens' chief motive
for retaining the poem, along with a sentimental memory of
what its composition had meant to the "exhausted realist" of
1922. At the end of "Anecdote of the Abnormal" (OP 23–24),
which Stevens must have written in 1922 and then rejected,
the poet breaks off his feeble variations on the stale theme of
colors and identity to invoke the hero of his mock-epic:

> Because new colors make new things
> And new things make old things again . . .
> And so with men.
>
> Crispin-valet, Crispin-saint!
> The exhausted realist beholds

> His tattered manikin arise,
> Tuck in the straw,
> And stalk the skies.

Here Stevens, not Crispin, has become the "exhausted realist," while his minuscule *persona* rises before him in an apotheosis which is both comic and invigorating.

VIII

Academic Discourses

Having postponed the publication of a volume of verse until his forty-fourth year, Stevens was determined to exercise "the most fastidious choice" in making a selection from his earlier work,[154] and he naturally threw the balance of the volume toward the poems of recent years. The years 1921–22 had been extraordinarily productive, yielding nearly half the material in the first edition of *Harmonium*, and when Stevens wrote to Harriet Monroe of his dissatisfaction with many of the poems he was referring mainly to his earlier works:

> All my earlier things seem like horrid cocoons from which later abortive insects have sprung . . . the reading of these outmoded and debilitated poems does make me wish rather desperately to keep on dabbling and to be as obscure as possible until I have perfected an authentic and fluent speech for myself.[155]

The writing of "The Comedian as the Letter C" had left him with a taste for the long poem, for doing "long stretches at a time," [156] but in the months after the completion of *Harmonium* Stevens' poetic activity began to decline. This falling off into the virtually silent years of 1925–30 had many causes, some of them personal; it is always difficult to explain the dry stretches in a poet's career. However, one thing is clear: after the process of self-examination involved in writing "The

Comedian as the Letter C" and selecting the poems for *Harmonium*, Stevens grew dissatisfied with even his latest theories and styles; yet he had great difficulty in finding the "authentic and fluent speech" which would take their place.

Three poems which appeared in the year after the publication of *Harmonium* (September 1923) compose a striking image of the uncertainty and depression that accompanied Stevens' efforts at a new speech.[157] "Red Loves Kit" (OP 30–32) was evidently to have been a long poem on the theme of elemental emotions between man and woman, a sort of latter-day "Le Monocle de Mon Oncle" cast in the fifteen-line meditative form of "Sunday Morning." The first stanza, after a flat opening, builds to a promising conclusion:

> Your yes her no, your no her yes. The words
> Make little difference, for being wrong
> And wronging her, if only as she thinks,
> You never can be right. You are the man.
> You brought the incredible calm in ecstasy,
> Which, like a virgin visionary spent
> In this spent world, she must possess. The gift
> Came not from you. Shall the world be spent again,
> Wasted in what would be an ultimate waste,
> A deprivation muffled in eclipse,
> The final theft? That you are innocent
> And love her still, still leaves you in the wrong.
> Where is that calm and where that ecstasy?
> Her words accuse you of adulteries
> That sack the sun, though metaphysical.

The stanza form, which combines the formality of the blank verse in "Sunday Morning" with the changing pace of the inner rhymes in "Le Monocle," seems adequate to the kind of sustained development found in those earlier poems, and the second part of "Red Loves Kit" does indeed begin such a development. But in the third and last stanza Stevens abandons his exploration of the "convulsive harmony" between man and woman, and tries to round the poem off with a complex twelve-line image of crows in moonlight followed by an appeal to the "galliard," the "milord," of the previous stanzas:

> And you, good galliard, to enchant black thoughts
> Beseech them for an overpowering gloom.
> It will be fecund in rapt curios.

The intent is obvious: to provide an elaborate summary image, as at the end of "Le Monocle," which will correspond to the mood of the lover. But the resemblance is not successful; the dramatic situation between man and woman has not been explored sufficiently to allow for such an ending, and the final Crispin-like line is a confession of failure. Like the deliberately trivial title, which is supposed to point up ironic resemblances between ordinary lovers and the grand lovers of the poem, it simply does not work. "Red Loves Kit" is a *pastiche*, almost self-imitation: the poem stands on the page as a ruin of former achievements.

"Academic Discourse at Havana" was written out of Stevens' visit to Havana in February 1923. In a long letter to his wife, full of delight in the sights and sounds of the place, Stevens mentions a Chinaman who came up to him on the street "with a big box swung over his shoulder and said 'Hot Peanuts!,'" the comic prototype for the "mythy goober khan" in the poem.[158] The contrast between the sensuous enthusiasm of Stevens' letter and the somber tones of the poem is striking, and shows how far he had moved from the world of "The Emperor of Ice-Cream." "Academic Discourse" (originally "Discourse in a Cantina at Havana") was begun in 1923 on commission, designed for a "collection of poems by various poets" which never materialized, and was "considerably longer" in that vanished early form.[159] Stevens then cut it down for magazine publication in late 1923, and it was reprinted without change in *Hound and Horn* for Fall 1929. When Stevens expanded *Harmonium* in 1930 he did not include the poem, "since it seems to be cramped," [160] but no changes were made when it was finally included in the first edition of *Ideas of Order* (1935). Stevens' continuing interest in the poem makes it an important link between *Harmonium* and the verse of the 1930's. With its darker tones and subdued emotions, "Academic Discourse at Havana" harmonizes closely with the elegiac pieces in *Ideas of Order*, and reminds us of how early Stevens was reacting against the gauds of *Harmonium*. His progress from 1923 to 1935 was slow and tentative, free of the dramatic turning-points dear to biographers, and "Academic Discourse" easily spans the years.

"Academic Discourse at Havana" (CP 142–45) is a poem about decadence, the decay of the seasons reflecting man's separation from nature and his loss of the great coordinating mythologies. Life is an "old casino," the swans that once "warded the blank waters of the lakes" are perishing. But just as the circus imagery borrowed from Laforgue and the poet-swan derived from the Symbolist tradition are made uniquely Stevens' own, so that our thoughts of "sources" drop away, so the poet's attitude toward this decadence is uniquely his. Unlike most American writers, Stevens does not eulogize a lost mythology, or regret that "the sustenance of the wilderness / Does not sustain us in the metropoles." He will accept the "metropoles" if they are our fate, and will celebrate the "grand decadence" of the present, not as a connoisseur of decadence in the manner of the 'nineties but as an unsentimental realist who knows that we live in "an old chaos of the sun." In this the poem does not differ from many of Stevens' earlier works; yet it has a more somber tone than most of *Harmonium*, and its discourse on the poet's role is subtly different. Just as the language of its last movement anticipates that of "The Idea of Order at Key West," so the aesthetic viewpoint seems more congenial to the later *Ideas of Order*.

"Canaries in the morning, orchestras / In the afternoon, balloons at night." Part I of "Academic Discourse" begins by contrasting these gauds with the darker superstitions of another climate or another age, "nightingales, / Jehovah and the great sea-worm." In the "metropoles" we are not sustained by elemental things. Instead, as Part II declares:

> Life is an old casino in a park
> The bills of the swans are flat upon the ground.
> A most desolate wind has chilled Rouge-Fatima
> And a grand decadence settles down like cold.

We live in a time like the death of the year, the summer-house of the imagination swept by chilling realities. The swans, now exhausted and part of the landscape, were once the proud subjects for generations of myth-makers. In four seasonal movements which mark stages in the history of man's myth-making, Stevens traces dispassionately and sometimes ironically man's relation to the swans. In the beginning, before "the chronicle / Of affected homage foxed so many books," the swans were part of the fabulous landscape, arraying the "twilights of the mythy goober khan." But then the toil of thought made the swans part of man's world, projecting our feeling into them: "The indolent progressions of the swans / Made earth come right; a peanut parody / For peanut people." Not content with this domesticating of nature, a later age in the summer-like plenitude of the imagination made an "urgent, competent, serener myth," perhaps the romantic swan of Mallarmé or Yeats, but this too "Passed like a circus." That age was broken when "Politic man ordained / Imagination as the fateful sin." Now the poet must find world enough in ordinary things, "Grandmother and her basketful of pears."

> The burgher's breast,
> And not a delicate ether star-impaled,
> Must be the place for prodigy, unless
> Prodigious things are tricks.

The historical cycle has led us to where the poem began, but with a subtle darkening in the setting: "Life is an old casino in a wood."

Part IV muses on the "function of the poet" in such a landscape. Is his work the equivalent of canaries and orchestras and balloons, to enliven the old casino with his sounds and colors? The answer is not the usual unequivocal "no," since Stevens knows our need for baubles and distractions. But the poet must do more, as speaker for all of us:

> His rarities are ours: may they be fit
> And reconcile us to our selves in those
> True reconcilings, dark, pacific words,
> And the adroiter harmonies of their fall.

"Close the cantina." The moonlit night is "older than its oldest hymn, / Has no more meaning than tomorrow's bread," yet the poet must speak of it if he is to reconcile us to ourselves. "Academic Discourse at Havana" mounts to its Yeatsian close in an effort to justify the poet's words:

> This may be benediction, sepulcher,
> And epitaph. It may, however, be
> An incantation that the moon defines
> By mere example opulently clear.
> And the old casino likewise may define
> An infinite incantation of our selves
> In the grand decadence of the perished swans.

The poet's speech may simply be a ceremonial form to ease our desolation, "benediction, sepulcher, / And epitaph." Yet it could be a true "incantation," a responsive inner singing, telling of our immediate lives with all the clarity and realistic compassion of moonlight that is "not yellow but a white." Just as the image of the old casino and its perished swans is "an infinite incantation of our selves," so the poet may reconcile us to our selves by embodying that image in "dark, pacific words."

"Academic Discourse at Havana" is not wholly successful, and it is easy to see why Stevens treated it with ambivalence: publishing the poem twice in journal form, withholding it from the second edition of *Harmonium*, then finally adding it to the canon in *Ideas of Order*. The structure is indeed "cramped," especially in the third part, where the history of man's myth-making is diffuse and imprecise compared to the pithy elegance of stanza III in "Sunday Morning." This movement of the poem was probably longer and more detailed in the original version, and in cutting it Stevens succeeded merely in cramping his argument. There are also cross-rubs of tone which work against the poem as a whole: the circus imagery and comic touches undermine, rather than reinforce, the meditation of Part IV. The atmosphere of Parts I to III is very much a " 'twenties" atmosphere, an unsentimental, flamboyant, almost raffish acceptance of decadence. The times are pressing in on Stevens, and on the fastidious aloofness of *Harmonium*. In this aspect, as in so many others, "Academic Discourse at Havana" is a shaky bridge between two stages in Stevens' poetic development. When compared with the brilliant and controlled "Sea Surface Full of Clouds," it may seem an unsuccessful performance: but "Academic Discourse" contained within it the germ of things to come, while "Sea Surface Full of Clouds" did not.

In October 1923 Stevens and his wife celebrated the publication of *Harmonium* by taking a cruise to California, via Havana and the Panama Canal, and late that month they passed through the Gulf of Tehuantepec, which became the setting for his last major poem of the 1920's. "Sea Surface Full of Clouds" is an extraordinary performance in every way, an exhibition of linguistic virtuosity which is something of a *coup de théâtre* in Stevens' poetic voyage. Anthologists have been attracted by its symmetrical design and overwhelming technical brilliance, qualities which thrust themselves upon the reader and mask the poem's essential exhaustion. For Stevens seems to have written "Sea Surface Full of Clouds" out of an exhausted imagination, with the intricate forms and elaborate word-play serving an almost ritualistic function: a ritual to revive his flagging interest in poetry. Many critics have seen the poem as the great triumph of Stevens' early verse, but if a victory it was a pyrrhic one. Beneath its brilliant surface the poem speaks of personal enigmas and artistic dilemmas, and before our eyes we see the poet painting himself into an aesthetic corner from which he will have great difficulty in escaping.

"Sea Surface Full of Clouds" (CP 98–102) consists of five scenes (five out of an infinite series of possible scenes) where the configurations of sea and sky both stimulate and reflect the moods of the poet.[161] The patterns linking the five sections together are so intricate, and so mechanical, that a reading of the poem is almost mesmeric. Each section opens with the same line, "In that November off Tehuantepec": the setting is always the same. The first stanza of each section describes how the essential sameness of the sea at night yielded to a day of different colors and moods, and this pattern of difference-within-sameness is reflected in the stanza form: the opening stanzas all have the same rhyme-scheme and rhyme-words, varying only in their internal structure. The second stanzas then elaborate on the setting with variants on the same metaphors ("rosy chocolate / And gilt umbrellas," "chop-house chocolate / And sham umbrellas," "porcelain chocolate / And pied umbrellas," "musky chocolate / And frail umbrellas," "Chinese chocolate / And large umbrellas"), which then find their responses in the "machine" of ocean. The repeated word-patterns and the rhyme-scheme, which is made up of identical rhyme-words as in the opening stanzas, continue the hypnotic effect of a monotonous sameness overlaid with surface differences.

In the third and fourth stanzas the projection of moods into the ocean's machine-like motion ("perplexed," "tense," "tranced," "dry," "obese") is completed, and the different sections of the poem begin to diverge from each other in interpretation of the scene and mood. The third and fourth stanzas, which pose questions about the power that transformed the amorphous sea and clouds into a particular scene, maintain the same rhyme-scheme (although not the same rhyme-sounds) until the final line of the fourth stanza, where the question that has been posed is answered in a line of precious French which evokes the nature of the scene's transfiguration. At the beginning of the poem these lines in French rhyme truly with their neighbors, but with the assonance of the third section ("clouds-*amour*") the pattern begins to break down, and as the imagination becomes suspect the rhyming in the later stanzas becomes less ordered. Stanzas five and six, which elaborate on the changes wrought by the infusing mind of the observer, are the most varied in the poem; but there is always a return to sameness, to the sea and sky upon which the imagination feeds, and this is accomplished in the last line of each section, which always rhymes truly with the last line of the preceding stanza. The effect of these intricate crosspatternings in rhyme and stanzaic form is a centripetal motion which works against the theme of refreshing transfigurations. The poem seems to collapse into itself. With thirty tercets and only thirty different rhymes, "Sea Surface Full of Clouds" possesses a claustrophobic form which belies the open gesture of its final lines.

The key to each scene in "Sea Surface Full of Clouds" is the answer given in French, where Stevens' love for "la légèreté, la grâce, le son et la couleur du français" is given free play.[162] By their very preciosity these lines declare that the balance of the poem is on the side of language and the imagination, not the "text" of the actual seascape. In the first section the transfiguring power seems wholly benign:

> Who, then, in that ambrosial latitude
> Out of the light evolved the moving blooms,
>
> Who, then, evolved the sea-blooms from the clouds
> Diffusing balm in that Pacific calm?
> *C'était mon enfant, mon bijou, mon âme.*

The seascape of section II is less comforting. The "malevolent sheen" of the ocean, lying in "sinister flatness," threatens the sea-blooms of reflected clouds: but still the imagination is a shaping force to be praised. "*C'était mon frère du ciel, ma vie, mon or*" that transformed the scene. By contrast, the moonlight imagination of section III, which changes all to pale uncertainty and dark mystery, evokes a more feminine fancy: "*Oh! C'était mon extase et mon amour.*"

Out of the "dry machine" of ocean, section IV weaves a pattern of sensuality: "musky chocolate," "loosed girdles," the "nakedness" of the green sea transformed by the "bluest seaclouds." The seascape is changed by a fortuitous and essentially arbitrary act of the mind, like the nonchalance with which "The Ordinary Women" flit from "dry catarrhs" to moonlight and guitars (CP 10).

> Who then beheld the figures of the clouds
> Like blooms secluded in the thick marine?
>
> Like blooms? Like damasks that were shaken off
> From the loosed girdles in the spangling must.
> *C'était ma foi, la nonchalance divine.*

Finally, the imagination of section V figures as a clown-comedian, turning the scene into a "turquoise-turbaned Sambo" juggling "sovereign clouds." The change comes not from the "cloudy-conjuring sea," but from the drollery and ingenuity of the mind: "*C'était mon esprit bâtard, l'ignominie.*" The poem has progressed from a transforming imagination which is soul to man, and brother of the sky, to a fancy which indulges in idle or comic transformations. The final promise of "fresh transfigurings of freshest blue" is never fulfilled.

"Sea Surface Full of Clouds" is usually thought of as a highpoint in *Harmonium*, one of Stevens' most persuasive statements of the imagination's powers; but it may also be seen as an artificial and somewhat pretentious effort to revive the exhausted imagination, a use of language as if it were a stimulant. In the passion which occasionally breaks through, as in stanza IV, there are tantalizing hints that the poem is a displaced and disguised treatment of emotions or occasions that never enter its public life. In the canon of *Harmonium*, "Sea Surface Full of Clouds" makes an interesting counter-statement to "Thirteen Ways of Looking at a Blackbird": in one the decorative imagination deals with a seascape of fluid color and motion, almost without form, while in the other an austere imagination works constantly from the concrete details of a perceived landscape. If "Thirteen Ways of Looking at a Blackbird" is like a series of Japanese prints rendering the same scene in different seasons or from different viewpoints, then "Sea Surface Full of Clouds" is more like Monet's Impressionistic renderings of Rouen cathedral in various lights, but with one crucial exception: whereas Monet tried to record the façade of Rouen cathedral as it struck the eye at different times of day, showing how light transforms the density and tactile details of the solid stone, Stevens took as his subject the most fluid of scenes, where the imagination could be sovereign over physical reality. Such an exercise actually ran counter to his evolving poetic, which pointed not in the direction of subjectivism but toward an imaginative realism, not toward the excesses of Monet but toward the Cézanne of Mont Sainte-Victoire. In a letter commenting on one of his late poems of the imagination, "Angel Surrounded by Paysans" (CP 496–97), Stevens told a critic that the "necessary angel" of the poem was the angel of reality.

> This is clear only if the reader is of the idea that we live in a world of the imagination, in which reality and contact with it are the great blessings. For nine readers out of ten, the necessary angel will appear to be the angel of the imagination and for nine days out of ten that is true, although it is the tenth day that counts.[163]

"I am the necessary angel of earth, / Since, in my sight, you see the earth again, / Cleared of its stiff and stubborn, man-locked set, / And, in my hearing, you hear its tragic drone . . ." (CP 496–97). This is exactly what "Sea Surface Full of Clouds," with its "man-locked set," cannot accomplish. Perhaps Stevens abandoned poetry for a time because his only visitations were from the angel of the imagination.

Notes to Part I

1. Quoted in William Carlos Williams, "Prologue to *Kora in Hell*," *Selected Essays of William Carlos Williams* (New York, 1954), pp. 12–13. First published in 1920, the "Prologue" is dated 1 September 1918. Omissions indicated by Williams; the original of the letter has not been located.

2. On 12 March 1923, Stevens wrote to Alfred A. Knopf: "I think that the following: THE GRAND POEM: PRELIMINARY MINUTIAE would be a better title for my book than its present one. It has a good deal more pep to it. If you agree, won't you change the title for me?" But evidently Knopf did not agree, and on May 18th Stevens wired: "USE HARMONIUM." (*Letters*, pp. 237–38).

3. Stevens' undergraduate verse has received thorough treatment in Robert Buttel, *Wallace Stevens: The Making of 'Harmonium'* (Princeton, 1967), Chapter I.

4. Many of these poems are quoted, in full or in part, by Buttel; others are to be found in *Letters*.

5. *The Autobiography of William Carlos Williams* (New York, 1951), pp. 134ff.

6. *Letters*, p. 320. WS to Ronald Lane Latimer, 6 May 1937.

7. *Letters*, p. 231. WS to Harriet Monroe, 28 October 1922.

8. *Letters*, p. 180. WS to his wife, 7 August 1913.

9. *Letters*, p. 165. 13 August 1914.

10. It seems likely that the exigencies of publishing separated "From a Junk" and "Home Again" from the other poems in the series. In the letter cited in the previous footnote Stevens speaks of "my stuff in The Trend" without any reference to two distinct groups of poems.

11. *Letters*, p. 157. WS to Elsie Moll, 19 August 1909.

12. *Letters*, p. 120. WS to Elsie Moll, 13 January 1909. It is interesting to compare this letter with Stevens' ironic treatment of "The Lake Isle of Innisfree" in his late poem, "Page from a Tale" (CP 421–23).

13. Buttel, p. 75. Prior to the "Little June Books" of 1908 and 1909 Stevens had thought of compiling a book of verse entitled "Vagabondia" (*Letters*, p. 106).

14. On 24 January 1909, Stevens sent Elsie Moll a short poem, later included in the 1909 "Little June Book," which he had "scribbled"—as he says in the letter containing the poem—"to the accompaniment of a line of Bliss Carman's" (*Letters*, pp. 128-29). And on January 31st he wrote to his fiancée that he had "skipped through a half-dozen little volumes of poetry by Bliss Carman" in order to refresh his imagination (*Letters*, p. 130).

15. *Letters*, p. 108. The poem is excerpted from a letter written shortly after 5 June 1908. Stevens retained a copy of the poem in the red folder which became a depository for those early verses he wished to save and perhaps revise.

16. *Letters*, p. 169.

17. For an account of these changes see Earl Miner, *The Japanese Tradition in British and American Literature* (Princeton, 1958), especially Chapter III.

18. *Egoist*, I (15 August 1914), 306.

19. *Letters*, pp. 137-38. WS to Elsie Moll, 18 March 1909.

20. For Stevens and the "Harvard Poets" of his generation, see Buttel, Chapters I and II; Joseph N. Riddel, *The Clairvoyant Eye* (Baton Rouge, 1965), p. 55; and Samuel French Morse, *Wallace Stevens: Poetry as Life* (New York, 1970), Chapter I.

21. Arthur Davison Ficke, *The Happy Princess and Other Poems* (Boston, 1907), p. 89.

22. Buttel, p. 70, and *Letters*, p. 137, fn. 6.

23. Buttel, p. 71.

24. F. S. Flint, "Imagisme," *Poetry*, I (March 1913), 199.

25. *Letters of Ezra Pound*, ed. D. D. Paige (London, 1951), p. 80.

26. "The History of Imagism," *Egoist*, II (1 May 1915), 71.

27. See fn. 1.

28. For the circumstances surrounding the publication of "Phases," and a reconstruction of the entire series Stevens sent to Miss Monroe, see Appendix B. Further information may be found in Harriet Monroe, *Poets and Their Art* (New York, 1932), pp. 39-45, and *A Poet's Life* (New York, 1938), pp. 342-43.

29. *Letters*, p. 117. WS to Elsie Moll, 10 January 1909.

30. In the typescript the last poem (XI) is followed by the pseudonym "Peter Parasol." Stevens used the name later as the title of one of the poems in "Pecksniffiana" (1919) which was excluded from *Harmonium* (OP 20).

31. Quoted in Buttel, p. 187.

32. Carl Van Vechten, "Rogue Elephant in Porcelain," *Yale University Library Gazette*, 38 (October 1963), 49. The poems Stevens read were "Cy Est Pourtraicte . . ." (CP 21), "Infernale" (OP 24-25), and "Dolls" (Buttel, p. 186).

33. It is difficult to reconstruct the group of poems rejected by Miss Monroe, but the "exploratory" verses which Stevens himself grew tired of would include: "To Madame Alda . . . ," "Dolls," "An Exercise for Professor X," "Headache," and "I have lived so long with the rhetoricians," all dating from 1914-15 and left in manuscript (Buttel, pp. 107, 186, 184, 188-189, 183); "The Silver Plough-Boy," "Bowl," and "Blanche McCarthy" (OP 6-7, 10); "The Florist Wears Knee-Breeches" and "Song" (see Appendix B); "Inscription for a Monument" (*Others*, March 1916; reprinted in *The Palm at the End of the Mind*, ed. Holly Stevens [New York, 1971], p. 17). Some of the more successful experiments—"Disillusionment of Ten O'Clock," "Tea," "Cy Est Pourtraicte. . . ," "Domination of Black," "Tattoo," "Six Significant Landscapes"—were included in *Harmonium*, both for their own sake and as a record of Stevens' poetic progress.

34. Ezra Pound, *The Spirit of Romance* (London, 1952), p. 14.

35. Ezra Pound, *Collected Shorter Poems* (London, 1968), p. 131.

36. Buttell, pp. 187–88.
37. Buttel, p. 183.
38. Buttel, p. 184.
39. Reprinted in T. E. Hulme, *Further Speculations,* ed. Sam Hynes (Lincoln, Nebraska, 1962), pp. 67–76.
40. *Ibid.,* p. 72. Italics mine.
41. Ezra Pound, *Umbra* (London, 1920), p. 125.
42. *Further Speculations,* pp. 72, 71, 73.
43. *Poetry,* I (March 1913), 199.
44. From *Adagia,* OP 161.
45. Buttel, p. 107. The typescript of "To Madame Alda. . . ," like that of "Domination of Black," bears the address 441 West 21st Street; the poem would seem to belong with the group published in *Others* for March 1916. Stevens left the West 21st Street address in May of that year.
46. Letter of 8 June 1916. Quoted in Buttel, p. 190.
47. Of the seven poems published in *Others* in March 1916, three were saved for *Harmonium:* "Domination of Black," "Tattoo," and "Six Significant Landscapes" (originally "Eight Significant Landscapes"; the rejected sections V and VII are printed in Buttel, p. 144). One other poem, "Bowl," was reprinted in *Opus Posthumous* (pp. 6–7), and "Inscription for a Monument" may be found in *The Palm at the End of the Mind* (p. 17). The remaining two—"The Florist Wears Knee-Breeches" and "Song"—are reprinted in Appendix B. Two other poems, "Blanche McCarthy" (OP 10) and "To Madame Alda . . ." (Buttel, p. 107), should probably be considered as part of the same phase in Stevens' work.
48. See Buttel, p. 144.
49. From "A Few Don'ts by an Imagiste," *Poetry,* I (March 1913), 200.
50. See *Letters,* p. 124. WS to Elsie Moll, 19 January 1909.
51. *Letters,* p. 42. Journal entry for 4 July 1900.
52. *Burnt Norton,* opening lines of Part V.
53. Joseph N. Riddel, *The Clairvoyant Eye* (Baton Rouge, 1965), p. 73.
54. *Letters,* p. 58. Entry for 10 August 1902.
55. William James, *Pragmatism* (New York, 1949), p. 123. The relevance of this passage to "Sunday Morning," and the general influence of James on Stevens, are discussed in an unpublished dissertation by Margaret L. W. Peterson, "Wallace Stevens and the Idealist Tradition: A Study of the Philosophical Background of Stevens' Poetry," Stanford University, 1965.
56. *Letters,* p. 183. WS to Harriet Monroe, 6 June 1915.
57. *Ibid.* WS to Harriet Monroe, 23 June 1915.
58. The facts about the two versions became known when the *Letters* were published in 1966, although a few scholars with access to the manuscripts had noted the situation earlier (not always with complete accuracy).
59. Reprinted in *In Defense of Reason* (New York, 1947), pp. 431–59.
60. Michel Benamou, "Wallace Stevens: Some Relations Between Po-

etry and Painting," in *The Achievement of Wallace Stevens*, ed. Ashley Brown and Robert S. Haller (New York, 1962), p. 240.

61. Buttel, p. 215. All of the poem that has survived is printed on pp. 214–16. Also reprinted in *The Palm at the End of the Mind*, pp. 12–14.

62. *Poetry*, VIII (June 1916), 160. Announcement of the award.

63. *Letters*, p. 194. WS to Harriet Monroe, 29 May 1916.

64. *Letters*, p. 194. WS to Harriet Monroe, 22 May 1916.

65. *Letters*, p. 291. WS to Ronald L. Latimer, 5 November 1935.

66. *Ibid.*

67. *Letters*, p. 194. WS to Harriet Monroe, 29 May 1916.

68. *Letters*, p. 200. WS to Bancel La Farge, 27 June 1917.

69. *Letters*, p. 216. WS to Harriet Monroe, 4 March 1920.

70. *Letters*, p. 203. WS to Harriet Monroe, 31 October 1917.

71. *Quarterly Review of Literature*, XVI (1969), 236–47. Reprinted in *The Palm at the End of the Mind*, pp. 24–34.

72. *Letters*, p. 195. WS to Harriet Monroe, 29 May 1916. The first quotation comes from a rejected section of "Eight Significant Landscapes" (Buttel, p. 144); the second occurs in the revised version of *Three Travelers*, but was never published.

73. *Letters*, p. 201. From a note that accompanied Stevens' letter of 27 June 1917 to his stage designer, Bancel La Farge.

74. Buttel, p. 70.

75. Laura Sherry to WS, 15 August 1917 (Stevens MSS). "The idea of making drama out of a picture and a preface appeals to me. I don't agree with Mr. Pach about its being a book review, it is drama."

76. *Letters*, p. 729. WS to Vincent Persichetti, 27 September 1951: "I gave up writing plays because I had much less interest in dramatic poetry than in elegiac poetry."

77. *Letters*, p. 189.

78. The first half of the series, "In the Northwest," was never reprinted in Stevens' lifetime; it is reproduced in its entirety in *Opus Posthumous* (7–9). Of the four poems entitled "In the South," numbers 6 and 8 (renumbered 7) end the sequence in OP. The original number 7 was reprinted in both editions of *Harmonium* under the title "In the Carolinas" (CP 4), while number 9 was reprinted in the 1931 edition of *Harmonium* as "Indian River" (CP 112). "To the Roaring Wind" is the final poem in *Harmonium* (CP 113).

79. "Valley Candle" (CP 51), "The Wind Shifts" (CP 83), "Gray Room" (reprinted in *The Palm at the End of the Mind*), and "Meditation" (uncollected; reprinted in Appendix B.) "Thirteen Ways" appeared almost simultaneously in *Others: An Anthology of the New Verse*, ed. Alfred Kreymborg (New York, 1917).

80. *Letters*, p. 251. WS to L. W. Payne, Jr., 31 March 1928.

81. Earl Miner, *The Japanese Tradition in British and American Literature* (Princeton, 1958), p. 196.

82. Ezra Pound, "Vorticism," *The Fortnightly Review*, 96 N.S. (1 September 1914), 463, 465, 467.

83. *Letters*, p. 340. WS to Henry Church, 1 June 1939.

84. *Letters*, p. 288. WS to Ronald Lane Latimer, 31 October 1935.

85. *The Oxford Anthology of American Literature,* ed. William Rose Benet and Norman Holmes Pearson (New York, 1938), p. 1325. From a note by Stevens on his poetry.

86. Stéphane Mallarmé, *Autobiographie: Lettre à Verlaine* (Paris, 1924). Letter of 16 November 1885.

87. First published in *Others: An Anthology of the New Verse* (New York, 1917) along with a gathering of old and new poems including "Thirteen Ways."

88. *Letters*, p. 209. WS to Carl Zigrosser, 10 July 1918. Originally "Earthy Anecdote" was the first part of a set entitled "Earthly Anecdotes," with "The Jack-Rabbit" (CP 50) as the second part.

89. *Letters*, p. 204. WS to Carl Zigrosser, 20 February 1918.

90. When "Earthy Anecdote" was reprinted in *Others* for July 1919, "Life Is Motion" was paired with it.

91. *Letters*, p. 202. WS to Harriet Monroe, 1 September 1917.

92. *Letters*, p. 205. WS to his wife, 14 March 1918.

93. The poems saved for *Harmonium* (1931) were "The Surprises of the Superhuman" (CP 98), "Negation" (CP 97–98), and "The Death of a Soldier" (CP 97). "Lunar Paraphrase" (CP 107) was published for the first time in 1931. For a discussion of the origins and significance of "Lettres d'un Soldat," see Samuel French Morse, "Lettres d'un Soldat," *Dartmouth College Library Bulletin,* 4 N.S. (December 1961), 44–50.

94. René Taupin, *L'Influence du symbolisme française sur la poésie américaine* (Paris, 1929), p. 276.

95. Morse, "Lettres d'un Soldat," p. 49.

96. The poems, in order of publication, are "Anecdote of Men by the Thousand" (CP 51–52), "Metaphors of a Magnifico" (CP 19), "Depression Before Spring" (CP 63), "Earthy Anecdote" (CP 3), "The Apostrophe to Vincentine" (CP 52–53), "Architecture for the Adoration of Beauty" (OP 16–18; published as "Architecture" in the first edition of *Harmonium*), "Nuances of a Theme by Williams" (CP 18), and "Anecdote of Canna" (CP 55).

97. See also "The Plot Against the Giant" (CP 6) and "Explanation" (CP 72–73), which had appeared in the October 1917 *Others: An Anthology of the New Verse.*

98. William Carlos Williams, *Collected Earlier Poems* (Norfolk, Conn., 1951), p. 140. From *Al Que Quiere!* (1917).

99. "Anecdote of the Prince of Peacocks" (Buttel, pp. 192–93), which is on the same paper and in the same hand as fragments of "Lettres d'un Soldat," and "Romance for a Demoiselle Lying in the Grass" (OP 23), which is on the same paper as "The Naked Eye of the Aunt," are manuscript poems which may be considered satellites of "Le Monocle."

100. *Letters*, p. 91. Journal entry of 27 April 1906.

101. See *Letters*, pp. 106 and 134.

102. Walter C. Arensberg, *Poems* (Boston and New York, 1914), pp. 100–101.

103. *Letters*, p. 390. WS to John Pauker, 3 June 1941.

104. *Letters*, p. 251.
105. *Letters*, p. 250.
106. *Letters*, p. 464. WS to Hi Simons, 18 April 1944, commenting on stanza VII of "Le Monocle."
107. As Robert Buttel has pointed out (p. 186), the manuscript poem "Dolls" (*c*. 1915) foreshadows stanza XI of "Le Monocle," especially in its opening lines: "The thought of Eve, within me, is a doll / That does what I desire, as, to perplex, / With apple-buds, the husband in her sire."
108. See *Letters*, p. 251 (WS to L. W. Payne, Jr., 31 March 1928), where Stevens denies that the "rose rabbi" stands for old age pursuing a philosophical ideal: "Not at all. One is a rose rabbi and pursues a philosophic ideal of life when one is young."
109. *Letters*, p. 230. WS to Harriet Monroe, 23 September 1922.
110. The "Pecksniffiana" series, which appeared in *Poetry* for October 1919, included: "Fabliau of Florida" (CP 23), "Homunculus et La Belle Étoile" (CP 25–27), "The Weeping Burgher" (CP 61), "Peter Parasol" (OP 20), "Exposition of the Contents of a Cab" (OP 20–21), "Ploughing on Sunday" (CP 20), "Banal Sojourn" (CP 62–63), "The Indigo Glass in the Grass" (OP 22), "Anecdote of the Jar" (CP 76), "Of the Surface of Things" (CP 57), "The Curtains in the House of the Metaphysician" (CP 62), "The Place of the Solitaires" (CP 60), "The Paltry Nude Starts on a Spring Voyage" (CP 5–6), "Colloquy with a Polish Aunt" (CP 84). Of these, "Peter Parasol" and "The Indigo Glass in the Grass" were excluded from *Harmonium*, while "Exposition of the Contents of a Cab" appeared only in the first edition. "Piano Practice at the Academy of the Holy Angels" (OP 21–22) properly belongs to the series, since it was set up in print for *Poetry* and then canceled at Stevens' request (see *Letters*, p. 214). The first draft of "Nomad Exquisite" (CP 95), which was not published until the 1923 *Harmonium*, dates from January 1919 (see *The Palm at the End of the Mind*, ed. Holly Stevens [New York, 1971], p. 401).
111. *Martin Chuzzlewit*, Chaps. II, VI.
112. Robert Buttel (pp. 126–28) has discussed the relation of this poem to Imagist works by Amy Lowell and H. D. Ironically, Stevens used his borrowings to express his discontent with the Imagist formula.
113. Norman Silverstein, "Stevens' 'Homunculus et la Belle Étoile,'" *The Explicator*, 13 (May 1955), item 40.
114. Quoted by Daniel Fuchs at the conclusion of his excellent analysis of the poem in *The Comic Spirit of Wallace Stevens* (Durham, N.C., 1963), pp. 132–35. Fuchs remarks (p. 134) that the imagination "out-Platos Plato."
115. *Letters*, p. 306. WS to Ronald Lane Latimer, 24 January 1936.
116. Quoted in John Unterecker, *Voyager: A Life of Hart Crane* (New York, 1969), p. 153.
117. "Invective against Swans" (an extension of "Banal Sojourn") and "Infanta Marina" (reminiscent of "The Paltry Nude . . .") were published in *Contact* for January 1921. "Lulu Gay" and "Lulu Morose," two trifling take-offs on a contemporary collection of anonymous poems

entitled *Lillygay*, were published in *Contact* later that year (see OP 26–27). The exceptions are "Cortège for Rosenbloom," which appeared in *Measure* for March 1921, and "The Man Whose Pharynx Was Bad," published in the *New Republic* for 14 September 1921.

118. See the controversy between Conrad Aiken and Louis Untermeyer over Untermeyer's *The New Era in American Poetry:* "The Ivory Tower—I and II," *The New Republic*, 19 (10 May 1919), 58–61.

119. *Letters*, p. 219.

120. Richard Ellmann, "Wallace Stevens' Ice-Cream," *Kenyon Review*, 19 (Winter 1957), 91. Ellmann provides a convincing reading of the entire poem.

121. *Letters*, p. 223. WS to William Stanley Braithwaite, 5 December 1921.

122. See *Letters*, p. 137 (18 March 1909), where Stevens speaks of "some antiquated musical instruments that were amusing."

123. "Sur Ma Guzzla Gracile" contained the following poems, in this order: "Palace of the Babies" (CP 77), "From the Misery of Don Joost" (CP 46–47), "The Doctor of Geneva" (CP 24), "Gubbinal" (CP 85), "The Snow Man" (CP 9–10), "Tea at the Palaz of Hoon" (CP 65), "The Cuban Doctor" (CP 64–65), "Another Weeping Woman" (CP 25), "On the Manner of Addressing Clouds" (CP 55–56), "Of Heaven Considered as a Tomb" (CP 56), "The Load of Sugar Cane" (CP 12), "Hibiscus on the Sleeping Shores" (CP 22–23). "The Man Whose Pharynx Was Bad" (CP 96) and "The Bird with the Coppery, Keen Claws" (CP 82), both published in late 1921, may be logically grouped with this series.

124. *Letters*, pp. 222–23. WS to Harriet Monroe, 29 October 1921.

125. *New Republic*, 28 (14 September 1921), 74. Reprinted in *The Palm at the End of the Mind*, pp. 51–52.

126. Although not published until June 1922, the style of "Stars at Tallapoosa" would seem to pre-date Stevens' work on "The Comedian as the Letter C."

127. R. P. Blackmur, "Examples of Wallace Stevens," in *Language as Gesture* (New York, 1952), p. 223.

128. *Letters*, p. 224. WS to Harriet Monroe, 21 December 1921.

129. Stevens MSS. Hervey Allen to WS, 20 April 1922.

130. *Letters*, p. 640. WS to Thomas McGreevy, 13 July 1949.

131. *Letters*, p. 230. WS to Harriet Monroe, 23 September 1922.

132. The "Schemata" are printed in Samuel French Morse, *Wallace Stevens: Life as Poetry* (New York, 1970), p. 129. A slightly different listing may be found in Morse, "Wallace Stevens, Bergson, Pater," in *The Act of the Mind*, ed. Roy Harvey Pearce and J. Hillis Miller (Baltimore, 1965), p. 73.

133. *Letters*, p. 227. WS to Gilbert Seldes, 3 April 1922 and 5 May 1922.

134. *The Dial* for July 1922 published "Bantams in Pine-Woods," "The Ordinary Women," "Frogs Eat Butterflies. . . ," "A High-Toned Old Christian Woman," "O Florida, Venereal Soil," and "The Emperor of Ice-Cream." The two "moonlight poems" that Seldes returned cannot

be surely identified, but they may have been two of the three that were first published in *Harmonium* ("Anecdote of the Prince of Peacocks," "The Virgin Carrying a Lantern," "Jasmine's Beautiful Thoughts underneath the Willow").

For the purposes of discussion I have grouped the shorter poems of this period as follows:

The Book of Moonlight

"The Ordinary Women" (CP 10–12)

"Hymn from a Watermelon Pavilion" (CP 88–89)

"Anecdote of the Prince of Peacocks" (CP 57–58)

"The Virgin Carrying a Lantern" (CP 71)

"Jasmine's Beautiful Thoughts underneath the Willow" (CP 79)

Revue

"New England Verses" (CP 104–6)

"Bantams in Pine-Woods" (CP 75–76)

"Frogs Eat Butterflies. Snakes Eat Frogs. Hogs Eat Snakes. Men Eat Hogs." (CP 78)

"A High-Toned Old Christian Woman" (CP 59)

"O Florida, Venereal Soil" (CP 47–48)

"Last Look at the Lilacs" (CP 48–49)

"The Emperor of Ice-Cream" (CP 64)

"Anecdote of the Abnormal" (OP 23–24)

"This Vast Inelegance" (OP 25–26)

"Saturday Night at the Chiropodist's" (OP 27–28)

"Mandolin and Liqueurs" (OP 28–29)

"The Shape of the Coroner" (OP 29–30)

"The Revolutionists Stop for Orangeade" (CP 102–3)

"Floral Decorations for Bananas" (CP 53–54)

"The Public Square" (CP 108–109)

"Sonatina to Hans Christian" (CP 109–10)

"In the Clear Season of Grapes" (CP 110–11)

"Two at Norfolk" (CP 111–12)

Of these poems, all were printed in the little magazines of 1922–23 or in the two editions of *Harmonium* except "Anecdote of the Abnormal" (OP 23–24), "This Vast Inelegance" (OP 25–26), and "Saturday Night at the Chiropodist's" (OP 27-28). "This Vast Inelegance" was rejected by at least one journal; Stevens tinkered with it a bit and then abandoned it, probably because he found the long fifteen-syllable lines and un-rhymed couplets a monotonous form.

135. Buttel, pp. 192-93. Reprinted in *The Palm at the End of the Mind*, p. 402. See fn. 99.

136. Buttel, p. 194.

137. "New England Verses" was complete in some form by mid-1922; on 14 July 1922 Stevens received a letter from Ridgely Torrence in which Torrence regretted that he could not find a place for the poem in the *New Republic* (Stevens MSS).

138. *The Collected Poems of W. B. Yeats* (New York, 1956), p. 31. "To the Rose Upon the Rood of Time" is the prelude to *The Rose*, and Stevens had read another poem in this volume, "The Lake Isle of Innisfree," as early as 1909 (*Letters*, p. 120. WS to Elsie Moll, 13 January 1909).

139. *Letters*, p. 231. WS to Harriet Monroe, 28 October 1922.

140. *Letters*, p. 778. WS to Renato Poggioli, 3 June 1953.

141. *Ibid.*

142. Helen Vendler, *On Extended Wings* (Cambridge, Mass., 1969), p. 38.

143. *Letters*, p. 640. WS to Thomas McGreevy, 13 July 1949.

144. Guy Davenport, "Spinoza's Tulips: A Commentary on 'The Comedian as the Letter C'," *Perspective*, 7 (Autumn 1954), 149-50. For a summary of various theories concerning the models for Stevens' Crispin, see Joseph N. Riddel, *The Clairvoyant Eye* (Baton Rouge, 1965), pp. 94-95, and especially fn. 42, p. 288, where Stevens is shown to have possessed a *History of Harlequinade* published in 1915.

145. This possible source has been explored by Samuel French Morse, "Wallace Stevens, Bergson, Pater," in *The Act of the Mind*, ed. Roy Harvey Pearce and J. Hillis Miller (Baltimore, 1965), pp. 74-75, and by Buttel, pp. 196-97.

146. *Letters*, pp. 351-352. WS to Hi Simons, 12 January 1940. See also p. 294 (WS to Ronald Latimer, 15 November 1935) and p. 778 (WS to Renato Poggioli, 3 June 1953).

147. Stevens MSS. R. P. Blackmur to WS, 2 December 1931.

148. *Letters*, p. 350. WS to Hi Simons, 12 January 1940.

149. *Ibid.*

150. Hi Simons, " 'The Comedian as the Letter C': Its Sense and Significance," in *The Achievement of Wallace Stevens*, ed. Ashley Brown and Robert S. Haller (New York, 1962), p. 98. Another extensive and illuminating reading of the poem may be found in Daniel Fuchs, *The Comic Spirit of Wallace Stevens* (Durham, N.C., 1963), pp. 31-61. A good summary of the poem's "doctrinal design" and of received critical opinion may be found in Ronald Sukenick, *Musing the Obscure* (New York, 1967), pp. 46-60.

151. Frank Kermode, *Wallace Stevens* (Edinburgh and London, 1960), p. 48.

152. Helen Vendler, *On Extended Wings* (Cambridge, Mass., 1969), p. 44.

153. *Letters*, p. 330. WS to Ronald Lane Latimer, 29 January 1938.
154. *Letters*, p. 232. WS to Harriet Monroe, 21 December 1922.
155. *Letters*, p. 231. WS to Harriet Monroe, 28 October 1922.
156. *Ibid.*
157. In order of publication, these are "Discourse in a Cantina at Havana" (*Broom*, November 1923), "Sea Surface Full of Clouds" (*The Dial*, July 1924), and "Red Loves Kit" (*Measure*, August 1924).
158. *Letters*, pp. 234–36. WS to his wife, 4 February 1923.
159. *Letters*, p. 335. WS to Hi Simons, 26 September 1938.
160. Unpublished letter from WS to R. P. Blackmur, 18 October 1930. Princeton University Library.
161. Excellent detailed analysis of the poem may be found in Joseph N. Riddel, " 'Disguised Pronunciamento': Wallace Stevens' *Sea Surface Full of Clouds*," *Texas Studies in English*, 37 (1958), 177–86. A condensed version of this analysis appears in *The Clairvoyant Eye* (Baton Rouge, 1965), pp. 44–47.
162. René Taupin, *L'Influence du symbolisme française sur la poésie américaine (1910–1920)* (Paris, 1929), p. 276. From a letter Stevens wrote to the author.
163. *Letters*, p. 753. WS to Sister M. Bernetta Quinn, 29 May 1952.

PART II

The Place of Poetry

T HE YEARS BETWEEN THE FIRST AND SECOND EDITIONS OF
Harmonium (1923–31) WERE A TIME OF GREAT ACTIVITY
in Stevens' personal and business lives. The birth in 1924 of his
only child, Holly, added new responsibilities, and made him
eager to establish financial security. As Holly Stevens has
pointed out in her edition of the *Letters,* working conditions
in the two-family house where Stevens lived were not good,
and the poet—like Crispin—spent a good part of his leisure
time tending his garden. Apparently "it was not a time or an
atmosphere conducive to creativity." [1] This is the period
Stevens was referring to in 1937 when he wrote a consoling
letter to Ronald Lane Latimer, who had published *Owl's Clover*
and was then closing The Alcestis Press:

> Giving up The Alcestis Press must be to you what
> giving up any idea of writing poetry would be to me.
> Nevertheless, a good many years ago, when I really was
> a poet in the sense that I was all imagination, and so
> on, I deliberately gave up writing poetry because, much
> as I loved it, there were too many other things I wanted
> not to make an effort to have them. . . . I didn't like
> the idea of being bedeviled all the time about money and

The Notes are to be found at the end of Part II, on page 296.

> I didn't for a moment like the idea of poverty, so I went
> to work like anybody else and kept at it for a good many
> years.[2]

There is no reason to doubt the substance of this declaration.
Years before, Stevens had told his fiancée that "I should like
to make a music of my own, a literature of my own, and
I should like to live my own life":[3] the labors of 1924-31
made it possible for him to do just that. Still, we may wonder
if the reasons given in the letter to Ronald Latimer tell a complete story. There is a certain irony in the recall of "when I
really was a poet," and the last chapters have shown that
Stevens, in "The Comedian as the Letter C" and the academic discourses which followed it, was working toward an
aesthetic impasse. "A change of style is a change of subject,"
as one of the *Adagia* puts it (OP 171), and Stevens had fallen
into a poverty of subjects. As he told Thomas McGreevy in
1950, after completing *The Auroras of Autumn*: "One grows
tired of being oneself and feels the need of renewing all one's
thoughts and ways of thinking. Poetry is like the imagination
itself. It is not likely to be satisfied with the same thing twice." [4]

Whatever the reasons may have been, only one poem—and
that a trifle—can be definitely attributed to the years 1925-
28.[5] Some of the new poems added to *Harmonium* in 1931
may have been written or revised during this period—"In the
Clear Season of Grapes" (CP 110-11) and "Two at Norfolk"
(CP 111-12) are the most promising candidates—but it is
more likely that they belong to the burst of poetic activity in
1921-23. Writing to R. P. Blackmur in October 1931 about
the new material added to the second edition of *Harmonium*,
Stevens remarked that "none of it was really new." [6] The first
definite signs of an awakening interest in verse are "The Sun
This March," published in the *New Republic* for 16 April
1930, and "Annual Gaiety," which appeared later that year in
Louis Untermeyer's anthology *Modern American Poetry* but
had been written before June 1929.[7] In these two poems of
the winter sun Stevens warmed himself into poetic life.

"Annual Gaiety" (OP 32–33) sings the delights of the winter sun, which gives solace enough by pinking "the ice-hard melanchole" with its "catholic" majesty. The exotic world of imagined Florida is flat and distasteful by comparison:

> Wherefore those prayers to the moon?
> Or is it that alligators lie
> Along the edges of your eye
> Basking in desert Florida?

The poem ends with an appeal to "Père Guzz," the father of "guzzly" delights:

> Père Guzz, in heaven thumb your lyre
> And chant the January fire
> And joy of snow and snow.

"The Sun This March" (CP 133–34) adapts the imagery and themes of "Annual Gaiety," but turns them into meditative couplets which are deeply confessional:

> The exceeding brightness of this early sun
> Makes me conceive how dark I have become,
>
> And re-illumines things that used to turn
> To gold in broadest blue, and be a part
>
> Of a turning spirit in an earlier self.
> That, too, returns from out the winter's air,
>
> Like an hallucination come to daze
> The corner of the eye. Our element,
>
> Cold is our element and winter's air
> Brings voices as of lions coming down.
>
> Oh! Rabbi, rabbi, fend my soul for me
> And true savant of this dark nature be.

The elegiac tone of this little poem was to become the ground-bass for *Ideas of Order*, as in "Sad Strains of a Gay Waltz" or "Anglais Mort à Florence." Like the "desert Florida" seen out of the corner of an eye in "Annual Gaiety," scenes that were once turned to gold by the blue imagination and became "part / Of a turning spirit in an earlier self" are now reilluminated by a colder light. Stevens told his Italian translator, Renato Poggioli, that he had always been attracted to the figure of the rabbi "because it is the figure of a man devoted in the extreme to scholarship and at the same time to making some use of it for human purposes." [8] Unlike the "dark rabbi" of youthful introspection invoked at the close of "Le Monocle de Mon Oncle," the rabbi of this poem is the late winter sun, a true savant of man's dark nature because he can redeem it from darkness and illuminate its world as a scrupulous scholar would gloss a text: "veracious page on page, exact" (CP 40). The mood of this poem, balanced between winter's darkness and spring's evanescent gold, and the almost metaphysical use of language (e.g. "conceive" in the second line), can be traced to parts of *Harmonium*, but the combination strikes a new if still minor note in Stevens' amassing harmony.

"The Sun This March" is the true prelude to *Ideas of Order*, but when Stevens prepared the second edition in 1936 he placed a recently composed poem, "Farewell to Florida," in the front as program-piece. This reversal of chronology has led to a general misapprehension of Stevens' poetic progress in the early 1930's. "Farewell to Florida" is a poetic manifesto of 1936, where the ship's voyage from Key West to a "leafless" North becomes an allegory of changes in style and subject. Its place at the head of *Ideas of Order* has encouraged the neat view that Stevens underwent a sudden transformation in the early 1930's, renouncing the gaudy South of *Harmonium* after a long silence and turning to the North of darker themes. Such a view falsifies both the complexities of *Harmonium* and the uneasy fluctuations which finally produced Stevens' major poems of the mid-1930's. After "The Sun This March" Stevens lapsed into silence again, telling Lincoln Kirstein in April 1931 that "nothing short of a coup d'état would make it possible for me to write poetry now," and he made the same confession to

Harriet Monroe in August 1932: "Whatever else I do, I do not write poetry nowadays."[9]

The paucity of Stevens' work at this time may be seen in the way he salvaged old materials. The expansion of *Harmonium* in late 1930 caused him to sort through the published and unpublished poems not included in the first edition, and at Christmas 1930 he sent Harriet Monroe a poem "for yourself alone" which later became the third stanza of "The Woman Who Blamed Life on a Spaniard" (OP 35).[10] Sometime in 1931–32 the new journal *Contempo* asked Stevens for a contribution and he obliged with the three-stanza version of this poem (OP 34–35).[11] Embarrassed that he had given a poem to another journal after telling Miss Monroe that he had nothing for *Poetry*, Stevens sent her "another scrap," published in *Poetry* for October 1932.[12] This fragment, entitled "Good Man, Bad Woman" (OP 33), appears to be a stanza left over from the "Red Loves Kit" sequence of 1924. It has the same dramatic situation, the same language, and is cast in the fifteen-line "Sunday Morning" stanza. The three stanzas of "The Woman Who Blamed Life on a Spaniard" must also be from this series: the stanza form and diction are identical, and the address to the man in both poems is the same. The opening stanza of "The Woman Who Blamed Life on a Spaniard" will give the flavor of the entire sequence:

> You do not understand her evil mood.
> You think that like the moon she is obscured
> But clears and clears until an open night
> Reveals her, rounded in beneficence,
> Pellucid love; and for that image, like
> Some merciful divination, you forgive.
> And you forgive dark broachings growing great
> Night after night because the hemisphere
> And still the final quarter, still the rim,
> And still the impassioned place of it remain.
> If she is like the moon, she never clears

But spreads an evil lustre whose increase
Is evil, crisply bright, disclosing you
Stooped in a night of vast inquietude.
Observe her shining in the deadly trees.

It is highly probable that "Red Loves Kit," "Good Man, Bad Woman," and "The Woman Who Blamed Life on a Spaniard" are fragments from an abortive long poem which could have been begun before 1924, and that Stevens pillaged this material when new poems were lacking. The reasons for abandoning the long project are obvious. The meditative style of "Sunday Morning," so successful with a generalized theme, becomes embarrassingly personal when applied to the subject of discord and alienation between man and woman. Unlike the "autobiographical" poems of *Harmonium*, "Le Monocle de Mon Oncle" and "The Comedian as the Letter C," the poems of this series provide no defenses in sustained irony or a comic *persona*. What irony there is has a bitter and sporadic quality, and the attempts to import protective effects from "Le Monocle" are failures. Samuel French Morse is surely right in his suggestion that Stevens never republished these fragments "because their bitterness was 'personal' in precisely the way he thought poetry ought not to be." [13]

Two poems from 1932–33 reached the *Collected Poems*, "Autumn Refrain" and "Snow and Stars," and each testifies to a renewed interest in "the essential gaudiness of poetry," a phrase Stevens used in 1933 to explain why "The Emperor of Ice-Cream" was his favorite poem.[14] When taken in conjunction with "The Sun This March," they define the twin poles of *Ideas of Order*. "Autumn Refrain" (CP 160) is a mock-sonnet, without rhyme or division, and its rejection of the traditional sonnet form is part of its rejection of the "nightingale." The plain grackle of autumn has become the spokesman for the American sublime of today, replacing Keats' nightingale and all its antecedents. Keats' ode "To Autumn" is also ironically in the background. In deliberately hesitant and elliptical lines that anticipate the form of such later poems as "The Man on the Dump" (CP 201–203), Stevens recovers his full poetic power.

> The skreak and skritter of evening gone
> And grackles gone and sorrows of the sun,
> The sorrows of sun, too, gone . . . the moon and moon,
> The yellow moon of words about the nightingale
> In measureless measures, not a bird for me
> But the name of a bird and the name of a nameless air
> I have never—shall never hear. And yet beneath
> The stillness of everything gone, and being still,
> Being and sitting still, something resides,
> Some skreaking and skrittering residuum,
> And grates these evasions of the nightingale
> Though I have never—shall never hear that bird.
> And the stillness is in the key, all of it is,
> The stillness is all in the key of that desolate sound.

The repeated "sorrows of the sun, / The sorrows of sun" and "the moon and moon" define the difference between things as emblems and things in themselves: "The sorrows of the sun" and "the moon" are realities, "sorrows of sun" and "moon" are poeticisms. The "yellow moon," which was rejected in "Academic Discourse at Havana" (CP 144), is the moonlight of the nightingale and evasive romanticism, "the name of a bird and the name of a nameless air / I have never—shall never hear." The death of evening has taken away "the skreak and skritter" of the grackles, just as the death of Romanticism has taken away its trappings. Yet "something resides, / Some skreaking and skrittering residuum" that grates with its reality the "evasions of the nightingale." The "stillness of everything gone" is in the "key of that desolate sound," just as this poem is written in the key of the desolate minimum. I wish to know if I can live with what I know, and with nothing else: these words might be a motto for "Autumn Refrain." It is one of the great poems by a realist of the imagination, and its greatness is rooted in our sense of tradition, a tradition that the poem deliberately evokes and then denies. In his preface to William Carlos Williams' *Collected Poems, 1921–1931,* published in 1934 (OP 254–57), Stevens spoke of the "anti-poetic" strain in Williams (much to that poet's annoyance), but the term applies with much more force to Stevens himself. "Autumn Refrain" is an "anti-poetic" poem, which does not mean that it is "anti-romantic" in Stevens' terminology. As he says in the preface to Williams' poems, the "romantic temperament" may appear in a rejection of "the accepted sense of things" (OP 255); all poetry is necessarily an interaction of the real and the unreal, the anti-poetic and the sentimental. These points are worth remembering, since the definition of a necessary romanticism is one of the major themes of *Ideas of Order.* "Autumn Refrain" provides a starting point for that process of definition in its desolate music of "everything gone."

"Autumn Refrain" was written in 1931, and published in the Winter 1932 issue of *Hound and Horn.* It was followed by "Snow and Stars" (CP 133), written sometime in 1932 and published in June 1933, which celebrates the grackle—the nightingale of the minimal American sublime—with all the gaiety of an Elizabethan song. The poem opens with a play on the archaic word spiss ("thick, dense"), and ends with a Shakespearean refrain ("ding, ding, dong"). In between, the "robe of snow and winter stars" is wished to the devil as "ransom for the willow." The first stanza will show how "Snow and Stars" acts as a contrasting pendant to "Autumn Refrain":

> The grackles sing avant the spring
> Most spiss—oh! Yes, most spissantly.
> They sing right puissantly.

Here is the "essential gaudiness" needed to offset more meditative verse.

The years 1930–33 had been lean years for the country as well as for Stevens' poetry (a comparison that will seem less grotesque when *Owl's Clover* is considered), and the edge of what William Carlos Williams called "the knife of the times" can be felt in *Ideas of Order*. By the end of 1933 Stevens was entering another period of intense creativity like that which preceded the publication of *Harmonium*, and the poems of this period often reflect indirectly but unmistakably the impact of an impoverished society. Two poems published as companion pieces in November 1933 bear witness to the impact: "The Brave Man" (CP 138) and "A Fading of the Sun" (CP 139). "The Brave Man" presents the familiar image of the sun as master of reality, the "brave man" who "walks without meditation" and banishes all illusions as the sunlight banishes the forms of night. In "A Fading of the Sun," on the other hand, any search for nobility in nature or "the poetic" is rejected: "Who can think of the sun costuming clouds / When all people are shaken . . ."

> The warm antiquity of self,
> Everyone, grows suddenly cold.
> The tea is bad, bread sad.
> How can the world so old be so mad
> That the people die?

If these outer supports have gone, if "joy shall be without a book," then the supports for joy must be found within.

> Within as pillars of the sun,
> Supports of night. The tea,
> The wine is good. The bread,
> The meat is sweet.
> And they will not die.

This simplistic and rather unsatisfactory poem was Stevens' early answer to the question of a poet's role in times of social and economic distress, a question that would soon come to the center of his poetry. "A Fading of the Sun" is a "variation" on the theme that was to occupy Stevens in *Owl's Clover*, the "essential conflict between Marxism and the sentiment of the marvellous," between the mundane preoccupations of a rising lower class and the "indulgences of an upper class" which was the natural audience for Stevens' kind of poetry (a poetry that one critic has called the perfect example of "conspicuous consumption" in language).[15] Stevens' own paraphrase of "A Fading of the Sun" does nothing to redeem it from didacticism (". . . we should look to ourselves for help. The exaltation of human nature should take the place of its abasement."),[16] but soon these notions would be embodied in more subtle structures and firmer rhythms.

I

Ideas of Order

The years 1934–37 mark a pivotal stage in Stevens' poetic life, the end of his "introspective voyage" and the beginning of a new pattern of poetic development. It was a time of intense creativity, where one poem gave impetus to another and each poem "proves another and the whole" (CP 441). As Stevens remarked while in the midst of these transitional years, "One of the essential conditions to the writing of poetry is impetus. This is a reason for thinking that to be a poet at all one ought to be a poet constantly." [17] His recent career had been a matter of "a good many fresh starts and each fresh start is a waste of time." [18] Now he could push his themes and techniques to their logical conclusions, secure in the knowledge that his muse had not left him (some of the poems in *Ideas of Order* were "better than anything in *Harmonium*")[19] and that his position in the business world was secure (he became a Vice-President of the Hartford Accident and Indemnity Co. in 1934).

A limited edition of *Ideas of Order* was published by the Alcestis Press in July 1935; a trade edition was issued by Knopf in October of the following year, augmented by three new poems ("Farewell to Florida," "Ghosts as Cocoons," and "A Postcard from the Volcano"). As was the custom at Knopf, the dust jacket contained a statement from the author on his poetic theories and his aims in this particular collection:

> We think of changes occurring today as economic changes, involving political and social changes. Such changes raise questions of political and social order.
>
> While it is inevitable that a poet should be concerned with such questions, this book, although it reflects them, is primarily concerned with ideas of order of a different nature, as, for example, the dependence of the individual, confronting the elimination of established ideas, on the general sense of order; the idea of order created by individual concepts, as of the poet, in "The Idea of Order at Key West"; the idea of order arising from the practice of any art, as of poetry in "Sailing after Lunch."
>
> The book is essentially a book of pure poetry. I believe that, in any society, the poet should be the exponent of the imagination of that society. *Ideas of Order* attempts to illustrate the role of the imagination in life, and particularly in life at present. The more realistic life may be, the more it needs the stimulus of the imagination.

Stevens' emphasis on the non-political nature of most of the poems in *Ideas of Order* is only partly true. Although some of the "poems of order" are concerned solely with the nature of the poet and the poetic process, others shade off into covert and even open political themes; *Ideas of Order* is a response to the intolerable disorder of the times, and its implications cannot be confined to a *secunda natura* of poetic forms. Probably Stevens' use of the term "pure poetry" on the dust jacket was most responsible for the subsequent attacks by left-wing critics and reviewers: in the midst of the Depression it appeared to be a deliberate provocation, and was perhaps intended as such. In fact, the term "pure poetry" as it is given meaning in the world of *Ideas of Order* has little to do with its ordinary significance, although Stevens would resort to that common meaning when speaking of *Harmonium:*

> . . . I was on the point of saying that I did not agree with the opinion that my verse is decorative, when I remembered that when *Harmonium* was in the making

there was a time when I liked the idea of images and images alone, or images and the music of verse together. I then believed in *pure poetry*, as it was called.[20]

What the term "pure poetry" actually meant to the Stevens of the mid-1930's is best defined in *Owl's Clover*: an imaginative construct, replacing the lost sanctions of religion and myth, which can make life tolerable or even—for a moment—joyous. As Stevens sums it up in his gloss to Part III of *Owl's Clover*, "if ideas of God are in conflict, the idea of pure poetry," that is, imagination "extended beyond local consciousness, may be an idea to be held in common by South, West, North and East." [21]

The chronology of Stevens' major work on *Ideas of Order* is so compressed that little can be gained from following the poems in some hypothetical order of composition. Of course, useful distinctions can be drawn between the poems written early in the period 1933–36 and those composed at the close of this period: the earlier poems are primarily concerned with poetic order, while social and political implications are more obvious in the later verses. Stevens began work on *Owl's Clover*, which he once thought of calling *Aphorisms on Society*, in the spring of 1935, and some poems published after that time—such as "Mozart, 1935" and "Dance of the Macabre Mice"—reflect his growing concern with the place of poetry in society. But it would be procrustean to force the poetry of these years into a strict sequence of development, and the best strategy is to allow the poems to group themselves under separate but interrelated "ideas of order."

The poems written at this time which were excluded from *Ideas of Order* are of more than usual interest.[22] Their quality, on the whole, is much higher than that of the *disjecta membra* from *Harmonium*, and it seems obvious that Stevens rejected them because of their light and playful tone. If they had been included in *Ideas of Order* they would have annulled the autumnal atmosphere, making the volume much more like

Harmonium in spirit and variety. In putting together *Ideas of Order* Stevens did much the same thing that Yeats did in shaping *The Tower*: poems that reflected his own complex personality at the time were sacrificed in favor of a unified "personality" for the volume. As it stands, *Ideas of Order* contains just enough witty or light verse to set off the dominant strain of darkening thoughts and darkening colors. Poems such as "The Pleasures of Merely Circulating" (CP 149–50), where the constant motion and disorder of the amusing verse becomes a kind of "classical" order in itself, or "Delightful Evening" (CP 162), where the "wormy metaphors" of the Germanic "Doktor" are mocked with an offhand wit, point up the themes of the darker poems without overwhelming them.

The orphans of *Ideas of Order* testify to the abundance of Stevens' imagination in these years. As always, he had to write a certain amount of light or self-mocking verse to help the more serious poems along, and some of these poems from *Opus Posthumous* are almost private amusements. Stevens' obsession with order of every kind—in his room, his office, his poetry, the world—is parodied in "A Room on a Garden" (OP 40–41), where "Order, the law of hoes and rakes, / May be perceived in windy quakes / And squalls." "Order is the end / Of everything," the poem declares, gently mocking the poet's current penchant for "poems of order." With a similar lightness, "Lytton Strachey, Also, Enters Into Heaven" (OP 38–39) makes an elegant protest against the social seriousness of Lenin and the poetic bombast of Vachel Lindsay's "General William Booth Enters Heaven":

> In this apologetic air, one well
> Might muff the mighty spirit of Lenin.
> That sort of thing was always rather stiff.
> Let's hope for Mademoiselle de Lespinasse,
> Instead, or Horace Walpole or Mrs. Thrale.
>
> He is nothing, I know, to me nor I to him.
> I had looked forward to understanding. Yet

> An understanding may be troublesome.
> I'd rather not. No doubt there's a quarter here,
> Dixhuitième and Georgian and serene.

Some of the excluded poems turn away the "old woman that knocks at the door," the symbol of depressed times used later in *Owl's Clover,* and insist that "The strong music of hard times . . . Must be played on the concertina" ("Outside of Wedlock," OP 76–77). "Polo Ponies Practicing" begins by announcing that "The constant cry against an old order, / An order constantly old, / Is itself old and stale," and then finds solace in the freshness of the moment which lies "Beyond any order, / Beyond any rebellion." "The Drum-Majors in the Labor Day Parade" (OP 36–37) march to a mechanical beat: "The parade's no good."

> They ought to be muscular men,
> Naked and stamping the earth,
> Whipping the air.
>
> The banners should brighten the sun.
> The women should sing as they march.
> Let's go home.

These light or comic treatments of the need for order in a changing society hold an underlying seriousness, but if they had been printed in *Ideas of Order* they would have both offended the public and spoiled the volume's consistency of tone and attitude. Yet one cannot help thinking that in some of the minor pieces Stevens comes closest to his essential, everyday self.

Table Talk

> Granted, we die for good.
> Life, then, is largely a thing
> Of happens to like, not should.
>
> And that, too, granted, why
> Do I happen to like red bush,
> Gray grass and green-gray sky?

What else remains? But red,
Gray, green, why those of all?
That is not what I said:

Not those of all. But those.
One likes what one happens to like.
One likes the way red grows.

It cannot matter at all.
Happens to like is one
Of the ways things happen to fall. (OP 40)

A delicate companion-piece to the more serious "Waving
Adieu, Adieu, Adieu" (CP 127–28), "Table Talk" speaks of
that spontaneous delight in things as they are which helped
Stevens to be his "singular self."

Referring to the arrangement of poems in the first edition
of *Ideas of Order*, Stevens denied that it was programmatic.
"Not every poem expresses a phase of order or an illustration
of order: after all, the thing is not a thesis." [23] The famous
anthology pieces from the volume give an impression of an
almost philosophical concern with the place of poetry, but
when *Ideas of Order* is read as a single complex statement—
the way Stevens intended it to be read—the ground-color is
seen to come from those poems which celebrate the cyclical
orders of nature or dramatize the personal dilemmas of an
aging poet in a chaotic world. These poems establish an emotional climate for the more theoretical poems of order, and
are in some ways the most satisfactory poems Stevens ever
wrote. Standing between the more mannered verses of *Harmonium* and the grand poems of Stevens' later life, which for
all of their greatness give the impression of existing in a
separate world co-existent with our own, the meditative or
elegiac poems of *Ideas of Order* hold the same special place in
the canon of Stevens' poetry that the poems of *The Wild
Swans at Coole* hold in Yeats' career: they are the fullest and
most satisfying treatments of our common experience, cast in
a language which is both traditional and distinctive.

Ideas of Order never allows us to forget that, in the words of a later poem, "The greatest poverty is not to live / In a physical world" (CP 325). Scattered through the volume are quiet reminders that a fundamental reality lies in our immediate experience of the turning seasons and the changing weather.

> Ever-jubilant,
> What is there here but weather, what spirit
> Have I except it comes from the sun? (CP 128)

In glossing the poem which these lines close, "Waving Adieu, Adieu, Adieu" (CP 127–28), Stevens commented that the " 'ever jubilant weather' is not a symbol. We are physical beings in a physical world; the weather is one of the things that we enjoy, one of the unphilosophical realities. The state of the weather soon becomes a state of mind." [24] Winter and summer are celebrated in "Meditation Celestial & Terrestrial" (CP 123–24), the "lustrous inundations" of the returning sun breaking down the "bluest season" of icy winter. The "Mud Master" of spring is "master of the mind" (CP 147–48), while in autumn "The Reader" must peruse the pages of that season (CP 146–47).

> No lamp was burning as I read,
> A voice was mumbling, "Everything
> Falls back to coldness,
>
> Even the musky muscadines,
> The melons, the vermilion pears
> Of the leafless garden."
>
> The sombre pages bore no print
> Except the trace of burning stars
> In the frosty heaven. (CP 147)

Autumn is the dominant season of *Ideas of Order,* and the poems of other climates and seasons are but souvenirs of poetry's other lives in happier days. The experience at the center of *Ideas of Order* is one of deprivation, a sense and acceptance of "Nothing that is not there and the nothing that is." The question which opens "Gallant Château" (CP 161), "Is it bad to have come here / And to have found the bed empty?," is given a simple answer: "It is good. The bed is empty, / The curtains are stiff and prim and still." The "desolate sound" of "Autumn Refrain" (CP 160) is good because it contains no "evasions of the nightingale." The epigraph from Mario Rossi which heads "Evening without Angels" (CP 136–38)—"*the great interests of man: air and light, the joy of having a body, the voluptuousness of looking*"—could head most of Stevens' early poems: the air and light around us give form to the motions of our minds. But for the mind of *Ideas of Order* "Bare night" and "Bare earth" are the best environment:

> Bare night is best. Bare earth is best. Bare, bare,
> Except for our own houses, huddled low
> Beneath the arches and their spangled air,
> Beneath the rhapsodies of fire and fire,
> Where the voice that is in us makes a true response,
> Where the voice that is great within us rises up,
> As we stand gazing at the rounded moon. (CP 137–38)

"Like Decorations in a Nigger Cemetery" (CP 150–58) is a collection of "true responses" to the bare realities of autumn and death. Opening with a "poetic" invocation to the passing autumn sun, a prophet-bard who—like Walt Whitman—"is singing and chanting the things that are part of him," the poem winds through fifty short stanzas which are only loosely connected by repeated images and common themes. The title, as Stevens told Morton Zabel when he submitted the sequence to *Poetry*, "refers to the litter that one usually finds in a nigger cemetery and is a phrase used by Judge Powell last winter in Key West." [25] In the poem's elliptical fashion the title may be translated, "This poem is a litter of observations on the theme of death." Stevens often had great difficulty in finding the time for extended composition, and as he told Zabel most of the "Decorations" were "written on the way to and from the office." They appear to be entries from a poetic notebook, as if the "Schemata" or *Adagia* had been turned into verse, and Stevens has made a virtue out of their disjointed nature. The three- and four-line stanzas are deliberately compressed, almost like short-hand entries in a notebook, and this condensation produces both a sense of immediacy and a controlled allusiveness. As Helen Vendler has remarked, "The oddest characteristic of *Decorations* is its abjuring of verbs. In at least a fifth of the poem the stanzas are syntactically incomplete, and verbs have been dispensed with. Partly, this yields a quality of epigram . . . and partly it strengthens the sense that these are jottings, *adagia*, epitaphs, the daily *pensées* of the inspector of gravestones." [26] Some of the stanzas have a *haiku*-like structure, evolving around a concrete image, but others are almost totally free of visual effects; and in these more "abstract" stanzas the central *pensée* takes the place of the image, giving us the same sense of thought made tangible.

The thematic center of "Decorations" lies at its structural center, in stanza XXV:

> From oriole to crow, note the decline
> In music. Crow is realist. But, then,
> Oriole, also, may be realist.

There is a realistic romanticism as well as a realistic fatalism, and both are present as the poem spreads out from this point in two directions. Many of the stanzas may be considered as *données* or glosses for the other poems in *Ideas of Order*. Stanza XXV, quoted above, is related to the redefinition of the romantic in "Sailing after Lunch." Stanza XXXII ("Poetry is a finikin thing of air / That lives uncertainly and not for long / Yet radiantly beyond much lustier blurs") compacts a theme that is examined at greater length in "The Idea of Order at Key West." Stanza XVIII is a perfect case in point:

> Shall I grapple with my destroyers
> In the muscular poses of the museums?
> But my destroyers avoid the museums.

In the Preface to Williams' *Collected Poems*, which had appeared a few months earlier, Stevens had compared the poet
to "that grand old plaster cast, Lessing's Laocoön: the realist
struggling to escape from the serpents of the unreal" (OP
256–57). Here in stanza XVIII that struggle is generalized, and
then ironically undercut: by grappling with the "unreal" as
imagined through poetic conventions the artist is simply
grappling with himself.

Stanza III declares "the eccentric to be the base of design,"
and the design of most of the stanzas in the poem is deliberately
off-center. The scattered glosses that Stevens supplied to Hi
Simons furnish the missing centers for a few of them, as in the
examples below:

XXXVI

The children will be crying on the stair,
Halfway to bed, when the phrase will be
    spoken,
The starry voluptuary will be born.

> Death is like this: A child will
> die halfway to bed. The phrase
> is *voice of death;* the *volup-
> tuary* is the child in heaven.

XXXVIII

The album of Corot is premature.
A little later when the sky is black.
Mist that is golden is not wholly mist.

> Do not show me Corot while it
> is still summer; do not show me
> pictures of summer while it is
> still summer; even the mist is
> golden; wait until a little later.

XLII

God of the sausage-makers, sacred guild,
Or possibly, the merest patron saint
Ennobled as in a mirror to sanctity.

> An anthropomorphic god is
> simply a projection of itself by
> a race of egoists, which it is
> natural for them to treat as
> sacred.[27]

In each case a key is missing: the voice as the "voice of death" in XXXVI, the dramatic situation in XXXVIII (a retrospect of summer from autumn), the proper reading of the syntax in XLII. Reading the "Decorations" is like following Leopold Bloom's interior monologue; we supply the missing connections and gloss the cryptic allusions. The result of Stevens' method is a poetic sequence which has the spontaneous appearance of a harrowing of the poet's mind. Many of the stanzas have the air of a poem caught in the process of composition, with the original perceptions and images not fully assimilated. It is this sense that we are dealing with the primordia of poetry that makes "Like Decorations in a Nigger Cemetery" such a pleasure to read; we as readers are implicated in the creation of the poem. Like the eccentric shapes of the trees in leafless November, the images and puzzles of the poem provide a base for the total design of *Ideas of Order*.

In a world marked by "the elimination of established ideas," as Stevens phrased it on the dust jacket, the strong spirit that can confront new realities without regret or outside support is the true hero. "How to Live. What to Do" (CP 125–26), the poem that Stevens preferred "to all the others" in *Ideas of Order* because "it so definitely represents my way of thinking," [28] celebrates those who can turn from the "impure" world of "unpurged" images to scale the "heroic height" of the rock, the ultimate reality. The measured quatrains, formal and serene, make the poem a kind of secular hymn:

> There was neither voice nor crested image,
> No chorister, nor priest. There was
> Only the great height of the rock
> And the two of them standing still to rest.

> There was the cold wind and the sound
> It made, away from the muck of the land
> That they had left, heroic sound
> Joyous and jubilant and sure. (CP 126)

But against this almost unobtainable heroic ideal we must balance the conditions of the times, which break down even the strongest will. "Anglais Mort à Florence" (CP 148), Stevens' great elegy for a lost independence of spirit, dramatizes the "states of helplessness or states of degeneration" [29] out of which new orders must come.

> A little less returned for him each spring.
> Music began to fail him. Brahms, although
> His dark familiar, often walked apart.
>
> His spirit grew uncertain of delight,
> Certain of its uncertainty, in which
> That dark companion left him unconsoled
>
> For a self returning mostly memory.
> Only last year he said that the naked moon
> Was not the moon he used to see, to feel
>
> (In the pale coherences of moon and mood
> When he was young), naked and alien,
> More leanly shining from a lankier sky.
>
> Its ruddy pallor had grown cadaverous.
> He used his reason, exercised his will,
> Turning in time to Brahms as alternate
>
> In speech. He was that music and himself.
> They were particles of order, a single majesty:
> But he remembered the time when he stood alone.
>
> He stood at last by God's help and the police;
> But he remembered the time when he stood alone.
> He yielded himself to that single majesty;
>
> But he remembered the time when he stood alone,
> When to be and delight to be seemed to be one,
> Before the colors deepened and grew small.

The sombre figuration made by this poem is one of a life sustained more and more by memory and external orders ("God's help and the police"). The gradual deprivation of self is expressed in slow tercets which become almost a dirge, as the last three stanzas pile one end-stopped line upon another. The failure of music (both in the life and the poem) is a triumph of rationality over imagination: "He used his reason, exercised his will, / Turning in time to Brahms as alternate / In speech." The separation of self and music ("He was that music and himself.") is in direct contrast to the "pale coherences of moon and mood / When he was young": self and music have become "particles of order," a single rather than an all-embracing majesty. The separation of "to be" and "delight to be" is the tragedy of the failed imagination, and the simple statement of regret repeated in each of the last three stanzas —"But he remembered the time when he stood alone"—makes a moving litany of lost independence.

"Anglais Mort à Florence" speaks of our need for some general sense of order, but that order must be vital, of the world and not of the schoolroom. The danger of classicism (and all rage for order is a classical rage) is that it will be satisfied with plaster casts, stale images from the past. In "Gray Stones and Gray Pigeons" (CP 140) and "Winter Bells" (CP 141) Stevens plays on this theme: the church without the bishop ("Globed in today and tomorrow, / Dressed in his colored robes.") is dead and dry; the synagogue, the "church without bells," may produce only "propriety" in its desire to regulate the spirit. This problem of old and new forms, of refreshing the past, is the theme of the amusing "Lions in Sweden" (CP 124–25). Those "sovereigns of the soul," the images we live by, soon grow stale with use and become mere "souvenirs" of the past, like the outworn turns of poetic diction: they are "sovereigns of the soul / And savings banks," like those dead classical images which decorate our public buildings.

> Fides, the sculptor's prize,
> All eyes and size, and galled Justitia,
> Trained to poise the tables of the law,
> Patientia, forever soothing wounds,
> And mighty Fortitudo, frantic bass.

The poet rejects most of the dead images that were once "sovereigns of the soul": they are mere souvenirs. "But these shall not adorn my souvenirs, / These lions, these majestic images," which answer to a universal need for the heroic. If they have become souvenirs they must be renewed.

> . . . the whole of the soul, Swenson,
> As every man in Sweden will concede,
> Still hankers after lions, or, to shift,
> Still hankers after sovereign images.
> If the fault is with the lions, send them back
> To Monsieur Dufy's Hamburg whence they came.
> The vegetation still abounds with forms.

"Lions in Sweden" is one of the few poems in Stevens' work that depends directly on a literary allusion. The lions which threaten to become souvenirs are like the heraldic lion which Dufy placed before the background of an imagined Hamburg (home of the Hagenbeck zoo, "the world's largest dealer in animals for circuses and zoos") in a woodcut for Guillaume Apollinaire's *Le Bestiaire ou le Cortège d'Orphée* (1911).[30] The woodcut interprets a wry quatrain by Apollinaire on the death of the Orphic imagination:

> O lion, malheureuse image
> Des rois chus lamentablement,
> Tu ne nais maintenant qu'en cage
> A Hambourg chez les Allemands.

If the lions have become souvenirs, send them back to the zoo of caged images where they belong: new ones are available. "The vegetation still abounds with forms," even in icy Sweden.

"The American Sublime" (CP 130–31) elaborates on the

same theme, the problem of finding a source for the sublime in an anti-heroic age. Andrew Jackson was faced with this paradox when he posed for his statue: should it be an image of classical eloquence, or an image of the backwoods President (we know from "The Noble Rider and the Sound of Words" [NA 10–11] that Stevens considered the actual statue of Jackson in Lafayette Square a piece of false-eloquence, a "work of fancy" that is "neither of the imagination nor of reality," but this sense of the statue hardly enters the poem). What does enter "The American Sublime," which was an offshoot from Stevens' work on the "statue" poems of *Owl's Clover*,[31] is a sense that the American sublime must avoid the evasions of the nightingale.

> How does one stand
> To behold the sublime,
> To confront the mockers,
> The mickey mockers
> And plated pairs?
>
> When General Jackson
> Posed for his statue
> He knew how one feels.
> Shall a man go barefoot
> Blinking and blank?
>
> But how does one feel?
> One grows used to the weather,
> The landscape and that;
> And the sublime comes down
> To the spirit itself,
>
> The spirit and space,
> The empty spirit
> In vacant space.
> What wine does one drink?
> What bread does one eat?

The ideas of order in "Lions in Sweden" and "The American Sublime" concern human behavior as well as poetic behavior, reminding us that in Stevens' *mundo* every theory of the poem is also a theory of how to live. The first edition of *Ideas of Order* was headed by "Sailing after Lunch" (CP 120–21), a poem specifically concerned with the meaning of the "romantic" in the modern world. It is easy to see why Stevens later replaced this quirky poem by a more formal program-piece, "Farewell to Florida," but in some ways "Sailing after Lunch" is closer to the central concerns of *Ideas of Order*. Just as Stevens wished not to abolish "pure poetry," but to redefine and enlarge it, so he wished to "re-state" the romantic. The opening line of "Sailing after Lunch"—"It is the word *pejorative* that hurts"—plunges into the middle of this argument. As Stevens wrote to the publisher of the first edition:

> When people speak of the romantic, they do so in what the French commonly call a *pejorative* sense. But poetry is essentially romantic, only the romantic of poetry must be something constantly new and, therefore, just the opposite of what is spoken of as the romantic. Without this new romantic, one gets nowhere; with it, the most casual things take on transcendence. . . . What one is always doing is keeping the romantic pure: eliminating from it what people speak of as the romantic.[32]

This theory was to become the framework for Stevens' essay on Marianne Moore, published in December 1935 (OP 247–54), which he acknowledged as an expression of the same ideas embodied earlier in "Sailing after Lunch." At the heart of his review of Miss Moore's *Selected Poems* is a distinction between the romantic "in the pejorative sense," an obsolescent use of standard trappings, and "the romantic in its other sense, meaning always the living and at the same time the imaginative, the youthful, the delicate and a variety of things which it is not necessary to try to particularize at the moment . . . the vital element in poetry" (OP 251–52). In the midst of this definition Stevens quotes the following passage from A. E.

Powell's *The Romantic Theory of Poetry*, remarking that when she describes the romantic poet the author "is surely not thinking of the romantic in a derogatory sense."

> He [the poet] seeks to reproduce for us the feeling as it lives within himself; and for the sake of a feeling which he thinks interesting or important he will insert passages which contribute nothing to the effect of the work as a whole. (OP 251)

In this description, which sheds a great deal of light on the design of Stevens' longer poems at this time (especially "Like Decorations in a Nigger Cemetery"), the crucial phrase is "the feeling as it lives within himself," as distinct from trite souvenirs of that feeling.

All these ideas are given form in "Sailing after Lunch," which opens with a wry portrait of the modern romantic poet as "A most inappropriate man / In a most unpropitious place."

> It is the word *pejorative* that hurts.
> My old boat goes round on a crutch
> And doesn't get under way.
> It's the time of the year
> And the time of the day.
>
> Perhaps it's the lunch that we had
> Or the lunch that we should have had.
> But I am, in any case,
> A most inappropriate man
> In a most unpropitious place.

The next two stanzas play on the distinction between the two romanticisms: the "heavy historical sail" through the "mustiest blue" of worn-out forms is a voyage out of Stevens' past.

> Mon Dieu, hear the poet's prayer.
> The romantic should be here.
> The romantic should be there.
> It ought to be everywhere.
> But the romantic must never remain,

> Mon Dieu, and must never again return.
> This heavy historical sail
> Through the mustiest blue of the lake
> In a really vertiginous boat
> Is wholly the vapidest fake. . . .

By contrast, the true romantic sail is a voyage of present feelings and impressions, a record of today's climate. By becoming a "pupil / Of the gorgeous wheel," which is both the wheel of the boat as it responds to changing winds and the "gorgeous wheel" of nature's seasonal and diurnal changes, the poet accomplishes his most cherished aim: to give a "slight transcendence to the dirty sail."

> It is least what one ever sees.
> It is only the way one feels, to say
> Where my spirit is I am,
> To say the light wind worries the sail,
> To say the water is swift today,
>
> To expunge all people and be a pupil
> Of the gorgeous wheel and so to give
> That slight transcendence to the dirty sail,
> By light, the way one feels, sharp white,
> And then rush brightly through the summer air.

The "slight transcendence" which Stevens desired is present everywhere in *Ideas of Order*, and occasionally it gives rise to noble rhetoric, as in the "sovereign" images of "Some Friends from Pascagoula" (CP 126–27). These rhetorical flights come perilously close to the old romantic, but are almost always saved by a realistic background or, as in this poem, an ironic contrast between the spectators ("a kinky clan") and the language. *Ideas of Order* is remarkably free of trite emotions or stale poetic diction, and even when Stevens undertakes a standard "romantic" subject, as in "The Idea of Order at Key West," the treatment is uniquely his own. Like "Academic Discourse at Havana," "The Idea of Order at Key

West" is concerned with the function of the poet, but in contrast to the earlier poem the setting is purely traditional. A girl, walking by the sea, sings of it and produces order out of chaos; like Orpheus or Arion, those mythic archetypes of the poet, she can master nature with her song. But even in the title a qualification is introduced which is quintessential Stevens: this "idea" of order is not a permanent paradigm, but a momentary product of one time and one place. It is not "romantic" in any pejorative sense of that word, but a complex tracing of one particular interaction encompassing singer and song, sea and audience.

"Re-statement of Romance" (CP 146) opens with a verse paragraph which might be a gloss on the first movement of "The Idea of Order at Key West":

> The night knows nothing of the chants of night.
> It is what it is as I am what I am:
> And in perceiving this I best perceive myself
>
> And you. . . .

The girl in "Idea of Order at Key West" sings "beyond the genius of the sea" because Stevens rejects the older romantic notions of the poet expressing the voice of nature. "The sea was not a mask. No more was she. / The song and water were not medleyed sound / Even if what she sang was what she heard, / Since what she sang was uttered word by word." The singer is not an aeolian harp, expressing the words of wind or sea, but a "maker" in the classical sense of the poet as "maker," the sense explored by Sir Philip Sidney in his *Apology for Poetry*:

> . . . indeed that name of "making" is fit for him [the poet], considering that whereas other Arts retain themselves within their subject, and receive, as it were, their being from it, the poet only bringeth his own stuff, and doth not learn a conceit out of a matter, but maketh matter for a conceit. . . .

The poet has made the song: "it was she and not the sea we heard." But if the "ever-hooded, tragic-gestured sea / Was merely a place by which she walked to sing," whose spirit infuses the song? The sound of the song may come from the sea, but its spirit is "More even than her voice, and ours, among / The meaningless plungings of water and wind." The maker has constructed an imaginative world of order, an artifice, which gives meaning to sea and sky as long as the music lasts. It is a response to nature, not an expression of nature.

> It was her voice that made
> The sky acutest at its vanishing.
> She measured to the hour its solitude.
> She was the single artificer of the world
> In which she sang. And when she sang, the sea,
> Whatever self it had, became the self
> That was her song, for she was the maker. Then we,
> As we beheld her striding there alone,
> Knew that there never was a world for her
> Except the one she sang and, singing, made.

But the mysterious effect of the song is its afterglow, the sharpened perceptions and sense of order which linger in the minds of the audience. Addressing the French critic Ramon Fernandez as the "type" of the aesthetician (Stevens knew Fernandez's writings, but Fernandez is evoked primarily because his Spanish name makes him an appropriate authority for order at Key West), the poet frames a question:

> Ramon Fernandez, tell me, if you know,
> Why, when the singing ended and we turned
> Toward the town, tell why the glassy lights,
> The lights in the fishing boats at anchor there,
> As the night descended, tilting in the air,
> Mastered the night and portioned out the sea,
> Fixing emblazoned zones and fiery poles,
> Arranging, deepening, enchanting night.

The answer is never given, because whatever explanation or paraphrase we offer will be "pale" by comparison to the actual transformation; and the poem closes with an apostrophe to the "rage for order" which made it.

> Oh! Blessed rage for order, pale Ramon,
> The maker's rage to order words of the sea,
> Words of the fragrant portals, dimly-starred,
> And of ourselves and of our origins,
> In ghostlier demarcations, keener sounds.

The deliberately chosen words from another romanticism ("fragrant portals, dimly-starred," "ghostlier demarcations, keener sounds"), like the surprising "enchanting" at the end of the previous movement, are neutralized by the "rage" of the maker, and in Stevens' special vocabulary they are anything but vague or trite. As in stanza XIX of "Like Decorations in a Nigger Cemetery," the "portals" are the mysterious gates of night and death, while "ghostlier" is used in the sense of "spiritual," not "insubstantial," with overtones of its darker meaning. "The Idea of Order at Key West" is an *ars poetica* for the romantic of the present, a modern rewriting of Wordsworth's "The Solitary Reaper." In Wordsworth's poem the Highland Lass is the poet as sayer, singing a "melancholy strain" out of her own feelings; in Stevens' poem the singer is a maker, building a verbal artifice out of the sound of the sea. The song in which the Highland Lass expresses her melancholy lingers in the heart of the listener, and becomes part of him:

> I listened, motionless and still;
> And, as I mounted up the hill,
> The music in my heart I bore,
> Long after it was heard no more.

Stevens' listeners, by contrast, do not carry away a song but a heightened sensibility and a deeper talent for "arranging" nature, as the painter arranges his scene. In their samenesses and divergences, the two poems illustrate Stevens' place in a tradition and his rage to "refreshen" it.

◇

Those points where the orders of poetry touch the orders of society are always difficult to locate, and the subject of Stevens as a political poet is especially tricky. Certainly much of his major poetry in the 1930's was written out of a deep sense of social change, and was designed as a counterattack against fashionable notions of the poet's responsibilities. The Stevens of *Owl's Clover* and some of the poems in *Ideas of Order* is outraged, on the defensive, and defensive poetry is never entirely satisfactory. But when Stevens sat down to write his poems of social order the initial impulses and frustrations were usually lost in the making of the poems, so that what began as a reaction to social disorder was often displaced into poetry on the larger theme of order in art and life. Beyond this, Stevens was essentially a poet of freedom and individuality, not of authoritarianism, and as a result his "political" poems are almost entirely free of the fascist impulse which flickers intermittently in the later poems of W. B. Yeats. Stevens may have admired Mussolini and been complacent about the invasion of Ethiopia,[33] but in his poetry he is the partisan of individuality, privacy, and spontaneity. If he was a capitalist of the imagination, at least he stuck to the motto of *laissez faire*. To him, "order" meant "peace."

> If poetry introduces order, and every competent poem introduces order, and if order means peace, even though that particular peace is an illusion, is it any less an illusion than a good many other things that everyone high and low now-a-days concedes to be no longer of any account? Isn't a freshening of life a thing of consequence?[34]

The more overtly "political" poems of *Ideas of Order* tend
to bear out these generalizations. "Botanist on Alp (No. 1)"
was published separately in October 1934, and taken alone it is
petulantly political: "Claude has been dead a long time," "Marx
has ruined Nature," and we are left with the spectacle of a
"boarded and bare" hotel which the poet does his best to
ignore. But when the poem was included in *Ideas of Order*
Stevens supplied it with a companion piece, "Botanist on Alp
(No. 2)," where the counterbalancing "poems" of earth and
death provide a long perspective for the original "Botanist on
Alp" (CP 135–36). Similarly, "Mozart, 1935" (CP 131-32) may
have been begun as a "variation" on the theme of the poet's
role in a time of Communism and class struggle,[35] but when it
reached the page it was a general poem of order which speaks
of the poet's dilemma. Caught between the demand that he
play the present ("Its shoo-shoo-shoo, its ric-a-nic, / Its en-
vious cachinnation.") and his sentimental desire for escape in
time, the poet must "Strike the piercing chord" of falling
snow, the chord of the romantic realist.

> Be thou the voice,
> Not you. Be thou, be thou
> The voice of angry fear,
> The voice of this besieging pain.
>
> Be thou that wintry sound
> As of the great wind howling,
> By which sorrow is released,
> Dismissed, absolved
> In a starry placating.
>
> We may return to Mozart.
> He was young, and we, we are old.
> The snow is falling
> And the streets are full of cries.
> Be seated, thou.

The "Be thou, be thou" of the address to the poet echoes
Shelley's "Ode to the West Wind" ("Be thou, Spirit fierce, /

My spirit! Be thou me, impetuous one!"), and there is a nice irony in the contrast between the two poems; but Stevens' address is equally serious, he would have the poet speak with the voice of his age, and his view of the poet's role is ultimately almost as grand as that of Shelley.[36] The "thou" of Shelley's "Ode" is all that is left of the old romanticism, but in its own way the new conception of the poet as realistic nightingale reaches just as far.

"Sad Strains of a Gay Waltz" (CP 121–22) and "Ghosts as Cocoons" (CP 119) are other poems which begin in social disillusionment and end in music. Spring is the time of "Ghosts as Cocoons," but the clumsy masses ("butcher, seducer, blood-man, reveller") have fashioned a "mangled, smutted, semi-world hacked out / Of dirt . . ." that moonlight cannot obscure: the bride of sun and music must come to blot it out. "Sad Strains of a Gay Waltz" is an elegy for the lost gaiety of the waltz and the lost forms of "mountain-minded Hoon," whose "Palaz" was reared in *Harmonium* (CP 65).

> There is order in neither sea nor sun.
> The shapes have lost their glistening.
> There are these sudden mobs of men,
>
> . . .
>
> Imposing forms they cannot describe,
> Requiring order beyond their speech. (CP 122)

"The epic of disbelief" demands a new poet, a "harmonious skeptic" who in "skeptical music"

> Will unite these figures of men and their shapes
> Will glisten again with motion, the music
> Will be motion and full of shadows.

Perhaps the most blatantly political of the poems in *Ideas of Order* is "Dance of the Macabre Mice" (CP 123), a "favor" that dropped from *Owl's Clover*. Here the statue of "The Founder of the State" is mocked by the mice that dance around it, just as the comic form of the poem mocks them. As always, the original social rage dissolves into one of the established forms of his poetry. But "Dance of the Macabre Mice" contains a greater residue of personal frustration than the other poems, and it is with relief that we turn to "A Postcard from the Volcano" (CP 158–59), the last of the poems of social order to be written, and the most sophisticated. The title suggests a postcard from Vesuvius, displaying the ruins of a vanished order, and the poem itself is a postcard written from the volcano of contemporary society. The double-vision of the poem is one source of its power: told for the most part in the imagined future tense, "A Postcard from the Volcano" keeps our attention fixed on the present, while between the two viewpoints there intrudes a constant sense of apocalyptic destruction.

> Children picking up our bones
> Will never know that these were once
> As quick as foxes on the hill;
>
> And that in autumn, when the grapes
> Made sharp air sharper by their smell
> These had a being, breathing frost;
>
> And least will guess that with our bones
> We left much more, left what still is
> The look of things, left what we felt
>
> At what we saw. The spring clouds blow
> Above the shuttered mansion-house,
> Beyond our gate and the windy sky
>
> Cries out a literate despair.
> We knew for long the mansion's look
> And what we said of it became
>
> A part of what it is . . . Children,
> Still weaving budded aureoles,
> Will speak our speech and never know,

> Will say of the mansion that it seems
> As if he that lived there left behind
> A spirit storming in blank walls,
>
> A dirty house in a gutted world,
> A tatter of shadows peaked to white,
> Smeared with the gold of the opulent sun.

Here the unrhymed tercets which Stevens had developed into his chief vehicle for meditative or elegiac verse are used with expressive flexibility, and the tetrameter lines gradually mount from a quick opening to the slow magnificence of the last verse. The first three tercets pose the mystery of the anonymous dead, who still managed to bequeath the "look of things," what they felt at what they saw. The shift back to the present tense in the fourth tercet anchors the poem in the despair of the present, reflected in a sky which is "literate" because we have given it words, just as what we said of the mansion (the world in which we live) "became / A part of what it is." Then the poem returns to the future, with the only assurance our knowledge that our speech will survive, and with it "what we felt / At what we saw." The children's description of the ruined mansion, which like the "perished swans" of "Academic Discourse at Havana" is an "infinite incantation of ourselves," can only be framed in the language that we made. The words that transform a "dirty house in a gutted world" into the magnificent artifice of color which crowns the poem are all that will remain of our feelings after the volcano's eruption: but they contain a great deal of our selves.

"Farewell to Florida" (CP 117–18), first published in July 1936 and reprinted three months later as the program-piece to the second edition of *Ideas of Order*, is more a valedictory than an introduction. It was almost certainly written after the other poems in the volume had been completed, and when *Owl's Clover* was nearly finished, so it stands as a coda to the most turbulent period in Stevens' poetic career. When read in this light, and with a recognition of Stevens' complex attitude toward "Florida" as place and symbol, "Farewell to Florida" becomes more than a simple account of the poet's voyage from tropical escapism into the turmoil of the mid-thirties. Louis Martz claimed that in this poem "Stevens renounces all that 'Florida' has symbolized in his earlier poetry: that world of vivid physical apprehension, where man created within the bounds of the natural order." [37] But what is rejected is not the natural order and physical sensation, it is that "Green barbarism turning paradigm" (CP 31) which threatened to overwhelm Crispin in Yucatan. Florida had always been recognized in Stevens' poetry as a "venereal soil," creative and self-destroying, and "Farewell to Florida" is the last phase of an ambivalent poetic courtship which began in 1917–18. After *Ideas of Order* the word "Florida" never appears again in Stevens' verse.

The style of "Farewell to Florida" is explicit and oratorical, akin to the "rhetoric" of *Owl's Clover* that Stevens ultimately rejected. But within the compass of the four tightly organized stanzas the style is extremely effective, appropriate to the high resolve which is Stevens' theme. The apostrophe to the "high ship," and the repeated image of transformation ("The snake has left its skin upon the floor"), frame the simplest language:

> The moon
> Is at the mast-head and the past is dead.
> Her mind will never speak to me again.
> I am free.

The second and third stanzas paint a vivid picture of a love affair turned bitter: all that was once seductive and entrancing now seems sterile and threatening. The poet seems intent upon denying the past, upon forgetting that the "ever-freshened Keys" and "vivid blooms" once warmed him into verse, until the very end of the third stanza:

> To stand here on the deck in the dark and say
> Farewell and to know that that land is forever gone

> And that she will not follow in any word
> Or look, nor ever again in thought, except
> That I loved her once . . . Farewell. Go on, high ship.

"I loved her once . . . Farewell." The poet stops just short of renouncing the past, and in the final stanza he turns from a selective retrospect of *Harmonium*'s South to a "leafless" North which was always there as the alternate climate of *Harmonium*.

> My North is leafless and lies in a wintry slime
> Both of men and clouds, a slime of men in crowds.
> The men are moving as the water moves,
> This darkened water cloven by sullen swells
> Against your sides, then shoving and slithering,
> The darkness shattered, turbulent with foam.
> To be free again, to return to the violent mind
> That is their mind, these men, and that will bind
> Me round, carry me, misty deck, carry me
> To the cold, go on, high ship, go on, plunge on.

The imagery of this concluding stanza is scarcely more attractive than the "sepulchral" imagery of stanzas II and III ("slime," "sullen," "slithering," "shattered," "turbulent"), but the poet embraces it as a new freedom. What he has renounced is not "vivid physical apprehension" and the "bounds of the natural order"—the figures of stanza IV are sufficient contradiction to that view—but a romanticism grown tired and sterile. The oriole must turn realist, and become like the crow. As a summation of Stevens' mood at the time when he was poised between *Owl's Clover* and *The Man with the Blue Guitar*, "Farewell to Florida" marks the balance-point of Stevens' poetic career. His poetic "voyage" was nearing an end, to be replaced by different and more self-contained patterns of artistic development.

II

The Statue

Early in 1935 Stevens was invited by a London publisher to "write a long poem for a series of long poems," and this invitation—like the announcement of the Blindman Prize that started his work on "The Comedian"—had a catalytic effect on his imagination.[38] The burst of creativity that produced *Ideas of Order* gave him the impetus needed for a long poem, and he must have welcomed the occasion to develop his themes within a larger and more flexible form. The resulting sequence of five poems, *Owl's Clover*, stands in the same relation to *Ideas of Order* as "The Comedian" does to *Harmonium*. But whereas "The Comedian as the Letter C" traces the spiritual and artistic career of an archetypal artist-hero, *Owl's Clover* deals with the immediate problem of the poet's place in a disordered society. Stevens' own dilemmas as a poet are painfully evident, exposed without the ironic protections of the earlier "disguised pronunciamento." In structure, too, *Owl's Clover* makes a sharp contrast to "The Comedian"; its development is thematic and spatial, not narrative, and the poems revolve around the "variable symbol" of the statue, which focuses the complex problems that beset "pure poetry" in an age without order or sanctions. As Stevens said in a talk on "The Irrational Element in Poetry" which grew out of his work on *Owl's Clover*, "The pressure of the contemporaneous from the time of the beginning of the World War to the present time has been constant and extreme" (OP 224):[39] *Owl's Clover* both embodies this pressure and responds to it.

The first and most satisfying part of *Owl's Clover*, "The Old Woman and the Statue" (OP 43–46), was finished before the middle of 1935 and published in the Summer issue of the *Southern Review*. Although the poem "deals specifically with the status of art in a period of depression," as Stevens later commented, "it is, when generalized, one more confrontation of reality (the depression) and the imagination (art). A larger expression than confrontation is: a phase of the universal intercourse. There is a flow to and fro between reality and the imagination." [40] The crucial term in this description is "generalized": like the best poems of political order in *Ideas of Order*, "The Old Woman and the Statue" makes a universal metaphor out of the tensions of the present. However, the relative equanimity and "objectivity" reflected in this poem were soon broken by Stanley Burnshaw's harsh review of the first edition of *Ideas of Order*, which appeared in the left-wing journal *New Masses* at the beginning of October. Bracketing Stevens with a minor poet, Haniel Long, Burnshaw delivered an attack on the irrelevance and confusion of *Ideas of Order*, contrasting it unfavorably with *Harmonium*. According to Burnshaw, Stevens is unaware of the "alternatives" facing the poet in a time of radical change. It is worth quoting at length from the review, which had a traumatic impact on Stevens' morale:

> Realists have been bitter at the inanity of Pope's "whatever is is right," but Stevens plunges ahead to the final insolence: "For realists, what is is what should be." And yet it is hard to know if such a line is not Stevens posing in self-mockery. One can rarely speak surely of Stevens' ideas.
>
> . . .
>
> . . . it is verse that Stevens can no longer write. His harmonious cosmos is suddenly screeching with confu-

sion. *Ideas of Order* is the record of a man who, having lost his footing, now scrambles to stand up and keep his balance. The opening poem observes

> . . . This heavy historical sail
> Through the mustiest blue of the lake
> In a really vertiginous boat
> Is wholly the vapidest fake. . . .

And the rest follows with all the ironical logic of such a premise. The "sudden mobs of men" may have the answer

> But what are radiant reason and radiant will
> To warblings early in the hilarious trees. . . .

Sceptical of man's desire in general, there is still much to be said for the ordering power of the imagination. But there remains a yearning—and escape is itself an irony. "Marx has ruined Nature, for the moment," he observes in self-mockery; but he can speculate on the wisdom of turning inward (*vide* Long), and a moment later look upon collective mankind as the guilty bungler of harmonious life, in "a peanut parody for a peanut people." What answer is there in the cosmic law—"everything falls back to coldness"? With apparent earnestness he goes a step beyond his former nature-man interfusing harmony:

> Only we two are one, not you and night,
> Nor night and I, but you and I, alone,
> So much alone, so deeply by ourselves,
> So far beyond the casual solitudes,
> That night is only the background of our selves. . . .

And in a long poem he pours out in strange confusion his ideas of order, among them

> If ever the search for a tranquil belief should end,
> The future might stop emerging out of the past,
> Out of what is full of us; yet the search
> And the future emerging out of us seem to be one.[41]

This review-notice disturbed Stevens out of all proportion to its tone or content, and we may suspect that it touched a fundamental insecurity in his attitude toward the social role of the poet, that Stevens was indeed a man off-balance. In the letters of the following weeks he returned again and again to the theme of "The Old Woman and the Statue," but now within the specific context of Marxism and the social revolution. Four years later he would be able to say with confidence that "pure poetry is rather older and tougher than Marx and will remain so," [42] but while he pushed toward the completion of *Owl's Clover* in 1935–36 he was less serene. "I hope I am headed left, but there are lefts and lefts, and certainly I am not headed for the ghastly left of *Masses*," he wrote on 9 October 1935.[43] At about this time the second poem of *Owl's Clover*, which had probably been underway before the *New Masses* review appeared, was given the title "Mr. Burnshaw and the Statue," a response to the topical which reveals the depth of Stevens' anxiety. The issues that troubled him were given full expression in a letter of 5 November 1935:

> The last question is whether I feel that there is an essential conflict between Marxism and the sentiment of the marvellous. I think we all feel that there is conflict between the rise of a lower class, with all its realities, and the indulgences of an upper class. This, however, is one of the very things which I at least have in mind in MR. BURNSHAW. My conclusion is that, while there is a conflict, it is not an essential conflict. The conflict is temporary. The only possible order of life is one in which all order is incessantly changing. Marxism may or may not destroy the existing sentiment of the marvellous; if it does, it will create another. It was a very common fear that Socialism would dirty the world; it is an equally common fear that Communism will do the same thing. I think that this is all nonsense. Of course, that would be the immediate effect, as any upheaval results in disorder.
> So that there may be no doubt about it, let me say that I believe in what Mr. Filene calls "up-to-date capitalism." I don't believe in Communism; I do believe in up-to-date capitalism. It is an extraordinary experience

for myself to deal with a thing like Communism; it is like dealing with the Democratic platform, or with the provisions of the Frazier-Lemke bill. Nevertheless, one has to live and think in the actual world, and no other will do, and that is why MR. BURNSHAW, etc. has taken a good deal of time.[44]

The writing of "Mr. Burnshaw and the Statue" was a catharsis for Stevens, and the remaining poems of *Owl's Clover* mark a partial return to the "generalized" discourse of "The Old Woman and the Statue." Yet it was not until the writing of "The Man with the Blue Guitar" in the winter of 1936–37 that Stevens was able to regain full confidence in his art.

Stevens had originally intended a "set of six or seven" poems on the statue, but by the beginning of 1936 he had settled on a sequence of five, and in May the five poems were finished.[45] Shortly before publication Stevens thought of altering the working-title, *Owl's Clover*, to *Aphorisms on Society*, but he wisely decided to "stick to *Owl's Clover*," [46] since his natural gift for the adage or aphorism is completely obscured in the winding rhetoric of the poems. *Owl's Clover* is an appropriate title because, as Stevens noted, it combines the "owlishness" and didacticism of the poems, their focus on the false issues of the present, with a suggestion that the poet has not completely abandoned his native style.[47]

In spite of his initial enthusiasm Stevens was soon dissatisfied with the long version of *Owl's Clover* published by the Alcestis Press in August 1936, and when the series was reprinted in *The Man with the Blue Guitar* (October 1937) it had been cut by nearly 200 lines (see Appendix C for a comparison of the two versions). Some of the changes were part of the "generalizing" process Stevens had originally adopted, such as the elimination of Mr. Burnshaw from the title and text of the second poem, but most of them were simple cuts aimed at tightening the argument and strengthening the verse-paragraphs. With the exception of Parts II and III of "A Duck for Dinner," Stevens did little rewriting; he simply eliminated whole sections and movements, and it is a sign of the work's diffuseness that these large cuts entailed little or no change in the syntax of surrounding passages. In most cases one line leads directly into another even though an intervening section has been jettisoned. With the exception of "The Comedian as the Letter C," where the narrative movement would prevent such cutting, most of Stevens' longer poems were pruned of substantial units: the rejected stanzas of "Le Monocle de Mon Oncle," "The Man with the Blue Guitar," and "Examination of the Hero in a Time of War" testify to this method of condensation. But it is one thing to eliminate separate units from an "orchestrated" poem written in regular stanzas, and quite another to cut chunks of verse from a dialectical poem such as *Owl's Clover*. The revisions of *Owl's Clover* were made possible by its loose syntax, weak pentameter lines, and lack of unifying repetitions in sound and imagery. The sprawling verse-paragraphs and sparse internal harmonies were probably just as important as the topical references in Stevens' ultimate decision to exclude *Owl's Clover* from the *Collected Poems*. Since the revisions did not make a substantial improvement in the poem, all quotations in this chapter will be taken from the full Alcestis Press version, which is reprinted in *Opus Posthumous*. It is in this version that Stevens' ambiguities and hesitations are more evident.

In the summer of 1940 the critic Hi Simons, who had won Stevens' confidence with his perceptive interpretation of "The Comedian as the Letter C," submitted a long list of questions concerning "The Man with the Blue Guitar" and *Owl's Clover*, and Stevens responded in a series of detailed letters.[48] The comments on *Owl's Clover* are especially full, amounting to an interpretation and gloss of the entire poem, and it would be foolish to substitute another paraphrase for Stevens' own, although he often talks more about the ideas behind the poem than those implicit in the text.[49] In contrast to his specific and often evasive remarks on other poems, Stevens' paraphrases of

Owl's Clover are general and "philosophical"; and this eager-
ness to explain is one sign of the disparity between intention
and achievement which mars the work. As Stevens' comments
suggest, our best approach to *Owl's Clover* is through the repeated uses of the statue as a "variable symbol," since the interactions between art and society are presented most clearly
in relation to this central icon.[50]

Two *Adagia* might stand as epigraphs to all of *Owl's Clover*,
but especially to "The Old Woman and the Statue."

> Poetry is not the same thing as the imagination taken
> alone. Nothing is itself taken alone. Things are because
> of interrelations or interactions. (CP 163)

> Poetry is a purging of the world's poverty and change
> and evil and death. It is a present perfecting, a satis-
> faction in the irremediable poverty of life. (OP 167)

The first of these *pensées* states the essential dynamic of the
poem: without the contrasting figure of the old woman, "the
bitter mind / In a flapping cloak" (OP 44), the description of
the statue's eloquence would be mere rhetoric. It is the interaction between art and the deprived mind, between imagination
and reality, that makes the subject live. Without that interaction
or interrelation neither the statue nor the old woman would
hold our attention as part of a larger order.

The second *pensée* sums up the poet's dilemma: how can
he offer "pure poetry" as a "purging of the world's poverty
and change and evil and death" in an age when these realities
press down with cruel force? How can he speak of spiritual
poverty when those around him are hungry, or of imaginative
freedom when those around him are faced with oppression?
How can he resist the way of Tolstoy in *What is Art?*, a rejection of useless "beauty" in favor of an art that is socially
relevant? What is the justification of a poetry that causes nothing to happen?

By being faithful to the first of these mottos, "The Old
Woman and the Statue" makes the second come true. The

key to the poem's success lies in its viewpoint: it is told in the past tense. Although the immediate occasion for the poem is Stevens' concern with "the status of art in a period of depression," that occasion is treated obliquely, and as a result the poem becomes a "generalized" treatment of one more phase in the universal interaction between reality and the imagination.[51] The old woman is not a specific victim of the Great Depression, like one of the figures in William Carlos Williams' proletarian portraits, but a timeless image of our desolate lives. This does not mean that she has become a "symbol," but simply that she speaks with the "desolate syllables" of universal poverty.

The poem opens with a deliberate "distancing" of the scene:

> Another evening in another park,
> A group of marble horses rose on wings
> In the midst of a circle of trees, from which the leaves
> Raced with the horses in bright hurricanes.

There follows in Part II a powerful evocation of the statue in autumn, the shapes thrusting into life, "The marble leaping in the storms of light." The work of art is dominant and superb against the autumn sky: "So much the sculptor had foreseen." What he had not foreseen (Part III) was the old woman, a "bitter mind / In a flapping cloak," a mind so "destitute that nothing but herself / Remained and nothing of herself except / A fear too naked for her shadow's shape." Before her all-encompassing misery the plunging statue "collapsed to marble hulk, / Stood stiffly, as if the black of what she thought / Conflicting with the moving colors there / Changed them, at last, to its triumphant hue." As Part IV progresses the light on the statue becomes false, the "clouds of bronze" subside to flatness, until the statue is a static form in a night that was her mind "so magnified / It lost the common shape of night and came / To be the sovereign shape in a world of shapes."

Part V moves from the past to the conditional tense, and imagines a world without her dark suffering.

Without her, evening like a budding yew
Would soon be brilliant, as it was, before
The harridan self and ever-maladive fate
Went crying their desolate syllables, before
Their voice and the voice of the tortured wind were one,
Each voice within the other, seeming one,
Crying against a need that pressed like cold,
Deadly and deep.

In this world the yew of death would be the yew of lunar
life, the statue would once more live.

There the horses would rise again,
Yet hardly to be seen and again the legs
Would flash in air, and the muscular bodies thrust
Hoofs grinding against the stubborn earth, until
The light wings lifted through the crystal space
Of night. How clearly that would be defined!

"The Old Woman and the Statue" may be a piece of
rhetoric, as many have claimed, but like "Farewell to Florida"
it is effective rhetoric, with both poverty and eloquence,
reality and imagination, evoked in moving language. It offers
no resolution other than that of its own form and harmonies,
but as a splendid drama of the confrontation between poverty
and art it tells more than a dozen proletarian novels.

In "Mr. Burnshaw and the Statue" (later "The Statue at
the World's End") the statue is used as a metonym for the
civilization in which it stands. The speaker in the first and third
parts is Mr. Burnshaw or someone like him, a fact that was
obscured in the revisions. Like an orthodox Marxist, the speaker
of Part I takes the work of art as product and symptom of a
society. The poem opens with a revolutionary litany:

The thing is dead . . . Everything is dead
Except the future. Always everything
That is is dead except what ought to be.
All things destroy themselves or are destroyed.

The horses of the sculptor have no relevance: "These are not even Russian animals. / They are horses as they were in the sculptor's mind." The statue is a relic of superstitious "moonlit muckers," it seems "a thing from Schwarz's, a thing / Of the dank imagination, much below / Our crusted outlines hot and huge with fact, / Ugly as an idea, not beautiful / As sequels without thought." The actual horses of autumn harvest are far more noble than "this jotting-down of the sculptor's foppishness."

Part II is an apostrophe to "all celestial paramours," a supplication for new music and new forms. If the marble horses are transformed "with lights / Astral and Shelleyan," nothing will really be changed, but at least the detritus of the past ("this gawky plaster") will have been cast away.

> Agree: the apple in the orchard, round
> And red, will not be redder, rounder then
> Than now. No: nor the ploughman in his bed
> Be free to sleep there sounder, for the plough
> And the dew and the ploughman still will best be one.
> But this gawky plaster will not be here.

Part III returns to the viewpoint of Mr. Burnshaw:

> The stones
> That will replace it shall be carved, "*The Mass*
> *Appoints These Marbles Of Itself To Be*
> *Itself.*" No more than that, no subterfuge,
> No memorable muffing, bare and blunt.

This monument to materialism is immediately counterpointed by another address to the "celestial paramours," the Muses, those who disclose "an eternal vista, manqué and gold / And brown, an Italy of the mind." But this is rejected as mere "poet's politics," and the section closes with an intimation that "even disorder may . . . have an order of its own."

> If ploughmen, peacocks, doves alike
> In vast disorder live in the ruins, free,

The charts destroyed, even disorder may,
So seen, have an order of its own, a peace
Not now to be perceived yet order's own.

In Part V a "solemn voice, not Mr. Burnshaw's" paints a majestic picture of the dump where all civilizations end, a picture which foreshadows such later poems as "The Man on the Dump" (CP 201–3) and recalls Stevens' description of the modern poet in his review of Williams' *Collected Poems:*

> What, then, is a romantic poet now-a-days? He happens to be one who still dwells in an ivory tower, but who insists that life would be intolerable except for the fact that one has, from the top, such an exceptional view of the public dump. . . . (OP 256)

The opening lines of this vision ("At some gigantic, solitary urn, / A trash can at the end of the world. . . .") bring together the two romantics in the clash of "urn" and "trash can," and the section proceeds to a scene of total desolation:

White slapped on white, majestic, marble heads,
Severed and tumbled into seedless grass,
Motionless, knowing neither dew nor frost.
There lies the head of the sculptor in which the thought
Of lizards, in its eye, is more acute
Than the thought that once was native to the skull . . .

All this is part of the "immense detritus of a world / That is completely waste, that moves from waste / To waste, out of the hopeless waste of the past / Into a hopeful waste to come." And out of this waste will rise a new life, so that "For a little time, again, rose-breasted birds / Sing rose-beliefs." Above the urn-dump "two lights commingle," the past and the future, "two immense / Reflections, whirling apart and wide away."

Parts VI and VII return to the "celestial paramours," the "Mesdames" addressed in II and IV, as the poet sings his final hymn of reconciliation. The reconciliations to the new and the strange celebrated in Parts II and IV are not enough:

neither a Shelleyan transformation nor a resignation to the strange order of disorder can suffice.

> It is only enough
> To live incessantly in change. . . .
> So great a change
> Is constant. The time you call serene descends
> Through a moving chaos that never ends. Mesdames,
> Leaves are not always falling and the birds
> Of chaos are not always sad nor lost
> In melancholy distances. You held
> Each other moving in a chant and danced
> Beside the statue, while you sang.

The song of the "celestial paramours" was a song of grief and loss, a song of devotion to the statue, but in Part VII the poet —in a prophetic measure reminiscent of stanza VII of "Sunday Morning"—urges the maidens to turn their backs upon the "vivid statue" and join the "drastic community" of change.

> Conceive that while you dance the statue falls,
> The heads are severed, topple, tumble, tip
> In the soil and rest. Conceive that marble men
> Serenely selves, transfigured by the selves
> From which they came, make real the attitudes
> Appointed for them and that the pediment
> Bears words that are the speech of marble men.

The motto is *"To Be Itself,"* and the poem ends with a vision of the "celestial paramours" joined to the "breathing earth," swept into "a storm blown into glittering shapes, and flames / Wind-beaten into freshest, brightest fire."

As Stevens says in his paraphrase, *"What this poem is concerned with is adaptation to change."* [52] Like the poems of *Ideas of Order*, which it touches at so many points, "Mr. Burnshaw and the Statue" speaks of the need to accept change or even chaos, to re-state the romantic and sing of things as they are. The dialectic of the poem's structure traces the necessary accommodation between imagination and reality, as each section qualifies its predecessor and builds toward a more complex statement. The heart of the argument lies in the most successful movement, Part V, where the new generation rises out of "the immense detritus of a world / That is completely waste," and

> For a little time, again, rose-breasted birds
> Sing rose-beliefs.

Stevens said that these lines were "a kind of summing-up of the whole poem," but around this simple statement of the cyclical romantic there rises a structure of uncertain tone and unintentional obscurity, qualities which were, if anything, enhanced by the 1937 revisions. The difficulty is the presence of Mr. Burnshaw and what he represents, and this presence so infected Stevens' imagination that it could not be removed by simple revisions. The theme of adjustment to change was one Stevens had already handled with great success in the early poems of *Ideas of Order*, but always with relation to a generalized sense of disorder. The specific introduction of Marxist attitudes into Parts I and III turned those sections into grotesque satires—Stevens' temperamental aversion to the attitudes pervades his imagery and language—and as a result the tonal harmonies of the poem were broken. The first addresses to the "celestial paramours," Parts II and IV, seem more ironic and precious than Stevens could have intended, and the final movement (VI and VII) degenerates into uncontrolled rhetoric: we do not believe in the prophetic dance because it is described, not presented. Only Part V remains in our minds as a successful poem whose bare imagery and muscular rhythms are totally appropriate to its subject. In trying to give his great themes of order and change a specifically contemporary grounding Stevens succeeded merely in trivializing them.

At first glance "The Greenest Continent" (OP 52–60) would appear to be a strategic retreat from the exposed position of "Mr. Burnshaw and the Statue," an impersonal review of Stevens' poetic set in a remote and imagined Africa. "Mr.

Burnshaw and the Statue" had been a "general and rather vaguely poetic justification of leftism," [53] by which Stevens meant the radical willingness to accept and accommodate change, not the particular "leftism" of the *New Masses;* but contemporary issues still raw on his sensibility invaded the poem and destroyed its perspective. As Stevens observed, a confrontation between Crispin and "the present-day unemployed" would have been a "catastrophe for him," [54] and parts of "Mr. Burnshaw and the Statue" remind us of such a confrontation. "The Greenest Continent" promises something very different: a rehearsal of familiar theories about man and his environment which can be traced back to the early poetry and experimental plays. In the words of the older Crispin, "The natives of the rain are rainy men" (CP 37). The god that rules over Africa will not be the god of the European imagination, but an "avuncular cloud-man beamier than spears."

There was a heaven once in Europe, "The spirit's episcopate, hallowed and high," but that heaven is now empty (Parts II and III). The Schlossbibliothek of European culture has had its books dispersed, the world of the statue is now a chaotic wasteland. But the statue cannot be given new life in Africa, "which had / No heaven, had death without a heaven, death / In a heaven of death." The statue is the product of a cold Northern clime, and in spite of what the "diplomats of the cafés expound," it cannot express another time and another place.

> If the statue rose,
> If once the statue were to rise, if it stood,
> Thinly, among the elephantine palms,
> Sleekly the serpent would draw himself across.
> The horses are a part of a northern sky
> Too starkly pallid for the jaguar's light,
> In which he and the lion and the serpent hide
> Even in sleep . . . (IV)

But if art is a product of local consciousness and each climate has its own god, what is the supreme fiction we must believe in, the supreme fiction which will take the place of a lost heaven? The final section of "The Greenest Continent" (VIII) chants a hymn to "Fatal Ananke" as the "common god."

> He looks upon the statue, where it is,
> And the sun and the sun-reek piled and peaked above
> The jostled ferns, where it might be, having eyes
> Of the shape of eyes, like blunt intaglios,
> And nothing more.

Ananke, the god of necessity and force against which none can stand, is Stevens' personification of the dark power which moves men and history. In a time of disorder and change when the imagination seeks a first cause, he is the "starless crown" of the world, and as such he is a creation of "pure poetry," that imagination "extended beyond local consciousness," which "may be an idea to be held in common by South, West, North and East." [55] "Ananke" is a fiction we create and then believe in willingly:

> The final belief is to believe in a fiction, which you know to be a fiction, there being nothing else. The exquisite truth is to know that it is a fiction and that you believe in it willingly. (*Adagia*, OP 163)

Summarized in this fashion, "The Greenest Continent" would appear to be a mature counterpart to *Three Travelers Watch a Sunrise*, a translation of familiar ideas into an exotic setting where they can be presented without the intrusion of personal or topical matters. But "The Greenest Continent" is constantly being invaded by contemporary life. The exemplars of cultural disintegration in Part II, reminiscent of Eliot's *Waste Land;* the angels "sighting machine-guns" in Part V; the "diplomats of the cafés" in Part VII—these keep the world of the 1930's in view. In fact, "The Greenest Continent" was Stevens' poetic reaction to the Italian invasion of Ethiopia in October 1935, and his assimilation of that historical disaster tells us a great deal about the current tensions in his art, especially when it is contrasted with the use of Mr. Burnshaw's Marxist beliefs in "Mr. Burnshaw and the Statue."

Stevens' initial response to the invasion of Ethiopia was ambivalent to say the least: on 31 October 1935 he declared that he was "pro-Mussolini, personally," and that the Italians had "as much right to take Ethiopia from the coons as the coons had to take it from the boa-constrictors," but three weeks later his attitude had changed:

> While it is true that I have spoken sympathetically of Mussolini, all of my sympathies are the other way: with the coons and the boa-constrictors. However, ought I, as a matter of reason, to have sympathized with the Indians as against the Colonists in this country? A man would have to be very thick-skinned not to be conscious of the pathos of Ethiopia or China, or one of these days, if we are not careful, of this country. But that Mussolini is right, practically, has certainly a great deal to be said for it.[56]

A social conservative devoted to the radical imagination, Stevens wished to balance his sympathetic indentification with change and freedom against his rational devotion to the "necessity" of things as they are. He believed "in leftism in every direction," calling it the "most magnificent cause in the world," but could not accept its shabby slogans or its programs for social change. As with the term "pure poetry," he redefined "leftism" in his own fastidious way, hoping to become part of the change all around him, although in each detail of behavior or speech he found himself in total opposition to those who had a better right to the title. On the level of personal convictions and practical politics, Stevens' claim to "leftism" would seem to be a sentimental evasion; but in his poetry it rings true as part of his lifelong progress toward an imaginative realism.

"The Greenest Continent" is, then, a poem about imperialism

and "the white man in Africa," but Stevens worked hard to make it more than "a collection of contemporary images."

> What I have been trying to do in the thing is to apply my own sort of poetry to such a subject. Is poetry that is to have a contemporary significance merely to be a collection of contemporary images, or is it actually to deal with the commonplace of the day? I think the latter, but the result seems rather boring.[57]

Stevens labored at the task of processing current events into his general theory of poetry, and "The Greenest Continent" is a more successful performance than "Mr. Burnshaw and the Statue." The occasion for the poem has been generalized, so that the actual invasion of Ethiopia is sunk in a general conflict between two cultures:

> Angels tiptoe upon the snowy cones
> Of palmy peaks sighting machine-guns? These,
> Seraphim of Europe? Pouring out of dawn,
> Fresh from the sacred clarities, chanters
> Of the pith of mind, cuirassiers against
> The milkiest bowman. This makes a new design,
> Filleted angels over flapping ears,
> Combatting bushmen for a patch of gourds,
> Loosing black slaves to make black infantry,
> Angels returning after war with belts
> And beads and bangles of gold and trumpets raised,
> Racking the world with clarion puffs. (V)

This is as close as the poem comes to its specific subject, and it is probably the least satisfactory movement in "The Greenest Continent." The paradox of *Owl's Clover* lies in the fact that the more Stevens generalizes, the more nearly he approaches the spirit of the times. The image of angels sighting machine-guns strains for relevance, but the hymn to "Fatal Ananke" (VIII) voices a general fatalism. Whether "an improvisation, or an importation from Italy," [58] the term is lifted far above the local context of Italian manifest destiny and turned into a dark expression of Stevens' determination to follow change wherever it might lead. In fact, his political ambivalence at times may be described as a wavering between a romantic attachment to the past and blind acceptance of historical necessity: the middle ground had not been located. "Ananke" was to appear once more in Stevens' poetry, in one of the discarded stanzas (OP 83) from "Examination of the Hero in a Time of War" (1941), but there it is the fatal rhythm against which the hero must struggle. Meanwhile, in 1935–36, "Ananke" was one of the fictions by which the poet lived.

The last two poems in *Owl's Clover*, "A Duck for Dinner" (OP 60–66) and "Sombre Figuration" (OP 66–71), continue to waver between the topical and the universal, between Stevens' raw response to immediate issues and his desire to construct a poetic of "pure poetry." The statue in each returns to something like its meaning in "The Old Woman and the Statue," becoming an emblem of sanity and light in a world of the masses and the "subman." "A Duck for Dinner" has the same opening structure as "Mr. Burnshaw and the Statue": The Bulgar, a spokesman for the evolving working class, will have nothing to do with the old romantic.

> The Bulgar said, "After pineapple with fresh mint
> We went to walk in the park; for, after all,
> The workers do not rise, as Venus rose,
> Out of a violet sea. They rise a bit
>
> On summer Sundays in the park, a duck
> To a million, a duck with apples and without wine.
> They rise to the muddy, metropolitan elms,
> To the camellia-chateaux and an inch beyond,
> Forgetting work, not caring for angels, hunting a lift,
> The triumph of the arcs of heaven's blue
> For themselves, and space and time and ease for the duck. . . .

The band of workers are evolving "inch / By inch" toward a state where, for once, all men will be "thinking together as one, thinking / Each other's thoughts, thinking a single thought." When that ideal is reached the individual will vanish into the single mind of society, and the ideal of pure poetry represented by the statue will no longer be needed. The gauds of life will be irrelevant.

> But that
> Apocalpyse was not contrived for parks,
> Geranium budgets, pay-roll water-falls,
> The clank of the carrousel and, under the trees,
> The sheep-like falling-in of distances,
> Converging on the statue, white and high. (III)

In contrast to the Bulgar's speeches in Parts I and III, Part II opens and closes with an apostrophe to the pioneers ("O buckskin, O crosser of snowy divides") for whom "men were to be ends in themselves." Inheritors of the "scholar's outline" of Europe, these individualists cherished "the print / Of London, the paper of Paris magnified / By poets, the Italian lives preserved / For poverty," but to those rising from actual poverty this is all "gaudy bosh." The contrast is between men of the frontier and men of the machine.

> For you,
> Day came upon the spirit as life comes
> And deep winds flooded you; for these, day comes,
> A penny sun in a tinsel sky, unrhymed,
> And the spirit writhes to be wakened, writhes
> To see, once more, this hacked-up world of tools,
> The heart in slattern pinnacles, the clouds,
> Which were their thoughts, squeezed into shapes, the sun
> Streamed white and stoked and engined wrick-a-wrack.
>
> . . .
>
> These lives are not your lives, O free,
> O bold, that rode your horses straight away.

After this précis of historical change, Part IV queries the future. Basilewsky's abortive "Concerto for Airplane and Pianoforte," the latest Soviet réclame, will not do; the future belongs to man, but the shape he will take is unclear.

> What man of folk-lore shall rebuild the world,
> What lesser man shall measure sun and moon,
> What super-animal dictate our fates?
> As the man the state, not as the state the man . . .

The progress from "man of folk-lore" to "super-animal" is an ascending one, rising toward the Nietzschean superman who may be our only hope if the future fails. But man is "the million and the duck," the mob, and the hero of the future may be orator to the masses, a compound of poet and dictator.

> The man in the band-stand could be orator.
> It may be the future depends on an orator,
> Some pebble-chewer practiced in Tyrian speech,
> An apparition, twanging instruments
> Within us hitherto unknown, he that
> Confounds all opposites and spins a sphere
> Created, like a bubble, of bright sheens,
> With a tendency to bulge as it floats away.
> Basilewsky's bulged before it floated, turned
> Caramel and would not, could not float. And yet
> In an age of concentric mobs would any sphere
> Escape all deformation, much less this,
> This source and patriarch of other spheres,
> This base of every future, vibrant spring,
> The volcano Apostrophe, the sea Behold?

The mixed tone of this passage is finally sorted out in "The Man with the Blue Guitar," where the poet-comedian who can juggle the world's changes like a seal with a ball (Poem XXV) is quite distinct from the false superman and orator of Poem X. It is a sign of Stevens' uncertainty in Owl's Clover that he can seriously consider "Some pebble-chewer practiced in Tyrian speech," some poetic Huey Long, as a possible and acceptable deformation of the imagination. If pure poetry, the "base of every future, vibrant spring" can produce this deformation, then poetry is empty rhetoric: "The volcano Apostrophe, the sea Behold." By trying to face as a realistic alternative a view of the future which violated his deepest sense of propriety, Stevens succeeded only in betraying himself. The fluctuation between Nietzschean superman and gimcrack orator in Part IV of "A Duck for Dinner" bespeaks not an openness to change but a weary fatalism.

In Part V the statue dominates, a "metropolitan of mind." The artist may be the true hero: "The statue is the sculptor not the stone. / In this he carved himself, he carved his age." Gazing at the statue, the people see more than its dynamic form: "They see and feel themselves, seeing / And feeling the world in which they live." Unlike the orator of Part IV, the maker of the statue is a true hero, "pater patriae," wearing the "diamond crown" of imagination which can from time to time obscure the "starless crown" of Ananke, making us "More of ourselves in a world that is more our own."

> Progenitor wearing the diamond crown of crowns,
> He from whose beard the future springs, elect.
> More of ourselves in a world that is more our own,
> For the million, perhaps, two ducks instead of one;
> More of ourselves, the mood of life made strong
> As by a juicier season; and more our own
> As against each other, the dead, the phantomesque.

Like the addresses to the "celestial paramours" in "Mr. Burnshaw and the Statue," Part V of "A Duck for Dinner" balances out the shabby alternatives, bringing the poem to a close on a note of stasis; but the stasis is that of cyclic change, not the stasis of man in the abstract. The Johnsonian concept of "general nature," that which is true of human psychology at all times and all places, is rejected as the worst sort of fiction:

> The civil fiction, the calico idea,
> The Johnsonian composition, abstract man,

> All are evasions like a repeated phrase,
> Which, by its repetition, comes to bear
> A meaning without a meaning. (VI)

Life is a process of change, which flares into imaginative dream from time to time and then subsides: "The envoi to the past / Is largely another winding of the clock." The final movement of "A Duck for Dinner" ends with a recognition of present-day deprivation:

> We walk
> In the park. We regret we have no nightingale.
> We must have the throstle on the gramophone.
> Where shall we find more than derisive words?
> When shall lush chorals spiral through our fire
> And daunt that old assassin, heart's desire?

In "Sombre Figuration" (OP 66–71) Stevens has almost disengaged himself from contemporary images. Only in Part III do we find a verse paragraph (and that cut for the 1937 edition) which confronts the particular demands of his generation. Yet the entire poem, like the final section of "The Greenest Continent," becomes a moving portent of its times precisely because it has been generalized. At the center of "Sombre Figuration" is a half-conscious foreboding of things to come, an imagination of disaster which is all the more terrible because it seems to belong to the racial memory. The disorders of the past are about to be re-enacted, but the form they will take is unclear to the rational mind.

> High up in heaven a sprawling portent moves,
> As if it bears all darkness in its bulk.
> But this we cannot see. The shaggy top
> Broods in tense meditation, constantly,
> On the city, on which it leans, the people there,
> Its shadow on their houses, on their walls,
> Their beds, their faces drawn in distant sleep.
> This is invisible. The supporting arms
> Reach from the horizons, rim to rim,

> While the shaggy top collects itself to do
> And the shoulders turn, breathing immense intent.
> All this is hidden from sight. (III)

Obsessed with the imagination of disaster, the poet seeks for an adequate terminology and finds it in the new language of psychoanalysis. In the world of "Sombre Figuration" the subconscious is in control, and irrationality is the hallmark of the times. The obvious companion piece to the poem is Stevens' essay on "The Irrational Element in Poetry" (OP 216–29), which was written at about the same time and is pervaded with a sense of overhanging disaster. Unlike the later essays and lectures of *The Necessary Angel*, "The Irrational Element in Poetry" shares with *Owl's Clover* a sprawling rhetorical structure and an obsession with the pressure of contemporary events. In it Stevens remarks that the origin of "The Old Woman and the Statue" lay in an atmosphere "charged with anxieties and tensions," which led him to seek a "confronting of the world as it had been imagined in art and as it was then in fact" (OP 219). It was the product of an age of anxiety.

> We are preoccupied with events, even when we do not observe them closely. We have a sense of upheaval. We feel threatened. . . . We are obsessed by the irrational. (OP 225)

Surrounded by evidences of the irrational, the poet naturally sees poetry as an irrational activity, the irrationality ranging from its capricious choice of subjects to its deep affinities with the subconscious. Freud is therefore one of the great figures of the century, since "he has given the irrational a legitimacy that it never had before" (OP 219). Fundamentally, the "irrational element in poetry is the transaction between reality and the sensibility of the poet from which poetry springs" (OP 217), and in "Sombre Figuration" this transaction is dramatized in language and imagery which stem from the new theories of the mind.

The figure who presides over the poem is the "subman," the subconscious mind which impresses its forms on even our most conscious acts.

> There is a man whom rhapsodies of change,
> Of which he is the cause, have never changed
> And never will, a subman under all
> The rest, to whom in the end the rest return,
> The man below the man below the man,
> Steeped in night's opium, evading day. (I)

The abiding "subman," Stevens' variant on the Jungian collective unconscious as well as the Freudian subconscious, becomes the hero in an age "grown weary of the man that thinks," an age betrayed by the sterile rationalists. For the purposes of this poem Stevens treats the imagination as "an activity of the sub-conscious," [59] the source of resemblances and remembrances, a constant surprise to "the sterile rationalist."

> Green is the path we take
> Between chimeras and garlanded the way,
> The down-descent into November's void.
> The spontaneities of rain or snow
> Surprise the sterile rationalist who sees
> Maidens in bloom, bulls under sea, the lark
> On urns and oak-leaves twisted into rhyme.
> The man, but not the man below, for whom
> The pheasant in a field was pheasant, field,
> Until they changed to eagle in white air,
> Lives in a fluid, not on solid rock. (II)

The subconscious, that unchanged cause of the "rhapsodies of change," is what we have instead of Johnsonian "general nature," and from its interactions with the conscious ("spontaneities of rain or snow") comes poetry ("the lark / On urns and oak-leaves twisted into rhyme").

The imagination of "Sombre Figuration" is a force so irrational, so out of touch with everyday reality, that it has become a begetter of "chimeras," a source of anxiety; and the poet naturally draws back toward the world of the conscious and normal. This is not the escape of a stale romanticism, but what Stevens calls "resistance to the pressure of the contemporaneous." The artist must establish himself on something explicable and tangible.

> The painter may establish himself on a guitar, a copy of *Figaro* and a dish of melons. These are fortifyings, although irrational ones. The only possible resistance to the pressure of the contemporaneous is a matter of herrings and apples or, to be less definite, the contemporaneous itself. In poetry, to that extent, the subject is not the contemporaneous, because that is only the nominal subject, but the poetry of the contemporaneous. Resistance to the pressure of ominous and destructive circumstance consists of its conversion, so far as possible, into a different, an explicable, an amenable circumstance. (OP 225)

Part IV of "Sombre Figuration" accomplishes this conversion, and brings us back to the statue standing in "hum-drum space."

> High up in heaven the sprawling portent moves.
> The statue in a crow's perspective of trees
> Stands brimming white, chiaroscuro scaled
> To space. (IV)

The statue here is neither a souvenir from the past, nor an embodiment of the imagination, nor an expression of the maker's personality, but an everyday object which restores us to the normal world of "hum-drum space": "The statue stands in true perspective." As Stevens comments in his paraphrase:

> I suppose it [the statue] stands for sanity. I thought of it as an impressive object of the normal world seen under abnormal conditions: not so much a work as an expression of the circumstances in which works are made. As such, in the poem, the statue is no part of the illimitable space of the sub-conscious. It is a normal

object that of itself brings everything back into true focus. . . . The truth is that, when the imagination no longer partakes to the degree that it should of the real, we reject it and restore ourselves in the hum-drum.[60]

In the end *Owl's Clover* returns to the base of all Stevens' poetry, the natural world of sensation, of air and space and light. The poem subsides into the comforts of the immediate world. "For the poet, the irrational is elemental," says Stevens in concluding "The Irrational Element in Poetry" (OP 229); "but neither poetry nor life is commonly at its dynamic utmost. We know Sweeney as he is and, for the most part, prefer him that way and without too much effulgence and, no doubt, always shall."

III

The Man with the Blue Guitar

Wallace Stevens' agonizing efforts to grapple with the "actuality" of 1935–36 resemble Ernest Hemingway's uneasy accommodations with the spirit of those years. *Owl's Clover* and *To Have and Have Not* give the same impression of a man working against the native grain of his talent, seeking expression for ideas that are too schematic and hypothetical for a sensibility that lives on observed fact. Even if Stevens and Hemingway had found the politics of the left congenial, their styles would have resisted its abstract disregard for the nuances of people and places. We should not be surprised to discover that when Stevens was asked, in 1942, to suggest a poet who could lecture on "Poetry and Actuality," his first choice was Ernest Hemingway: "Most people don't think of Hemingway as a poet, but obviously he is a poet and I should say, offhand, the most significant of living poets, so far as the subject of *Extraordinary Actuality* is concerned." [61] Stevens, like Hemingway, was a stylist of the actual, and it seems likely that he turned away from the kind of poetry he was writing in *Owl's Clover* not so much because he tired of the subject as because he found himself driven toward a style that was not his own. The long verse-paragraphs of *Owl's Clover*, with their lack of organized progression (as witnessed by the revisions) and their loose rhythms, were alien to his natural gift for the self-contained stanza. But in the longer perspective of his entire career the writing of *Owl's Clover* can be seen as a crucial turning-point, perhaps the most important phase in his poetic development. Under the intense pressure from without and within that produced the poems, Stevens exposed and questioned his most fundamental artistic assumptions, thus making possible the triumphant synthesis of "The Man with the Blue Guitar."

The first poem to appear after *Owl's Clover*, "The Men That Are Falling" (CP 187–88),[62] marks a return to the clipped stanzas that Stevens had used so effectively in the past. The occasion of the poem is political—the Spanish Civil War— but its central theme is a confrontation between the helpless romantic and the man of action. Taking his leading image from the Veronica of the Spanish bullfight and Saint Veronica's napkin, the "sudarium," Stevens invokes "The head of one of the men that are falling" in the war. This is not a face upon the linen, a pale image of the dreamer himself, but a "head upon the pillow in the dark, / More than sudarium, speaking the speech / Of absolutes, bodiless, a head / Thick-lipped from riot and rebellious cries." The grotesque situation is softened by the easy five-beat couplets, and in "immaculate syllables" without sound the hero of action declares himself: "he spoke only by doing what he did."

> God and all angels, this was his desire,
> Whose head lies blurring here, for this he died.
>
> Taste of the blood upon his martyred lips,
> O pensioners, O demagogues and pay-men!
>
> This death was his belief though death is a stone.
> This man loved earth, not heaven, enough to die.
>
> The night wind blows upon the dreamer, bent
> Over words that are life's voluble utterance.

"The Men That Are Falling" is one of Stevens' most moving poems, telling as it does of a simple and instinctive heroism which defies all theories. "A Thought Revolved" (CP 184–87), on the other hand, is merciless in its satiric treatment of typical "ideas" of life.[63] The "thought" revolved through four phases is in each case an evasion of reality. In "The Mechanical Optimist" the dying lady, having found the "idea of god" and the "idea of the Alps" too difficult, drifts away into a nirvana of illusion, "Like the night before Christmas and all the carols." The modern poet of Poem II, "Mystic Garden & Middling Beast," strides through a world of cigar stores and lunch rooms, yet he sings of a classical "idea of man" in language from another day. The speaker of Poem III, "Romanesque Affabulation," seeks an earthly leader whose qualities, listed in an interminable catalogue, soon become a burlesque of the original thought. And in the fourth poem, "The Leader," we are introduced to a "moralist hidalgo" whose idea of man's nobility is undermined by his own seediness:

> He sat among beggars wet with dew,
> Heard the dogs howl at barren bone,
> Sat alone, his great toe like a horn,
> The central flaw in the solar morn.

The notions of heroism expressed in each of the four poems are undermined by the verse-forms, which range from witty quatrains reminiscent of *Hugh Selwyn Mauberley* to parodies of Stevens' own style in *Owl's Clover* (Poem II). In each case the language betrays the idea of man or god that it expresses, and this renewal of Stevens' wit and irony is a sure sign of returning poetic vitality. Perhaps the most successful of the four poems is "The Mechanical Optimist," where the mechanical rhythms and predictable rhymes imitate the dying lady's thought.

> A lady dying of diabetes
> Listened to the radio,
> Catching the lesser dithyrambs.
> So heaven collects its bleating lambs.

> Her useless bracelets fondly fluttered,
> Paddling the melodic swirls,
> The idea of god no longer sputtered
> At the roots of her indifferent curls.

It is but a short step from these witty quatrains to the taut couplets of "The Man with the Blue Guitar."

The poems of "The Man with the Blue Guitar" were written in the winter and spring of 1936–37. In March 1937 Stevens announced that he had "written something like 35 or 40 short pieces, of which about 25 seem to be coming through," [64] and by summer the entire sequence was finished. On the dust jacket of *The Man with the Blue Guitar and Other Poems*, which was published that October, Stevens drew a distinction between his new poems and *Owl's Clover:*

> In one group, *Owl's Clover*, while the poems reflect what was then going on in the world, that reflection is merely for the purpose of seizing and stating what makes life intelligible and desirable in the midst of great change and great confusion. The effect of *Owl's Clover* is to emphasize the opposition between things as they are and things imagined; in short, to isolate poetry.
>
> Since this is of significance, if we are entering a period in which poetry may be of first importance to the spirit, I have been making notes on the subject in the form of short poems during the past winter. These short poems, some thirty of them, form the other group, *The Man with the Blue Guitar*, from which the book takes its title. This group deals with the incessant conjunctions between things as they are and things imagined. Although the blue guitar is a symbol of the imagination, it is used most often simply as a reference to the individuality of the poet, meaning by the poet any man of imagination.

The distinction is clear: in its constant emphasis on the flux of the present, the change and confusion of contemporary life, *Owl's Clover* tended to isolate the poetic activity. Although the meanings attached to it may vary, the statue does stand aloof in each of the poems. "The Man with the Blue Guitar," on the other hand, embraces the enigmas and disparities of *Owl's Clover* and constructs out of them a tenable world for poetry. It is the centerpiece of Stevens' poetic career, the end to one long process of development and the beginning of a later stage where the principles of growth and change are quite different. "The Man with the Blue Guitar" contains the "materia poetica" of the later Stevens, the matrix of ideas and themes out of which the major poems of the 1940's and 1950's evolved. Concise, self-confident, filled with a sense of new beginnings, it differs in every way from the rhetorical perplexities of *Owl's Clover*, yet it cannot be fully understood unless we place it in the context of Stevens' total achievement in the mid-thirties.

The serenity and buoyancy of "The Man with the Blue Guitar" are reflected in its verse-form. The taut couplets are a conscious reaction against the high rhetoric of *Owl's Clover* and "Farewell to Florida"; it is almost as if Stevens, determined to "pull himself together," did so by drawing on the most controlled form in his verse repertoire. The gift for adage and aphorism which is a fundamental of his poetry lies behind the condensed couplets, and the poems of "The Man with the Blue Guitar" constantly remind us of entries in the *Adagia*. They have the pithy quality of a proverb or saying, so that each line seems to demand expansion or interpretation. In two series of letters Stevens provided an extended gloss on "The Man with the Blue Guitar," and it is instructive to compare these comments with his remarks on *Owl's Clover*.[65] The letters to Hi Simons concerning *Owl's Clover* are essentially paraphrase; Stevens reduces the long rhetorical movements to simple statement, and is basically concerned with the "ideas" behind the poem. His comments on "The Man with the Blue Guitar" are, by contrast, mostly particular and expansive, a glossing of individual phrases and an elaboration of ambiguous metaphors. It is a sign of the fundamental difference between

the two works that he should wish to paraphrase *Owl's Clover*
and elaborate upon "The Man with the Blue Guitar." Whole
sections of *Owl's Clover* can be reduced to an aphorism,
while each aphorism in "The Man with the Blue Guitar" demands detailed explication. Writing to a would-be interpreter
in 1953, Stevens declared his opposition to the kind of explanations that serve so well with *Owl's Clover:*

> I do not think that a thesis should be based on questions
> and answers like an interview. On the contrary, I believe
> in pure explication de texte. This may in fact be my
> principal form of piety.[66]

One sign of Stevens' success in "The Man with the Blue
Guitar" is the poem's resistance to paraphrase. Only by an
emphasis on nuance and implication can we come to an understanding of its central design.

Speaking of the order of the poems, Stevens told Hi Simons
that they "are printed in the order in which they were written
without rearrangement. There were a few that were scrapped.
I kept them in their original order for my own purposes, because one really leads into another, even when the relationship
is only one of contrast." [67] This apparently disingenuous explanation may well be true. The pattern described by the
poems is one of variation and recapitulation on a series of related themes, and the inner harmonies of the sequence are far
more precise and subtle than its general structure. Sometimes
a group of poems will build variations on a single theme
(e.g. Poems XXII–XXVIII); at other times the movement from
poem to poem is one of deliberate contrasts. Poems are linked
to each other by *leitmotifs*, by similarities in imagery, and
occasionally by likenesses in rhyme structure (e.g. Poems IV
and VI). In short, the progression of the sequence is musical,
and individual poems may be linked with several others by a
complex network of formal and thematic resemblances. But
the real subtlety of "The Man with the Blue Guitar" occurs
within the individual poems, where the same term may be

given a total shift in meaning in the space of a few lines
(e.g. "things as they are" in Poem IV), or where an aphoristic
opening ("Poetry is the subject of the poem," Poem XXII)
may soon lose its apparent dogmatism. The structure of the
individual poems is essentially dramatic, either a confrontation
between two voices (as in Poem I) or between two attitudes
(Poem XIX). The result is a long poem whose general structure appears to be carefree and haphazard, but whose local
units have an amazing density and range of implication, so that
a complex theory is often implicit in the simplest line. In
contrast to "Like Decorations in a Nigger Cemetery," where
the density comes from elision and compression of language,
"The Man with the Blue Guitar" possesses the density of condensed thought. What appears at first reading to be a musical
revue of Stevens' aphorisms on art and life, the *Adagia* ver-
sified, is ultimately revealed as an *ars poetica* of stunning complexity. These spare couplets provide the scaffolding for much
of his later poetry.

In contrast to his elaborate schema for *Owl's Clover*, Stevens' comments on his intentions in "The Man with the Blue
Guitar" (CP 165–84) are simple and direct. Just as each poem
in the series plays intricate variations on a simple motif, so
the entire series is devoted to a subject which is easily stated
but whose ramifications have no end: "the incessant conjunctions between things as they are and things imagined."
Writing to Renato Poggioli in July 1953, Stevens defined his
central themes, which are in fact but one grand theme:

> The general intention of the *Blue Guitar* was to say
> a few things that I felt impelled to say 1. about reality;
> 2. about the imagination; 3. their inter-relations; and 4.
> principally, my attitude toward each of these things.
> This is the general scope of the poem, which is con-
> fined to the area of poetry and makes no pretense of
> going beyond that area.[68]

This limitation of scope and subject was the key to Stevens'
achievement in "The Man with the Blue Guitar." By refusing

to confront the issues of politics and social behavior on their own ground, where his expertise could be no greater than that of the sociologist or historian, and by translating them into his chosen area of the poem and its activities, Stevens managed to compress all of the subjects which engaged his mind in *Ideas of Order* and *Owl's Clover* into a defense of poetry that is also a major statement on "things as they are."

> Poetry increases the feeling for reality.
>
> The theory of poetry is the life of poetry.
>
> The theory of poetry is the theory of life. (OP 162, 178)

These aphorisms from the *Adagia*, which may seem facile and pretentious in isolation, are proved upon the pulse in "The Man with the Blue Guitar."

The emotional center of "The Man with the Blue Guitar" is Poem V, which was published separately in *Twentieth Century Verse* (April 1937) under the heading, "The Place of Poetry."

> Do not speak to us of the greatness of poetry,
> Of the torches wisping in the underground,
>
> Of the structure of vaults upon a point of light.
> There are no shadows in our sun,
>
> Day is desire and night is sleep.
> There are no shadows anywhere.
>
> The earth, for us, is flat and bare.
> There are no shadows. Poetry
>
> Exceeding music must take the place
> Of empty heaven and its hymns,
>
> Ourselves in poetry must take their place,
> Even in the chattering of your guitar.

This poem gives eloquent voice to a theme sounded as early as Stanza IV of "Sunday Morning," and as late as Parts II and III of "The Greenest Continent": the great other-worldly mythologies are dead, earth is the only heaven we can know, and poetry sings its only hymns. We have a poetic instead of a theology.

> The relation of art to life is of the first importance especially in a skeptical age since, in the absence of a belief in God, the mind turns to its own creations and examines them, not alone from the aesthetic point of view, but for what they reveal, for what they validate and invalidate, for the support that they give. (From *Adagia*, OP 159)

The first three lines of Poem V echo the vanished hymns to heaven in their sublime diction and long, five-beat lines, but at the end of the second couplet the verse narrows to the plain, four-beat norm of "The Man with the Blue Guitar," and present-day reality asserts itself. If poetry is no longer the music that celebrates a transcendental faith, then it must "exceed" music and provide a humanistic belief (based on "ourselves") that will "take the place / Of empty heaven and its hymns." The experience of reading this poem is an experience of initial impoverishment, as the heroic diction of the first three lines is withdrawn, and then of renewed hope as the last two couplets sketch a possible alternative. "After one has abandoned a belief in god, poetry is that essence which takes its place as life's redemption" (From *Adagia*, OP 158).

The nature of our shadowless earth, the rock upon which poetry builds, is imaged at the center of "The Man with the Blue Guitar" in Poem XV:

> Is this picture of Picasso's, this "hoard
> Of destructions," a picture of ourselves,
>
> Now, an image of our society?
> Do I sit, deformed, a naked egg,
>
> Catching at Good-bye, harvest moon,
> Without seeing the harvest or the moon?

> Things as they are have been destroyed.
> Have I? Am I a man that is dead
>
> At a table on which the food is cold?
> Is my thought a memory, not alive?
>
> Is the spot on the floor, there, wine or blood
> And whichever it may be, is it mine?

Here the sense of contemporary disorder and destruction that pervades *Ideas of Order* and *Owl's Clover* enters the poem obliquely, through Picasso's comment on his own pictures, but gains in power and generality by this displacement. Obviously Stevens had been disturbed by the Picasso paintings reproduced in *Cahiers d'Art* for 1935, with their radical deformations and reformations of the human figures, and intrigued by Picasso's comment to Christian Zervos:

> Formerly paintings evolved toward their final form by progression. Each day brought something new. A painting was a sum of additions. But for me, a painting is a sum of destructions [*une somme de destructions*]. I make a painting, then I destroy it. But ultimately nothing is lost; the red that I removed from one part can be found in some other part.[69]

If "things as they are," reality, is in a state of constant self-destruction, has man become simply a "hoard of destructions," living by slogans and dead metaphors ("Catching at Good-bye, harvest moon") without hope of re-integration?

> Is the spot on the floor, there, wine or blood
> And whichever it may be, is it mine?

The poem ends with a hidden reference to the Christian miracle of transubstantiation or transfiguration, which is used throughout the poem as a secular metaphor for the imagination's power to transform. With their realistic acknowledgment that earth is all we have, bare, shadowless, and in a state of social distintegration, Poems V and XV present the challenge that the imagination must face.

The opening poem of "The Man with the Blue Guitar" chants the refrains which will be repeated and elaborated through most of the sequence.

> The man bent over his guitar,
> A shearsman of sorts. The day was green.
>
> They said, "You have a blue guitar,
> You do not play things as they are."
>
> The man replied, "Things as they are
> Are changed upon the blue guitar."
>
> And they said then, "But play, you must,
> A tune beyond us, yet ourselves,
>
> A tune upon the blue guitar
> Of things exactly as they are."

The man with the blue guitar sits in the cross-legged posture of Picasso's "The Old Guitarist," trying to fit reality to his instrument as the tailor ("shearsman") tries to fit cloth to his pattern. The simplicity of the scene is deliberate, the "green" of things as they are and the "blue" of things imagined standing distinct and without subtlety; and the simplicity of the debate between guitarist and audience is reinforced by the almost childish rhymes. "Things as they are" and "things as they are . . . upon the blue guitar" seem to require no definition, until the audience demands "A tune beyond us, yet ourselves." It is this demand that poetry must not detach itself from reality, but present a credible version of it, which initiates the endless complications of creating a fiction that we know to be a fiction and yet believe in willingly.

The immense difficulty of giving reality an imaginative shape without distortion is confessed at the outset of Poem II ("I cannot bring a world quite round, / Although I patch it as I can"), and in poem after poem the problem is taken up and worried in different ways. In Poem IV, as Stevens comments, "reality changes into the imagination (under one's very eyes) as one experiences it, by reason of one's feelings about it." [70]

> A million people on one string?
> And all their manner in the thing,
>
> And all their manner, right and wrong,
> And all their manner, weak and strong?

The buzzing of life's diversity becomes the buzzing of the blue guitar, a statement of one aspect of reality. For a moment at least the imagination can seize upon reality and give it a place "in space," beyond time's "compass of change." In an age when the "thinking of god is smoky dew" the "thinking of art seems final," and the "senses of the guitar"—its transformations—may compose from time to time into a supreme fiction.

> A tune beyond us as we are,
> Yet nothing changed by the blue guitar;
>
> Ourselves in the tune as if in space,
> Yet nothing changed, except the place
>
> Of things as they are and only the place
> As you play them, on the blue guitar,
>
> Placed, so, beyond the compass of change,
> Perceived in a final atmosphere;
>
> For a moment final, in the way
> The thinking of art seems final when
>
> The thinking of god is smoky dew.
> The tune is space. The blue guitar
>
> Becomes the place of things as they are,
> A composing of senses of the guitar. (VI)

Poem VI leaps to the ideal resolution, a sustaining fiction which embodies "things as they are" while retaining all of the satis-

factions of that other reality, the poem. But the process by
which this is accomplished remains to be defined, and most
of the poems in "The Man with the Blue Guitar" are devoted
to that definition.

Several poems speak of the dangers inherent in emphasizing
the imagination at the expense of reality. Poem VII hypoth-
esizes a reversal in the normal relation between moon and
sun. What if it were possible to stand in the sun and "call it
merciful," to call it "The immaculate, the merciful good, /
Detached from us, from things as they are?" The music of
transformation would fade: "The strings are cold on the blue
guitar." In an even more extreme example, Poem XIII "deals
with the intensity of the imagination unmodified by contacts
with reality, if such a thing is possible." [71]

> The pale intrusions into blue
> Are corrupting pallors . . . ay di mi,
>
> Blue buds or pitchy blooms. Be content—
> Expansions, diffusions—content to be
>
> The unspotted imbecile revery,
> The heraldic center of the world
>
> Of blue, blue sleek with a hundred chins,
> The amorist Adjective aflame . . .

Here the broken syntax and the pejorative adjectives ("pale,"
"corrupting," "pitchy," "imbecile," "sleek") mock a world
where the imagination is unrestrained, where the "amorist
Adjective aflame"—the word "blue" as a heraldic personification—merely consumes itself. Poem XIII embodies one of
Stevens' central aphorisms: "In poetry at least the imagination
must not detach itself from reality" (OP 161).

The imagination as a free activity is willful and self-destruc-
tive; it must always depend on "things as they are," but that
dependence can take many forms and be felt with various
degrees of intensity. In Poem VIII the vivid motion and
colors of a storm evoke only a laconic response, a "leaden

twang" from the blue guitar, yet that faint response "like the reason in a storm" is enough to bring "the storm to bear." It is a point of order, the minimal reaction to a scene which should excite the full imagination:

> The vivid, florid, turgid sky,
> The drenching thunder rolling by,
>
> The morning deluged still by night,
> The clouds tumultuously bright
>
> And the feeling heavy in cold chords
> Struggling toward impassioned choirs,
>
> Crying among the clouds, enraged
> By gold antagonists in air—
>
> I know my lazy, leaden twang
> Is like the reason in a storm;
>
> And yet it brings the storm to bear.
> I twang it out and leave it there. (VIII)

In contrast to the sullen response of Poem VIII, the imagination in Poem IX dominates the scene, taking on the moods and colors of an essential dullness and making them memorable. As in "Sea Surface Full of Clouds" or "The Idea of Order at Key West," the poet is the maker, the active principle in a world which is nearly formless. The figure of the poet emerges from the drab landscape dressed in its weather, its "tragic robe," and becomes its spokesman.

> And the color, the overcast blue
> Of the air, in which the blue guitar
>
> Is a form, described but difficult,
> And I am merely a shadow hunched
>
> Above the arrowy, still strings,
> The maker of a thing yet to be made;
>
> The color like a thought that grows
> Out of a mood, the tragic robe

Of the actor, half his gesture, half
His speech, the dress of his meaning, silk

Sodden with his melancholy words,
The weather of his stage, himself. (IX)

Stevens referred to these two poems as "companion pieces;
they demonstrate the law of opposites." [72] It would seem that
the relationship between imagination and reality is a symbiotic
one, containing a fixed amount of energy. When "things as
they are" become most spectacular (as in the storm of Poem
VIII) the imagination need only provide a counterpoint; but
when the subject is flat and bare the imagination must absorb
every detail if it is to infuse life and order.

Stevens' variations on the theme of imagination and reality
reach a climax in Poems XVIII–XXIII. Poem XVIII postulates
an imaginative construct, "a dream" so overmastering that it
can stand "in face of the object" it depends upon, a dream
that has become a "thing" of "things as they are": music
that has become pure feeling, as in "Peter Quince at the
Clavier." It is like daylight on the shimmering cliffs above the
sea, which seems more real than the empty "sea of ex" beneath. Only such a dream-become-fact can master the stubborn
chaos of nature, which Stevens confronts in Poem XIX.

That I may reduce the monster to
Myself, and then may be myself

In face of the monster, be more than part
Of it, more than the monstrous player of

One of its monstrous lutes, not be
Alone, but reduce the monster and be,

Two things, the two together as one,
And play of the monster and of myself,

Or better not of myself at all,
But of that as its intelligence,

> Being the lion in the lute
> Before the lion locked in stone.

The almost heraldic image with which this poem closes provoked one of Stevens' most eloquent glosses:

> Monster = nature, which I desire to reduce: master, subjugate, acquire complete control over and use freely for my own purpose, as poet. I want, as poet, to be that in nature, which constitutes nature's very self. I want to be nature in the form of a man, with all the resources of nature = I want to be the lion in the lute; and then, when I am, I want to face my parent and be his true part. I want to face nature the way two lions face one another —the lion in the lute facing the lion locked in stone. I want, as a man of the imagination, to write poetry with all the power of a monster equal in strength to that of the monster about whom I write. I want man's imagination to be completely adequate in the face of reality.[73]

Out of this confrontation between poet and nature will come the fictions "exceeding music" that will take the place "Of empty heaven and its hymns." These fictions will not be "ideas" (Poem XX) but something as intimate as the air we breath, supreme abstractions which partake of "One's self and the mountains of one's land, / Without shadows, without magnificence, / The flesh, the bone, the dirt, the stone" (Poem XXI). They must be, in the words of *Notes toward a Supreme Fiction*, abstractions that are "blooded," filled with a vitality that comes from the incessant change of life.

The tableau which ends Poem XIX, "the lion in the lute / Before the lion locked in stone," was too static an emblem for Stevens' purpose, and in Poems XXII and XXIII he plays variations on that aphorism from the *Adagia* which comes closest to summing up his poetic:

> Poetry is not the same thing as the imagination taken alone. Nothing is itself taken alone. Things are because of interrelations or interactions. (OP 163)

The first line of Poem XXII, "Poetry is the subject of the poem," is often quoted in isolation as proof that Stevens' art was a reflexive one, taking always as its subject the imaginative process, but in context the meaning is more complicated. "Poetry," by which Stevens meant "pure poetry," [74] is the ordering of words and sounds which gives us a "pure" satisfaction; but it is the "absence in reality" that validates this pure construction, giving it the truth of our perishing earth. From reality the poem takes its substance, but it also gives in the "universal intercourse," bestowing a freshness and individuality on our familiar world.

> Poetry is the subject of the poem,
> From this the poem issues and
>
> To this returns. Between the two,
> Between issue and return, there is
>
> An absence in reality,
> Things as they are. Or so we say.
>
> But are these separate? Is it
> An absence for the poem, which acquires
>
> Its true appearances there, sun's green,
> Cloud's red, earth feeling, sky that thinks?
>
> From these it takes. Perhaps it gives,
> In the universal intercourse.

As Stevens comments on this poem, the imagination "does not create except as it transforms. There is nothing that exists exclusively by reason of the imagination, or that does not exist in some form in reality. Thus, reality = the imagination, and the imagination = reality. Imagination gives, but gives in relation." [75] The relationship is reciprocal, unlike that described by Coleridge in Chapter XIV of *Biographia Literaria*. Stevens could never exclaim "O Lady! we receive but what we give," since for him the vital impulse lay equally with the observer and the observed. Although accepting the Col-

eridgean belief that "pure poetry" is the balance or reconciliation of opposite or discordant qualities, Stevens refuses
to give primacy to either the imagination or its materials,
preferring to locate the soul of poetry in a "universal intercourse." [76]

Poem XXIII provides a series of equations for the poem's
"absence in reality," a duet between imagination and fact:

> A few final solutions, like a duet
> With the undertaker: a voice in the clouds,
>
> Another on earth, the one a voice
> Of ether, the other smelling of drink,
>
> The voice of ether prevailing, the swell
> Of the undertaker's song in the snow
>
> Apostrophizing wreaths, the voice
> In the clouds serene and final, next
>
> The grunted breath serene and final,
> The imagined and the real, thought
>
> And the truth, Dichtung und Wahrheit, all
> Confusion solved, as in a refrain
>
> One keeps on playing year by year,
> Concerning the nature of things as they are.

The poem begins as a duet, but ends as a single refrain.[77] The
exchange between clouds and earth, ether and undertaker,
is a constant struggle for supremacy which narrows as the
poem progresses, until in "Dichtung und Wahrheit" the opposition becomes an equation. As a student at Harvard in
1898–99 Stevens took a course in "Goethe and His Time"
where *Dichtung und Wahrheit* was required reading, and a
half-century later he spoke of Goethe as a former idol.[78] In
Goethe's autobiography the term for "poetry" or "fiction,"
Dichtung, has become so identified with his recaptured and
re-ordered life that the title may be read as an equation:

Dichtung = Wahrheit, Poetry = Fact or Truth. In Stevens' world, "the imagined and the real" are ultimately reconciled because they form a timeless refrain of "things as they are."

⌣

From the perspective of "The Man with the Blue Guitar," the phases of Stevens' previous career fall into a comprehensible pattern. His work on *Harmonium* constantly fluctuated between the excesses of imagination and fact, as Crispin's voyage described an oscillating pattern between these two poles. Just as the proportions between imagination and reality may vary from age to age, so they may vary within a single career, with some works being "favorable to the imagination" and others "favorable to what is real." [79] If we look back over Stevens' works before 1937, the landmarks in his poetic progress mark a steady interchange between extremes. The grotesque is balanced by the delicate, the primordial by the fictive, and the major statements of poetic theory—"To the One of Fictive Music," "The Idea of Order at Key West," "The Old Woman and the Statue"—rehearse various combinations of fact and fiction. It should not be surprising, therefore, to find the major concerns of Stevens' poetic development restated in "The Man with the Blue Guitar" as corollaries to the great theme of *Dichtung und Wahrheit*. For the purposes of illustration we can isolate three of these corollaries: man and his weather, the old romantic and the new, and the "idea of man."

Our weather, our climate, our environment: these form the stage upon which the poet performs. Poem XI quizzes the relationship:

> Slowly the ivy on the stones
> Becomes the stones. Women become
>
> The cities, children become the fields
> And men in waves become the sea.

It is the chord that falsifies.
The sea returns upon the men,

The fields entrap the children, brick
Is a weed and all the flies are caught,

Wingless and withered, but living alive.
The discord merely magnifies.

Deeper within the belly's dark
Of time, time grows upon the rock.

Both chord and discord are false, since man is neither absorbed by his environment nor overwhelmed by it: instead the two exist in easy harmony, and within the mystery of time "time grows upon the rock." The ideal balance between life and its environment is figured in the balance of the ideal poem. "The poetic view of life is larger than any of its poems," says Stevens in one of his *Adagia* (OP 174), and the poetic in life means man's adjustment to his climate and setting.

I am a native in this world
And think in it as a native thinks,

Gesu, not native of a mind
Thinking the thoughts I call my own,

Native, a native in the world
And like a native think in it.

In this opening to Poem XXVIII the obsolete form "Gesu" was chosen for its sound,[80] but also for its connotations: like the speaker in "Sunday Morning," the poet will not live in an obsolete past of another mind, but be a "native" in the only world he knows.

The urge to be "a native in this world" naturally leads to a rejection of all encrusted rhetoric, as in the "tattery hues" and "muffling mist" of Poem XIV. The romantic is always with us, but it must be of our time and our climate. Ideally, we would live "in space" (see Poems VI and XXVI) not in time, free of the past and attuned to every spontaneity of the moment. This desire to become, in Stevens' words, "one of the jocular procreations of the dark, of space," [81] is a longing after impossibility, but a necessary longing because it defines the ultimate limits of Stevens' romanticism. Against it we must balance his desire for the general, the "abstract," that which is true at all times and all places—his classicism, if you will—which is forever present in the traditional aspects of his language and verse-forms. Stevens' poetry exhibits constant impulses toward the extremes of romanticism and classicism, combined with a faith that these may one day be reconciled; and this tension is nowhere more apparent than in his quest for a tenable "idea of man" which will be liberating rather than restricting.

One of the principal trends in Stevens' poetry of the mid-1930's is his reluctant approach to an "idea of man" which might serve as an adequate fiction, taking the place "Of empty heaven and its hymns." The fear of abstractions was deep-rooted in his language and the genres of his poetry ("Go in fear of abstractions" was one of the slogans of Imagism), but Stevens knew that unless his poetry could deal with abstractions and general nature it would remain a mosaic of individual perceptions. An abstraction or essence can, of course, range from the purity of an individual perception (an object viewed without any preconceptions derived from myth or poetry) to the definition of a class or type, and it was this latter abstraction that Stevens feared. His poetry had always made attempts at the elemental abstraction, the isolation of irreducible feelings or impressions, but had shied away from such categories as "man," "nature," "the poem." Caught between the extreme romantic's passion for the individual sensation and the philosopher's desire for permanent classes or species, Stevens had taken a familiar escape-route in his early verse: the cycles of mutability are the source of permanence within change, as in "Peter Quince" or "Sunday Morning." But this notion of patterned change proved unequal to the pressures of a later time, and in the poems of *Ideas of Order* Stevens is

trying on various solutions, ranging from the heroic indi-
vidualism of "How to Live. What to Do" and "The Brave
Man" to the responsive effects of language in "The Idea of
Order at Key West" and "A Postcard from the Volcano."
These provisional orders, consoling in themselves, could not
fully satisfy the intense pressures of the age, and in *Owl's
Clover* Stevens found himself adrift without coordinating fictions to replace those he had so scrupulously rejected in his
earlier career. The formulations of *Adagia* and "The Man
with the Blue Guitar" reflect a self-conscious attempt to discover such fictions, and among the most important was the
fiction or abstraction of major man: "Man without variation.
Man in C Major. The complete realization, of the idea of
man. Man at his happier normal." [82]

The opening poem of "The Man with the Blue Guitar,"
with its demand for "A tune beyond us, yet ourselves," leads
directly to the dilemma of Poem II:

> I cannot bring a world quite round,
> Although I patch it as I can.
>
> I sing a hero's head, large eye
> And bearded bronze, but not a man
>
> Although I patch him as I can
> And reach through him almost to man.

The "hero's head" represents the inevitable displacement or
distortion of art, the fiction which must stand for the idea
of man that eludes the poet's reach. Like the sphere juggled by
the orator-hero of "A Duck for Dinner," it always has a
"tendency to bulge as it floats away" (OP 63). In making our
convincing fictions of man, the "fictive"—the artificial—seems
always to intervene.

"Ah, but to play man number one . . ." The third poem
begins on a wistful note, but as the ideal song of "man number
one" is developed Stevens' ambivalence breaks through. The
aim is "To strike his living hi and ho, / To tick it, tock it,

turn it true," to express man as he is "in the liveliness of lively experience, without pose," [83] without convention or artifice. The imagery, on the other hand, is that of destruction and dissection:

> Ah, but to play man number one,
> To drive the dagger in his heart,
>
> To lay his brain upon the board
> And pick the acrid colors out,
>
> To nail his thought across the door,
> Its wings spread wide to rain and snow,
>
> To strike his living hi and ho,
> To tick it, tock it, turn it true,
>
> To bang it from a savage blue,
> Jangling the metal of the strings . . .

The poem of "man number one" would be a savage poem, bitter and disturbing; after "his living hi and ho" has been abstracted man is like a hawk nailed to a barn door, the bloodless effigy of a living thing. The final couplet trails off into a silent acknowledgment of the apparent contradiction between abstraction and change, between the poem as idea and the poem as sensation.

The paradox inherent in Poem III of "The Man with the Blue Guitar" explains Stevens' stubborn reluctance, in the years 1934–37, to embrace the notion that poetry must be abstract. As the pressures of the times and the pressures within his own art drove him toward a general theory of poetry, his native bent for the particular and the accidental caused him to question each stage in the journey. He shared with Ezra Pound a distrust of abstract definitions which are not based on the particulars of experience. As Pound puts it in the first chapter of *ABC of Reading:*

> In Europe, if you ask a man to define anything, his definition always moves away from the simple things

that he knows perfectly well, it recedes into an unknown region, that is a region of remoter and progressively remoter abstraction.

Thus if you ask him what red is, he says it is a "colour."

If you ask him what a colour is, he tells you it is a vibration or a refraction of light, or a division of the spectrum.

And if you ask him what vibration is, he tells you it is a mode of energy, or something of that sort, until you arrive at a modality of being, or non-being, or at any rate you get in beyond your depth, and beyond his depth.[84]

Pound's solution to the problem of "generality"—patterns of concrete particulars modeled after his understanding of the Chinese ideogram—could never be that of Stevens, whose "rage for order" took a more philosophical bent, but the distrust of abstraction is a repeated theme in *Ideas of Order* and *Owl's Clover*. In "Like Decorations in a Nigger Cemetery" (Poem XXXV) Stevens mocks the "pundit of the weather" who is so absorbed in "man the abstraction, the comic sum" that he is unconcerned with "Men and the affairs of men." Type-figures are the substance of comedy, since they caricature man as he is, and many of the ideas of major man explored in *Owl's Clover* turn into caricature, like the "pebble-chewer practiced in Tyrian speech" (OP 63) of "A Duck for Dinner." Nonetheless, *Owl's Clover* exhibits a thirst for abstraction: "Fatal Ananke," the "metropolitan of mind," the "man of folklore," the "super-animal," the "subman," all are thrusts toward something beyond local order. Yet running counter to these attempts is a persistent suspicion of the bland ideal, whether that be the "general nature" of classical theory ("The civil fiction, the calico idea, / The Johnsonian composition, abstract man") or the more fashionable "collective unconscious" of modern psychology. All are seen as procrustean theories which "nail his thought across the door, / Its wings spread wide to rain and snow."

A way-station in Stevens' revolving of this problem is

Poem II of "A Thought Revolved" (CP 185), where the poet striding through an unheroic world of contemporary trivia "Denies that abstraction is a vice except / To the fatuous" and escapes into a "space of stone" where the "idea of man" is the true measure.

> One man, the idea of man, that is the space,
> The true abstract in which he promenades.
> The era of the idea of man, the cloak
> And speech of Virgil dropped, that's where he walks,
> That's where his hymns come crowding, hero-hymns,
> Chorals for mountain voices and the moral chant . . .

Attractive as the rhetoric may be, this "idea of man" is an evasion of the realities of time and change; it is possible to read the poem as another critique of the New Humanism, which in its emphasis on the norm of Johnsonian "general nature" neglected the facts of contemporary life and art. The "moral chant" was not to be the ground-bass of Stevens' "hero-hymns."

These experiments with abstraction provide the context for the poems in "The Man with the Blue Guitar" where Stevens fashions various images of his hero, "man number one." Poem X, for example, conjures up the image of a popular hero "whom none believes, / Whom all believe that all believe," the major man as demagogue; and then declares him to be the adversary. Stevens' gloss is unusually precise:

> If we are to think of a supreme fiction, instead of creating it, as the Greeks did, for example, in the form of a mythology, we might choose to create it in the image of a man: an agreed-on superman. He would not be the typical hero taking part in parades (columns red with red-fire, bells tolling, tin cans, confetti), in whom actually no one believes as a truly great man, but in whom everybody pretends to believe, someone completely outside of the intimacies of profound faith, a politician, a soldier, Harry Truman as god. *This second-rate creature is the*

adversary. I address him but with hostility, hoo-ing the
slick trombones.[85]

The popular hero of Poem X is one caricature of major
man; another would be the comedian-poet of Poem XXV,
who is the permanent master ("the nose is eternal") of a
changing world.

> He held the world upon his nose
> And this-a-way he gave a fling.
>
> His robes and symbols, ai-yi-yi—
> And that-a-way he twirled the thing.
>
> Sombre as fir-trees, liquid cats
> Moved in the grass without a sound.
>
> They did not know the grass went round.
> The cats had cats and the grass turned gray
>
> And the world had worlds, ai, this-a-way:
> The grass turned green and the grass turned gray.
>
> And the nose is eternal, that-a-way.
> Things as they were, things as they are,
>
> Things as they will be by and by . . .
> A fat thumb beats out ai-yi-yi.

The tone of this poem is half admiration and half mockery:
the idea of man as a sleight-of-hand artist is balanced against
the idea of man as the one perceiver of cyclic change. More
sombre is the provisional fiction of Poem XXI, where the
world of anthropomorphic myth ("that gold self aloft") gives
way to an adequate "substitute for all the gods," one's self
as personified in an actual mountain ("Chocorua") of an actual
land: "The flesh, the bone, the dirt, the stone."

Poem XXI leads easily into the climactic movement of "The
Man with the Blue Guitar," the end-point of all Stevens'
variations on the idea of man.

From this I shall evolve a man.
This is his essence: the old fantoche

Hanging his shawl upon the wind,
Like something on the stage, puffed out,

His strutting studied through centuries.
At last, in spite of his manner, his eye

A-cock at the cross-piece on a pole
Supporting heavy cables, slung

Through Oxidia, banal suburb,
One-half of all its installments paid.

Dew-dapper clapper-traps, blazing
From crusty stacks above machines.

Ecce, Oxidia is the seed
Dropped out of this amber-ember pod,

Oxidia is the soot of fire,
Oxidia is Olympia. (XXX)

This poem is Stevens' "Ecce Homo": Behold the Man. The
"old fantoche," man as puppet or stage comedian, is the
"comic sum" of our accumulated ideas about man: he is an
adaptable figure like Crispin, who has strutted through the
centuries playing different roles, and as we think of his past
performances he becomes a mere abstraction, what Stevens
called "one of the fantoccini of meditation." [86] At last, "in
spite of his manner," he is brought face-to-face with present-
day reality: "his eye / A-cock at the cross-piece on a
pole . . ." The image is complex and exact: the old actor has
become an actual lineman on the pole, "an employe of the
Oxidia Electric Light & Power Company," as Stevens wryly
remarked; but he is also a crucified man, the archetypal image
of man translated into contemporary reality. "Ecce, Oxidia
is the seed / Dropped out of this amber-ember pod, / Oxidia
is the soot of fire, / Oxidia is Olympia." These lines are dense

with implication. "Amber-ember," like the title "Amber Um-
ber" which Stevens wished to give to his last poems,[87] points
in two directions: toward change and gritty reality ("ember"),
toward permanence and exaltation ("amber"). Like "Dichtung
und Wahrheit," the two halves of the term balance out the
major oppositions of the poem. "Oxidia," the banal suburb,
is both the "seed" dropped from the blazing pod of the
machines and the "soot," the drab residue, of a flame-like
past. The very word "Oxidia" suggests a conversion or trans-
valuation: "Oxidia" is the only "Olympia" we have, and out
of it all our fictions of man must be evolved. "Oxidia" and its
major men are abstractions that have been blooded by present-
day reality.

After the climactic resolution of Poem XXX "The Man
with the Blue Guitar" draws to a close. Poems XXXI and
XXXII insist on the contemporary, the "rhapsody of things as
they are," and lead directly into the final poem, which is not
so much a conclusion as a re-enactment of familiar themes.

> That generation's dream, aviled
> In the mud, in Monday's dirty light,
>
> That's it, the only dream they knew,
> Time in its final block, not time
>
> To come, a wrangling of two dreams.
> Here is the bread of time to come,
>
> Here is its actual stone. The bread
> Will be our bread, the stone will be
>
> Our bed and we shall sleep by night.
> We shall forget by day, except
>
> The moments when we choose to play
> The imagined pine, the imagined jay.

"That generation" would be the generation of the thirties,
whose grand dream of social and economic amelioration—
now degraded and popularized—was a dream of inaccessible

Utopia, "Time in its final block," not the "wrangling" of dream and reality which is our life in time. Stevens returns to the tension which produced *Owl's Clover*, the demand that the poet play a useful role, and compares it by implication with Satan's demand that Jesus turn stone into bread. The temptation is clear: if you are a poet, give us the bread of illusions that will make our lot more tolerable. But Stevens' reply is unequivocal. "The bread / Will be our bread, the stone will be / Our bed and we shall sleep by night." Poetry cannot alter reality except in those moments when we "choose" to create fictions which remind us of reality:

> The moments when we choose to play
> The imagined pine, the imagined jay.

The open sounds of the final rhyme, in contrast to the closed sounds with which the work began ("are-guitar"), form a last gesture of freedom and creative irresponsibility. The "moments" are points of order, chosen, not ordained; they are the evidence of our freedom. The word "play" must be taken in all its senses—the senses of the guitar, the senses of an actor's role, and the ultimate sense of poetry as a liberating game with words which renews our feeling for reality. As R. P. Blackmur once said, "Poetry is a game we play with reality; and it is the game and the play—the game by history and training, the play by instinct and need—which make it possible to catch hold of reality at all." [88] Like the elements of a secular mass, the bread and stone of life remain unchanged, and yet they are powerfully transformed.

IV

Parts of a World

In form if not in substance, the artistic careers of Wallace Stevens and Henry James are strikingly similar. Each writer developed slowly, passing through an extended period of imitative and apprentice writing before producing his first characteristic masterpieces. Each writer went through an extensive phase of readjustment and self-examination at mid-career, responding not only to the evolving demands of his art but to the insistent pressures of his time. Each writer, however "mandarin" his work might appear, was deeply affected by the contemporary world, but this impact of the contemporary found its most profound expression when deflected into a general theory of life and art. Most significantly, each writer passed from the turmoil of mid-career into a final phase where his art became self-contained and self-sufficient, with its own "poetics" and sacred gloss (the prefaces to the New York edition for James, the essays of *The Necessary Angel* for Stevens). In this last phase the traditional pattern of chronological development took on less importance, and the structures of an achieved artistic world were presented over and over again with keener discriminations, finer tones. It is as if at a certain point the shape of the artist's development became spatial rather than linear: when reading the later works of Stevens and James we have the sense of a fluent world which has "stopped revolving except in crystal" (CP 407).

This last and major phase of each writer's development is a cyclic rehearsal and refinement of themes developed long before.

The years between the publication of "The Man with the Blue Guitar" (1937) and *Notes toward a Supreme Fiction* (1942) were those when Stevens' poetic development underwent this radical change. The poet of *Harmonium* was constantly reacting to the manners and styles of contemporary poetry, seeking for his own idiom; the poet of *Ideas of Order* and *Owl's Clover* was reacting to the external pressures and general disorder of the practical world around him. "The Man with the Blue Guitar" marked a point of consolidation. After its composition Stevens was a poet who reacted mainly to his own achievements and theories, building the self-referring world of the later poems which often appears mannered and repetitive until we are reminded by a sudden moment of simplicity that it is still a version of the world in which we live. The entire question of a poet's development is difficult to handle, since the temptation is always to force random or wandering explorations into a dialectical pattern. As Stevens remarked in his talk on "The Irrational Element in Poetry" (OP 220), "We say that we perfect diction. We simply grow tired."

> Manner is something that has not yet been disengaged adequately. It does not mean style; it means the attitude of the writer, his bearing rather than his point of view. His bearing toward what? Not toward anything in particular, simply his pose.

Without falsifying this irrational aspect of the poet's development, without minimizing the effects of fashion or boredom, it is still possible to say that Stevens' progress after "The Man with the Blue Guitar" was more spatial than temporal, and demands methods of criticism different from those appropriate to the earlier poetry. As themes are deepened and refined, techniques sharpened and perfected, the reader finds it more and more necessary to treat the poems as parts of a single imaginative construct whose vigor and consistency overcome the occasional *longueurs* of too-perfect accomplishment. We could all wish for fewer poems about poetry, perhaps, but for Stevens these provided the essential context to his poems of naked experience. The nature of the poetry written in the last fifteen years of Stevens' life, as well as its bulk and complexity, make it a special subject in itself. Already it has elicited major criticism: the works of Helen Vendler, Harold Bloom, and James Baird, to name only a few, have increased our understanding of the structures that Stevens created when his poetic development ceased to be a voyage of self-discovery and became the building of a single edifice. The present chapter can only look ahead, suggesting some important differences and similarities between the later Stevens and the "introspective voyager."

In brief, it is the contention of this study that the nature of Stevens' sensibility or vision did not change significantly after "The Man with the Blue Guitar." The materials of the later poetry are there in 1937, accompanied by an accumulated repertoire of verse-forms ready for refinement. The flexible blank-verse stanzas of "Esthétique du Mal," the more formal stanzas of "To an Old Philosopher in Rome," the tercets of *Notes toward a Supreme Fiction*, which illustrate Stevens' penchant for a relatively free verse-line controlled by a fixed stanza form—all are developed out of the poetry of the 1920's and 1930's. In the same way, the subtle aesthetic arguments of *Notes toward a Supreme Fiction* and the meditations of *The Auroras of Autumn* have their sources in the earlier poetry, especially *Owl's Clover* and "The Man with the Blue Guitar." George Santayana once said of Whitman's poetry that it was "the imaginary experiment of beginning the world over again," [89] and this is the impression that Stevens seeks to give —through artifice and deliberate improvisation—in his last works. But the raw materials for this final act of integration, which appears to be so self-sufficient and self-contained, were the earlier poems.

If we examine representative cross-sections of Stevens' work published between 1937 and 1942, the changes in the nature of his poetic development become clear. The poems which appeared in Autumn 1938 under the title "Canonica" (CP 191–205) are all extensions of themes encountered in *Owl's Clover* and "The Man with the Blue Guitar." "Idiom of the Hero" (CP 200–201) denies that the chaos of life can ever be mended or ameliorated on a permanent basis, thus echoing the last stanza of "The Man with the Blue Guitar." "Study of Two Pears" (CP 196–97) and "The Glass of Water" (CP 197–98) are two "pedagogical" works which discourse with pleasant dogmatism on the familiar themes of the irreducible world of sense ("The pears are not seen / As the observer wills") and the insatiable desire for a center of composition, a central idea. "The Poems of Our Climate" (CP 193–94) also uses the pedagogical setting of the painter's studio to refine a paradox already sketched in the earlier poetry: the paradox that we desire nature to be composed, "still," as in a painter's still-life, yet the "never-resting mind" cannot be satisfied with anything less than poems of our climate, reflecting its imperfection and change.

> There would still remain the never-resting mind,
> So that one would want to escape, come back
> To what had been so long composed.
> The imperfect is our paradise.
> Note that, in this bitterness, delight,
> Since the imperfect is so hot in us,
> Lies in flawed words and stubborn sounds.

In effect, this final stanza rejects the poem's delicate opening stanza, rejects the "pure poetry" of the early Stevens ("the idea of images and images alone, or images and the music of verse together") in favor of the later conception of pure poetry as a poetry of order-within-change, true to all the imperfections and stubborn facts of a flawed world.

The poems which form *Parts of a World* are, for the most part, theoretic explorations of the *materia poetica* found in "The Man with the Blue Guitar." A series published in July 1939, entitled "Illustrations of the Poetic as a Sense" (CP 221–27), plays variations on the theme of the old romantic and the new, the need for a *Dichtung* which is *Wahrheit*. "The Man on the Dump" (CP 201–2), published the year before in "Canonica," had rejected the evasions of the nightingale in favor of the grackle, a poetry of the irreducible minimum, "The the."

> One sits and beats an old tin can, lard pail.
> One beats and beats for that which one believes.
> That's what one wants to get near. Could it after all
> Be merely oneself, as superior as the ear
> To a crow's voice? Did the nightingale torture the ear,
> Pack the heart and scratch the mind? And does the ear
> Solace itself in peevish birds? Is it peace,
> Is it a philosopher's honeymoon, one finds
> On the dump? Is it to sit among mattresses of the dead,
> Bottles, pots, shoes and grass and murmur *aptest eve:*
> Is it to hear the blatter of grackles and say
> *Invisible priest;* is it to eject, to pull
> The day to pieces and cry *stanza my stone?*
> Where was it one first heard of the truth? The the.

Now in "The Common Life" (CP 221) Stevens revolves the problem and dramatizes the world without imagination. In the flat light of two-dimensional "reality," the "men have no shadows / And the women have only one side." The effect is that of a savage modern painting, a "hoard of destructions."

> It is a morbid light
> In which they stand,
> Like an electric lamp
> On a page of Euclid.

By way of balance, "The Sense of the Sleight-of-Hand Man"
(CP 222) and "Of Hartford in a Purple Light" (CP 226–27)
speak of the freshening imagination. The accidental revelations
of nature ("Could you have said the bluejay suddenly / Would
swoop to earth?") can be matched by spontaneous flights of
the imagination ("To think of a dove with an eye of grenadine
/ And pines that are cornets, so it occurs"). The sun, "Master
Soleil," is ever the same and ever new, making us abhor the
"souvenirs" of empty rhetoric with the light of constant transformation. All of these theoretic poems, which reach back as
far as *Harmonium,* can be seen as developing out of individual
stanzas in "The Man with the Blue Guitar." They culminate
in the two poems published in May 1940 under the title "Two
Theoretic Poems"—"Man and Bottle" (CP 238–39) and "Of
Modern Poetry" (CP 239–40).

"Man and Bottle" celebrates poetry as a destructive force,
and the poet as a warrior against the old romantic and the old
mythologies.

> The poem lashes more fiercely than the wind,
> As the mind, to find what will suffice, destroys
> Romantic tenements of rose and ice.

Similarly, "Of Modern Poetry" constructs an elaborate metaphor for the poetry of the present, using the familiar figures
of the poet as "actor" and the poetic activity as "the act of the
mind."

> The poem of the mind in the act of finding
> What will suffice. It has not always had
> To find: the scene was set; it repeated what
> Was in the script.
> > Then the theatre was changed
> To something else. Its past was a souvenir.
>
> > . . .
>
> > The actor is
> A metaphysician in the dark, twanging
> An instrument, twanging a wiry string that gives

> Sounds passing through sudden rightness, wholly
> Containing the mind, below which it cannot descend,
> Beyond which it has no will to rise.
>   It must
> Be the finding of a satisfaction, and may
> Be of a man skating, a woman dancing, a woman
> Combing. The poem of the act of the mind.

This poem and the others like it in *Parts of a World* are resonant with themes and phrases which were sounded as early as "Sunday Morning" and "For an Old Woman in a Wig," but the specific "theoretic" content has been evolved from the works of the mid-thirties. The essential background for understanding the later Stevens is a close reading of *Ideas of Order* and the two long poems which are its companions.

A recurrent theme in this study has been Stevens as a "war poet," seeking to find a place in his poetic world for the major catastrophes of the contemporary mind. "Man and Bottle" and "Of Modern Poetry" are, curiously enough, poems of war which declare that the mind, that "great poem of winter," has "to content the reason concerning war."

> It has to persuade that war is part of itself,
> A manner of thinking, a mode
> Of destroying, as the mind destroys,
>
> An aversion, as the world is averted
> From an old delusion, an old affair with the sun,
> An impossible aberration with the moon,
> A grossness of peace. (CP 239)

In short, modern poetry "has to think about war / And it has to find what will suffice" (CP 240). The Stevens of "Phases" and "Lettres d'un Soldat" had failed for several reasons: partly because he treated war as an expression of the old romanticism, with the soldier as romantic hero; partly because the violence and carnage could not be adequately described in his fastidious language; but most of all because the experience was remote from his sensibility. In "The Men That Are Falling," however, the fact of war found a place in Stevens' evolving theories of poetic behavior, opening the way for some of the most moving war poems of the Second World War. By displacing and generalizing the subject, turning the soldier into a "major man" and war into the destructive force which poetry both shares and controls, Stevens absorbed the experience of war into his poetic. Stated in this way the process sounds like the worst kind of hypocritical evasion, but the experience of reading Stevens' war poems is quite different. Such apparently diverse works as "Man and Bottle," "Of Modern Poetry," "Asides on the Oboe," "Examination of the Hero in a Time of War," *Notes toward a Supreme Fiction*, "Dutch Graves in Bucks County," "A Woman Sings a Song for a Soldier Come Home," and "Flyer's Fall" form a chorus on the war which is unsentimental and immensely powerful. Perhaps the finest of these poems, "Dutch Graves in Bucks County" (CP 290–93), unites the poet's dead ancestors with those then dying on the desert battlefield of North Africa: "And you, my semblables, are doubly killed / To be buried in desert and deserted earth." Any paraphrase of the poem will make it seem as unreal as "Phases": a wartime sermon on the necessary interdependence of violence and freedom. But under Stevens' hands a theme which is inherently sentimental becomes fresh and startling, as the dead are denied and the living celebrated. The poem speaks of the inevitable violence inherent in our need to make the world over again at every moment, yet the dead persist—like the vanished civilization of "A Postcard from the Volcano"— because it is their speech we still employ.

Stevens at last became a successful "war poet" because he had learned from *Owl's Clover* the poetic uses of the contemporary, and had fashioned in "The Man with the Blue Guitar" a tenable hero. The coda to *Notes toward a Supreme Fiction*, which links the poet and soldier as heroes in two wars that depend on each other, is usually dismissed as an "anticlimax," a false ending inserted to justify "pure poetry" in a time of war,[90] but in fact it is the emotional anchor of the entire poem. *Notes toward a Supreme Fiction,* a work which is systematic in structure but musical in its local developments, may be seen from one viewpoint as an elaborate working-out and testing of certain leading ideas which were evolved in the earlier poetry and first juxtaposed in "The Man with the Blue Guitar." The war between "thought and day and night" (CP 407), between the rage for abstraction and the fact of change, was the central tension of the "Blue Guitar," and the general drift of *Notes* will be familiar to any reader of the earlier poem. The entire argument turns on the notion of a necessary inter-course between opposites, like a poem's necessary "absence in reality":

> Two things of opposite natures seem to depend
> On one another, as a man depends
> On a woman, day on night, the imagined
>
> On the real. This is the origin of change.
> Winter and spring, cold copulars, embrace
> And forth the particulars of rapture come.
>
> Music falls on the silence like a sense,
> A passion that we feel, not understand.
> Morning and afternoon are clasped together
>
> And North and South are an intrinsic couple
> And sun and rain a plural, like two lovers
> That walk away as one in the greenest body. (CP 392)

This powerful evocation of cyclic change, embedded at the very center of *Notes toward a Supreme Fiction,* culminates in a passionate address to the compound figure of reader-muse, the poet's other self.

> Follow after, O my companion, my fellow, my self,
> Sister and solace, brother and delight.

The accomplished reader of English poetry, coming to this canto without a knowledge of its context in *Notes* or in Stevens' middle career, would naturally think that the poet was indulging in the traditional consolations of "Peter Quince" or "Sunday Morning," singing the permanence to be found in the unchanging pattern of seasonal change. The canto would appear to be a variant on Spenser's description of the immortal Adonis:

> . . . for he may not
> For ever die, and ever buried be
> In baleful night, where all things are forgot;
> All be he subject to mortalitie,
> Yet is eterne in mutabilitie,
> And by succession made perpetual . . . (*F.Q.* III. vi. 47)

In fact, just the opposite is true. The structure of *Notes*, and of many of Stevens' later poems, may be a cyclic one, but the poetry celebrates eternal change and freshness, not the stale pattern of "eterne in mutabilitie." The constant in time is change, not sameness: "this beginning, not resuming" (CP 391). The interchange between opposites, between fact and fiction, the real and the imagined, is the source of pleasure, whether in poetry or in life. "The partaker partakes of that which changes him" (CP 392).

The cyclic structure of *Notes* suggests that this central canto (II. iv) should be flanked by similar cantos in Parts I and III. Part I, "It Must Be Abstract," is concerned with the "first ideas" of nature and man, the radical perceptions which precede our later anthropomorphic reasoning, and this theme reaches its most luminous expression in canto iv:

> The first idea was not our own. Adam
> In Eden was the father of Descartes
> And Eve made air the mirror of herself,
>
> Of her sons and of her daughters. They found themselves
> In heaven as in a glass; a second earth;
> And in the earth itself they found a green—
>
> The inhabitants of a very varnished green.
> But the first idea was not to shape the clouds
> In imitation. The clouds preceded us

There was a muddy centre before we breathed.
There was a myth before the myth began,
Venerable and articulate and complete.

From this the poem springs: that we live in a place
That is not our own and, much more, not ourselves
And hard it is in spite of blazoned days.

We are the mimics. Clouds are pedagogues.
The air is not a mirror but bare board,
Coulisse bright-dark, tragic chiaroscuro

And comic color of the rose, in which
Abysmal instruments make sounds like pips
Of the sweeping meanings that we add to them.

The penultimate stanza, harking back to "On the Manner of Addressing Clouds" and "The Idea of Order at Key West," sums up Stevens' long divergence from traditional concepts of expression and mimesis. Anthropomorphic myths are but mirrors of ourselves, and produce the "varnished green" of an image removed from the real. "There was a muddy centre before we breathed. / There was a myth before the myth began": the first idea, reality itself, is the ultimate subject of the poem, and the poet who can refresh our sense of reality is a major man because he does not imitate or express, but "adds to" our sense of things.

The poem refreshes life so that we share,
For a moment, the first idea . . . It satisfies
Belief in an immaculate beginning

And sends us, winged by an unconscious will,
To an immaculate end. We move between these points . . .
                                                    (I. iii)

The successful poem is a metaphoric union of "an immaculate beginning" (unvarnished reality) and "an immaculate end" (a fictive construct, with a life and unity of its own: the second world of the pure poem). The poem is an "actor" upon the bare boards of things as they are.

Canto iv of Part III builds on the sense that our time and feelings are ours alone, and ours for only a little while. The "mystic marriage" of the great captain and the maiden Bawda is a figure for the adequate poem. It is a marriage of love, not convenience or convention; each partakes of the other and of the actual place of their lives ("Catawba" in South Carolina). "They married well because the marriage-place / Was what they loved." The marriage is like the union of sun and earth at mid-summer, each separate and each part of the other.

> There was a mystic marriage in Catawba,
> At noon it was on the mid-day of the year
> Between a great captain and the maiden Bawda.
>
> This was their ceremonial hymn: Anon
> We loved but would no marriage make. Anon
> The one refused the other one to take,
>
> Foreswore the sipping of the marriage wine.
> Each must the other take not for his high,
> His puissant front nor for her subtle sound,
>
> The shoo-shoo-shoo of secret cymbals round.
> Each must the other take as sign, short sign
> To stop the whirlwind, balk the elements.
>
> The great captain loved the ever-hill Catawba
> And therefore married Bawda, whom he found there,
> And Bawda loved the captain as she loved the sun.

Love precedes understanding, feeling precedes reason. The opening tercet of Part III, canto iv, "We reason of these things with later reason / And we make of what we see, what we see clearly / And have seen, a place dependent on ourselves," echoes the close of the first canto:

> But the difficultest rigor is forthwith,
> On the image of what we see, to catch from that
>
> Irrational moment its unreasoning,
> As when the sun comes rising, when the sea
> Clears deeply, when the moon hangs on the wall

Of heaven-haven. These are not things transformed.
Yet we are shaken by them as if they were.
We reason about them with a later reason. (III. i)

These passages bring together and harmonize two persistent
strains from "The Man with the Blue Guitar": the need to
wash away preconceptions, accepting the fortuitous gifts of
reality; and the need to transform and order. The imagination
is a "later reason," which must work upon reality but not
intrude upon it, and the easy courtship of the captain and
Bawda, sun and moon, is a figure for the making of the major
poem.

~

Connections such as these between the poetry of the mid-
1930's and *Notes toward a Supreme Fiction* could be multi-
plied at will. Stevens' work of 1937–42 was a refining and flesh-
ing-out of theories adumbrated in "The Man with the Blue
Guitar," and although it would be foolish to speak of a
simple "argument" in such a subtle and personal construction
as *Notes toward a Supreme Fiction*, we can say that it has its
life within the limits of subject-matter and theme mapped out
in the earlier poem. Taken together, the essays of *The Necessary Angel*, the pedagogical poems of *Parts of a World*, and
the individual cantos of *Notes toward a Supreme Fiction* may
be viewed as intricate dances around the "points of order"
established by Stevens' transitional verse of 1934–37.

The differences in kind and degree between Stevens' "introspective voyage" of 1914–37 and his later poetic development are clearly evident in his elaborations on the concept of
"man number one." The advent of World War Two focused
Stevens' attention on the figure of the hero, but unlike the
external events of 1914–18 and the mid-1930's it did not cause
Stevens to question his aesthetic assumptions or experiment
with new formulations of order. The "idea of man" explored
in "The Man with the Blue Guitar" and parts of *Owl's Clover*

could easily evolve into an adequate response. "Asides on the Oboe" (CP 250–51), which was first published in December 1940, stands squarely between "The Man with the Blue Guitar" and *Notes toward a Supreme Fiction,* demonstrating their essential sameness. In "The Greenest Continent" the "Fatal Ananke" had been Stevens' improvised fiction in which we choose to believe,[91] but by the time he had finished "The Man with the Blue Guitar" that particular improvisation had given way to the notion of major man, which "Asides on the Oboe" queries and affirms. The opening "prologue" is short and to the point:

> The prologues are over. It is a question, now,
> Of final belief. So, say that final belief
> Must be in a fiction. It is time to choose.

The choice in a time of "death and war" is clear. The older fictions, such as "the gods that Boucher killed," must give way to the "impossible possible philosophers' man,"

> The man who has had the time to think enough,
> The central man, the human globe, responsive,
> As a mirror with a voice, the man of glass,
> Who in a million diamonds sums us up.

This "man of glass" is the "transparence of the place in which / He is," the man who can cry: " 'Thou art not August unless I make thee so.' " As the fiction of his time and place, the "central man" is an "impossible possible": like Aristotle's "probable impossibility," we recognize him as the sum of ourselves although he remains a fiction. At a time of crisis, when "death and war prevented the jasmine scent / And the jasmine islands were bloody martyrdoms," the central man remained our spokesman. Unlike the finiky creations of Stevens' early poems, those "jasmine islands," the "man of glass" endured because he spoke for a time and a place.

"Examination of the Hero in a Time of War" (CP 273–81), written in 1941, accomplishes the impossible possible by bridging the space between Poems II and III of "The Man with the Blue Guitar." The "hero's head" of old romance is dismissed as an irrelevant souvenir, a piece of "Chopiniana": the "common man is the common hero," and the poet must devise a credible form out of the ruck of the present.

> Unless we believe in the hero, what is there
> To believe? Incisive what, the fellow
> Of what good. Devise. Make him of mud,
> For every day. In a civiler manner,
> Devise, devise, and make him of winter's
> Iciest core, a north star, central
> To our oblivion, of summer's
> Imagination, the golden rescue . . . (VI)

The common man as hero is a feeling, not a personification: certainly not the shabby public hero of Poem X in "The Man with the Blue Guitar," who is explicitly rejected. The hero is not a personification or image but an "it," an abstraction: "It is not an image. It is a feeling."

> There is no image of the hero.
> There is a feeling as definition.
> How could there be an image, an outline,
> A design, a marble soiled by pigeons?
> The hero is a feeling, a man seen
> As if the eye was an emotion,
> As if in seeing we saw our feeling
> In the object seen and saved that mystic
> Against the sight, the penetrating,
> Pure eye. Instead of allegory,
> We have and are the man, capable
> Of his brave quickenings, the human
> Accelerations that seem inhuman. (XII)

The central man in a time of war is a state of mind, not an icon; but it must be blooded with the reality of ordinary life. As "Examination of the Hero in a Time of War" draws to a close (XV–XVI) the abstraction threatens to overreach itself, to claim its own reality, and that "false empire" is rejected like all its predecessors. "These are the works and pastimes / Of the highest self: he studies the paper / On the wall, the lemons on the table." Just as each season has its own self, each nation its own personality, the hero is like "summer" or "America," a thing too real to be personified. "Examination of the Hero in a Time of War," which is almost discursive in its early and middle sections, ends on a less assertive note. Each age has its proper hero, and heroic summer only seems false when autumn stands in the doorway. Like the ancient dead of "Dutch Graves in Bucks County," the heroes of other seasons have an exemplary role.

Part I, canto x of *Notes toward a Supreme Fiction* refines on the terminology of "The Man with the Blue Guitar" and "Asides on the Oboe."

> The major abstraction is the idea of man
> And major man is its exponent, abler
> In the abstract than in his singular,
>
> More fecund as principle than particle,
> Happy fecundity, flor-abundant force,
> In being more than an exception, part,
>
> Though an heroic part, of the commonal.
> The major abstraction is the commonal,
> The inanimate, difficult visage. Who is it?
>
> What rabbi, grown furious with human wish,
> What chieftain, walking by himself, crying
> Most miserable, most victorious,
>
> Does not see these separate figures one by one,
> And yet see only one, in his old coat,
> His slouching pantaloons, beyond the town,
>
> Looking for what was, where it used to be?
> Cloudless the morning. It is he. The man
> In that old coat, those sagging pantaloons,

> It is of him, ephebe, to make, to confect
> The final elegance, not to console
> Nor sanctify, but plainly to propound.

Major man, the poet, is an "exponent" of the "idea of man," both in the sense that he interprets that "major abstraction" and in the sense that he represents or embodies it. An exponent is also that factor which raises a number to a higher power, and it is the duty of the poet to raise the common man to the power of abstraction. The tramp in sagging pantaloons is the common man and yet "the idea of man," as the poet's words raise him to the level of the commonal. As "the idea of man," he is an abstraction blooded by the life of our times. Like Crispin or a Chaplin hero, he is both valet and saint.

The evolution of the "idea of man," from "The Man with the Blue Guitar" through *Notes toward a Supreme Fiction*, illustrates the self-sufficient quality which marked Stevens' poetic life after 1937. The entire process of refining the abstraction and re-examining the hero takes place within a frame of reference established by the poems of the mid-1930's, which themselves consolidated the major aspects of Stevens' early achievement. The poet is no longer fluctuating between alternatives, or trying on new fashions in speech, but seeking to expand and understand a poetic world which has taken on the contours of his own mind. "How simply the fictive hero becomes the real" (CP 408); how easily the poet can now take the measure of changing reality. The prose statement on the poetry of war which concluded *Parts of a World* (1942) reflects a consciousness of "heroic fact" that would have overwhelmed the younger poet, but now "the poetry of a work of the imagination" seems adequate to this immense reality.

> The immense poetry of war and the poetry of a work of the imagination are two different things. In the presence of the violent reality of war, consciousness takes the place of the imagination. And consciousness of an immense war is a consciousness of fact. If that is true, it

follows that the poetry of war as a consciousness of the victories and defeats of nations, is a consciousness of fact, but of heroic fact, of fact on such a scale that the mere consciousness of it affects the scale of one's thinking and constitutes a participating in the heroic.

It has been easy to say in recent times that everything tends to become real, or, rather, that everything moves in the direction of reality, that is to say, in the direction of fact. We leave fact and come back to it, come back to what we wanted fact to be, not to what it was, not to what it has too often remained. The poetry of a work of the imagination constantly illustrates the fundamental and endless struggle with fact. It goes on everywhere, even in the periods that we call peace. But in war, the desire to move in the direction of fact as we want it to be and to move quickly is overwhelming.

Nothing will ever appease this desire except a consciousness of fact as everyone is at least satisfied to have it be.[92]

"The fundamental and endless struggle with fact" had become the basis of Stevens' poetic, and was to be the center of the cyclic progress of his later poetry. The late poems fan out in all directions from this point, and to it they return. The poet who wrote *Notes toward a Supreme Fiction* had established his genre, his language, his viewpoint. The interest we have in tracing the development of an individual poet is replaced by the fascination of a developing poetic universe.

No poem is more expressive of Stevens' final poetic than "To an Old Philosopher in Rome" (CP 508–11), where in his tribute to George Santayana, the old philosopher dying in Rome, the poet seems to be speaking covertly of his own "total edifice" of life and art. Although Stevens never attended Santayana's lectures at Harvard, nor took any of his courses, the philosopher was obviously aware of Stevens' poetic gifts, and in the manner of that easier day they came to know each other fairly well. "I read several poems to him," Stevens remembered in 1945, "and he expressed his own view of the subject of them in a sonnet which he sent me, and which is in one of his books." [93] Four years later Stevens was more specific: "Once he asked me to come and read some of my things to him. I read one of them in which the first line was 'Cathedrals are not built along the sea.' He must have spent the evening writing his reply because the next morning in my mail there was a sonnet from him entitled 'Answer To A Sonnet Commencing Cathedrals Are Not Built, etc.' " [94] The contrast between the two sonnets is instructive: Stevens' poem, one of the finest of his undergraduate publications, has a vigor of conception and freshness of diction that make Santa-yana's academic exercise seem stale and exhausted, yet the austere sense of deprivation in Santayana's reply would ulti-mately become Stevens' own.

> Cathedrals are not built along the sea;
> The tender bells would jangle on the hoar
> And iron winds; the graceful turrets roar
> With bitter storms the long night angrily;
> And through the precious organ pipes would be
> A low and constant murmur of the shore
> That down those golden shafts would rudely pour
> A mighty and a lasting melody.
>
> And those who knelt within the gilded stalls
> Would have vast outlook for their weary eyes.
> There they would see high shadows on the walls
> From passing vessels in their fall and rise;
> Through gaudy windows there would come too soon
> The low and splendid rising of the moon.
>
>   . . .
>
> For aeons had the self-responsive tide
> Risen to ebb, and tempests blown to clear,
> And the belated moon refilled her sphere
> To wane anew—for, aeons since, she died—
> When to the deeps that called her earth replied
> (Lest year should cancel unavailing year)

And took from her dead heart the stones to rear
A cross-shaped temple to the Crucified.
Then the wild winds through organ-pipes descended
To utter what they meant eternally,
And not in vain the moon devoutly mended
Her wasted taper, lighting Calvary,
While with a psalmody of angels blended
The sullen diapason of the sea.

Whatever the influence of Santayana on Stevens may have been,[95] it is certain that in the late 1940's Stevens' interest in the old philosopher began to quicken, an interest not based on his specific writings or ideas but on his exemplary role as a philosopher-poet. In April 1946 Edmund Wilson, recently returned from a visit to Rome, published an account of a meeting with Santayana that Stevens must have read.[96] Called "Santayana at the Convent of the Blue Nuns," the profile contains the hints and images which coalesced five years later in "To an Old Philosopher in Rome." The setting of the interview is immensely expressive: Santayana, dressed in a plain gown with cord "like a Franciscan friar's," cared for by the Blue Nuns in their "decorative and fantastic" headdresses of deepest blue, discourses on history and art. Although he is able to view the brawling events around him as if they were part of history, giving a long perspective to the present, he is "still in the world of men, conversing with them through reading and writing, a section of the human plasm that, insulated by convent walls and by exceptional resistances of character, still registers the remotest tremors." Alone, "with his plain table and his narrow bed," remote from the worlds of Spain and Harvard, he appears to be "a shell of faded skin and frail bone, in which the power of intellect, the colors of imagination" still burn, perhaps more brightly because the end is near. He is a man poised between "two civilizations," who can speak ironically and yet with relish of the chance recently offered him to become a Roman citizen, *civis Romanus*. His rejection of idealism in the conversation with Wilson has a startling similarity to the major themes of *Notes toward a Supreme Fiction*, which opens with the "inconceivable idea of the sun" and meditates on the death of Phoebus ("Phoebus was / A name for something that never could be named.")

> "For me," he said, "our conception of the flaming sun is a sensation of the same order—an essence [in the special sense that he has assigned to this word in his system]—as the older conception of Apollo with his golden rays. Neither is an object that we know, as the idealistic philosophers believe."

As Santayana jokingly remarked to Wilson, the "fact of our grandfather" must come before "the idea of our grandfather." His comments on the "three crucial false steps" in the history of Western philosophy could be Stevens' own: Socrates' subjugation of the physical world to the metaphysical; the Reformation's penchant for "all that had been bad in paganism," and its failure to revive, like the Renaissance, the "elements that had been good"; and finally the error of the German idealistic philosophers "in adopting the impossible position that the order of discovery of objects comes before the order of their genesis."

Throughout his interview Wilson was struck with the ability of Santayana to process all experience into his personal world.

> It would not be precisely true to say that Santayana is narcissistic, but he is interested in his own thought as a personal, self-contained system, and in his life as a work of art which owes its integrity and harmony partly to a rigorous avoidance of indiscriminate human relationships. The objective materials with which his mind works have been the systems of other thinkers and the assumptions of civilizations. It is easy to see when one meets him how his attitude toward the world has derived from his personal characteristics and from the circumstances of his life.

Alone and dying, Santayana still cherished every detail of the physical world around him, and Wilson came away with the final impression that "he reposes in his shabby chaise longue like a monad in the universal mind."

Stevens must have seen in this intense portrait an image of himself. Every detail is applicable to the creator of *The Auroras of Autumn* and the last poems, and the sense of Santayana as alter ego was clearly before Stevens in the summer of 1948 while he was writing his English Institute lecture on "Imagination as Value" (NA 133–56).

> Again in life the function of the imagination is so varied that it is not well-defined as it is in arts and letters. In life one hesitates when one speaks of the value of the imagination. Its value in arts and letters is aesthetic. Most men's lives are thrust upon them. The existence of aesthetic value in lives that are forced on those that live them is an improbable sort of thing. There can be lives, nevertheless, which exist by the deliberate choice of those that live them. To use a single illustration: it may be assumed that the life of Professor Santayana is a life in which the function of the imagination has had a function similar to its function in any deliberate work of art or letters. We have only to think of this present phase of it, in which, in his old age, he dwells in the head of the world, in the company of devoted women, in their convent, and in the company of familiar saints, whose presence does so much to make any convent an appropriate refuge for a generous and human philosopher. To repeat, there can be lives in which the value of the imagination is the same as its value in arts and letters. . . .
> (NA 147–48)

This passage is the text for "To an Old Philosopher in Rome," but Stevens' passionate involvement with Santayana as alter ego is better revealed in a letter of May 1949:

> Finally, about Santayana. . . . I knew him quite well. That was almost fifty years ago when he was quite a

different person from the decrepit old philosopher now living in a convent in Rome. A week or two ago he wrote a letter to a friend of mine who sent it to me to look at and in that letter he said:

> "I have always bowed, however sadly, to expediency or fate."

For the last week or two I have been repeating that sentence.[97]

"To an Old Philosopher in Rome" was first published in the autumn of 1952, at almost the exact time of Santayana's death.[98] In majestic blank-verse stanzas the poem constructs a theatrical setting where the city of the mind and the actual city of Rome are joined in a single perspective, as our two eyes make one in sight. Before Stevens had settled on his five-line stanza form the second stanza contained an extra line which attributed this convergence to "a common maker, not divine":[99] the poet is both subject and source of the poem's final order, since he is the major exponent of the imagination. The two worlds of the poem are a secularization of Augustine's City of Man and City of God, "The threshold, Rome, and that more merciful Rome / Beyond," the real and the imagined. At the moment of death the self approaches most nearly to that threshold between the real and the imagined which had become the focus of Stevens' art.

> On the threshold of heaven, the figures in the street
> Become the figures of heaven, the majestic movement
> Of men growing small in the distances of space,
> Singing, with smaller and still smaller sound,
> Unintelligible absolution and an end—
>
> The threshold, Rome, and that more merciful Rome
> Beyond, the two alike in the make of the mind.
> It is as if in a human dignity
> Two parallels become one, a perspective, of which
> Men are part both in the inch and in the mile.

"How easily the blown banners change to wings . . ." How easily the mind can accomplish its work of metaphoric enlargement. Yet that enlargement is made by the "common maker, not divine," is made out of "The bed, the books, the chair, the moving nuns," the consolations of a physical world.

> The newsboys' muttering
> Becomes another murmuring; the smell
> Of medicine, a fragrantness not to be spoiled . . .

Rome is "A shape within the ancient circles of shapes, / And these beneath the shadow of a shape," like a Platonic shadow of reality: but in Stevens' world the reality flows from the particular to the idea. The grandeur that the dying philosopher seeks can only be fashioned from "misery, the afflatus of ruin, / Profound poetry of the poor and of the dead . . ." In a line derived from "Academic Discourse at Havana" (CP 144), the speech of poverty is declared to be "older than the oldest speech of Rome": it is the irreducible fact which sets "the tragic accent of the scene."

As the poem mounts to a close, oscillating between the comforts of the two Romes, the philosopher-poet becomes that long-sought major abstraction, "the idea of man," the naked majesty. "How easily the blown banners change to wings" has already recalled the moving close of *Notes toward a Supreme Fiction*: "How simply the fictive hero becomes the real" (CP 408). At the end of "To an Old Philosopher in Rome" the two Romes become one, and for an eloquent moment fiction and fact are held in a single image.

> It is a kind of total grandeur at the end,
> With every visible thing enlarged and yet
> No more than a bed, a chair and moving nuns,
> The immensest theatre, the pillared porch,
> The book and candle in your ambered room,
>
> Total grandeur of a total edifice,
> Chosen by an inquisitor of structures

> For himself. He stops upon this threshold,
> As if the design of all his words takes form
> And frame from thinking and is realized.

The development of Stevens' later poetry differs from that of his earlier precisely because of those qualities displayed by "To an Old Philosopher in Rome": at the center of his final poetic is the possibility of a supreme fiction, and all his explorations of the relation between the real and the imagined radiate from it. Stevens acknowledged this in the brief biographical note that he wrote to accompany a reprinting of "The Auroras of Autumn."

> The author's work suggests the possibility of a supreme fiction, recognized as a fiction, in which men could propose to themselves a fulfillment. In the creation of any such fiction, poetry would have a vital significance. There are many poems relating to the interactions between reality and the imagination, which are to be regarded as marginal to this central theme.[100]

This central theme is the axis around which all the later poems revolve, as if they were satellites of one major idea, and the reader soon becomes enfolded in a cyclic recapitulation and refinement of themes and images that reach back to the earliest phases of Stevens' poetic life. Although Stevens denied that he was writing "a seasonal sequence" in his last years, preferring to speak of the "drift of one's ideas," the major poems of 1945–55 describe a seasonal pattern. As he commented in May 1949 in a letter to a would-be explicator:

> From the imaginative period of the Notes I turned to the ideas of Credences of Summer. At the moment I am at work on a thing called An Ordinary Evening in New Haven. . . . here my interest is to try to get as close to the ordinary, the commonplace and the ugly as it is possible for a poet to get. It is not a question of grim reality but of plain reality. The object is of course to purge oneself of anything false. I have been doing this

since the beginning of March and intend to keep studying
the subject and working on it until I am quite through
with it. This is not in any sense a turning away from
the ideas of Credences of Summer: it is a development
of those ideas. That sort of thing might ultimately lead to
another phase of what you call a seasonal sequence but
certainly it would have nothing to do with the weather:
it would have to do with the drift of one's ideas.[101]

"Credences of Summer" (CP 372–78), completed in July 1946,
is the emotional center of *Transport to Summer* (1947), and
in it Stevens embodies his most sustained vision of the reality
of summer. "At the time when that poem was written," he
later remarked, "my feeling for the necessity of a final accord
with reality was at its strongest: reality was the summer of the
title of the book in which the poem appeared." [102] The ten
sections of "Credences of Summer," cast in a slow and measured form reminiscent of Keats' Odes, speak of that moment
of ripeness when the "personae of summer" are

> Free, for a moment, from malice and sudden cry,
> Complete in a completed scene, speaking
> Their parts as in youthful happiness. (X)

Throughout the poem Stevens meditates on the "rock of
summer," half green earth and half placid air, half visible and
half audible, which is the rock of summer reality as seen by
the imagination of that season. Abstract interpretation and
mere description are rejected in favor of the composite reality:

> Postpone the anatomy of summer, as
> The physical pine, the metaphysical pine.
> Let's see the very thing and nothing else. (II)

As it vacillates back and forth between the "limits" of summer's
reality, the poem tests the validity of words and concrete
particulars. In section IV, one of Stevens' two "favorite sections," [103] the remembered landscape of a Pennsylvania summer
defines the ultimate extension of sensuous reality. The land-

scape is "the very thing and nothing else," presented without "evasion by a single metaphor" (II). The "secondary senses" of the Romantic eye and ear no longer are needed, and the region stands forth as a particular place where "accord with realities is the nature of things." [104]

> One of the limits of reality
> Presents itself in Oley when the hay,
> Baked through long days, is piled in mows. It is
> A land too ripe for enigmas, too serene.
> There the distant fails the clairvoyant eye
>
> And the secondary senses of the ear
> Swarm, not with secondary sounds, but choirs,
> Not evocations but last choirs, last sounds
> With nothing else compounded, carried full,
> Pure rhetoric of a language without words.
>
> Things stop in that direction and since they stop
> The direction stops and we accept what is
> As good. The utmost must be good and is
> And is our fortune and honey hived in the trees
> And mingling of colors at a festival.

In contrast to section IV, which speaks paradoxically of a natural language beyond words, Stevens' other favorite section (VII) celebrates the singers who brave the difficulty of singing "in face / Of the object."

> The singers had to avert themselves
> Or else avert the object. Deep in the woods
> They sang of summer in the common fields.
>
> They sang desiring an object that was near,
> In face of which desire no longer moved,
> Nor made of itself that which it could not find . . .

Yet only through a constant interchange between fact and fiction can the poem achieve an image of "the rock." Section VII breaks off its despairing argument at midpoint, and in the second movement Stevens celebrates the near-miracle of poetic creation. Incantation replaces argument as "Credences of Summer" speaks of its own origins.

> Three times the concentred self takes hold, three times
> The thrice concentred self, having possessed
>
> The object, grips it in savage scrutiny,
> Once to make captive, once to subjugate
> Or yield to subjugation, once to proclaim
> The meaning of the capture, this hard prize,
> Fully made, fully apparent, fully found.

Caught in an apparently unresolvable division between "self" and "object," mind and fact, Stevens resorts to a threefold poetic figure which combines a magical spell with overtones of the original creation. The embrace between fact and imagination is more savage than loving, a marriage in which the only choice is "to subjugate / Or yield to subjugation," and the entire passage which closes section VII borders on rhetorical evasion. In "Credences of Summer" Stevens seems so overwhelmed by the richness of the landscape that the delicate equilibrium between fact and fiction is momentarily threatened; but in "An Ordinary Evening in New Haven" the plain and barren scene restores our sense of the imagination's essential role.

Stevens' lifelong preoccupation with our response to climates and seasons reached its finest expression in his last poems. *Notes toward a Supreme Fiction* explores the springtime of the imagination, the poet as ephebe, while *Transport to Summer, The Auroras of Autumn,* and the poems of *The Rock* complete the cycle of moods and perceptions, bringing the poet to a stark reality of winter which is still an activity of the imagination. "I like a world in which the passing of the season (or the passing of the seasons) is a matter of some importance," Stevens wrote in 1951, and at the time when he was composing *The Auroras of Autumn* he remarked in a letter of early October that "We are just entering what is the most moving part of our calendar: the early autumn." [105] Autumn and winter, with their darker landscapes, bring a more pensive imagination, as in "The Auroras of Autumn" (CP 411–21) or "An Ordinary Evening in New Haven" (CP 465–89). But this sombre tone is "not in any sense a turning away from the ideas of Credences of Summer: it is a development of those ideas." In the self-contained manner of Stevens' final poetic, the poems of summer and winter complement each other as two facets of a total edifice.

"An Ordinary Evening in New Haven" exists in two versions: a sequence of eleven poems read before the Connecticut Academy of Arts and Sciences in 1949, and a longer suite of thirty-one poems which first appeared in *The Auroras of Autumn*. Although Stevens printed the longer version in *Collected Poems*, he decided to include the shorter version in *Selected Poems by Wallace Stevens*, a carefully chosen anthology designed to present Stevens' verse to the English audience. Unlike the two versions of "Sunday Morning," the two versions of "An Ordinary Evening in New Haven" are true alternatives, and the shorter sequence followed in this chapter is often more revealing.[106] In their easy relationship with each other, the two versions of "An Ordinary Evening" point up an important difference between the long poems of Stevens' early career and those of his last volumes. With the notable exception of "The Comedian as the Letter C," none of Stevens' longer poems has a conventional narrative structure; but in the earlier ones there is a logical progression of thought, if not of plot, which makes the ending of the poem a distinct advance over its beginning, and gives us a sense of the meditative poet moving through time toward some temporary synthesis. The general structure in these poems need not be exact: the individual lyric is the precise unit, and stanzas are often discarded or rearranged, so that even the most "argumentative" of the early poems, "Sunday Morning," is more precise in local effects than in general design. Nonetheless, the longer poems of *Harmonium* and the early 1930's (with the significant exception of "Like Decorations in a Nigger Cemetery") have a clear pattern of development: we feel that the poem possesses a dialectical argument as well as a logic of imagery and feeling. But the later poems of some length no longer convey this sense of an exploration through time. Beginning with "Like Decorations in a Nigger Cemetery" and "The Man with the Blue Guitar," Stevens began to construct long poems which, like Henry James' house of fiction, have a commanding center which controls a multiplicity of related points-of-view. Poems such as "Credences of Summer" are held together by a presiding mind or sensibility, not by a developing argument, and the internal harmonies convey a sense of thought revolved rather than developed. The long poems of Stevens' last years are spatial structures which surround a central "idea" with a multitude of alternate statements, each reaching almost to the truth. Thus the shorter version of "An Ordinary Evening" concludes with a poem that throws the balance toward language and the shaping mind ("an alteration / Of words that was a change of nature"), while the longer version relegates this poem to a penultimate movement and gives pride of place to another poem (X in the original version) which takes a more tentative view of "final form." The next-to-last poem of the shorter version has been transferred into a concluding statement (XXXI), in which the "edgings and inchings of final form," the unending attempts to find "formulae" for reality, are seen as inevitably partial and incomplete, "Like an evening evoking the spectrum of violet, / A philosopher practicing scales on his piano, / A woman writing a note and tearing it up."

> It is not in the premise that reality
> Is a solid. It may be a shade that traverses
> A dust, a force that traverses a shade.

This section may be thought a more appropriate ending because of its delicate tone and tentative attitude, but in no sense does it alter the validity of the earlier ending. Both are versions of that reality which is a "force," not a "solid." The long poems of Stevens' final years do not derive their extraordinary consistency from an argument which builds toward a conclusion, but from the integrity of a presiding mind which rehearses again and again the premises and possibilities of an achieved vision.

All these qualities of Stevens' later verse are on display in the first version of "An Ordinary Evening in New Haven." In its barren setting and austere lines, the poem confronts the "total leaflessness" of old age. But unlike "To an Old Philosopher in Rome," where the approach of death is treated in the high style of traditional elegiac poetry, "An Ordinary Evening" meditates upon the consolations and deprivations of age within the framework of a "theory of poetry" which might be a "theory of life." The poem begins where all Stevens' speculations begin: with primordia, the "eye's plain version" of things, the "vulgate of experience." But this irreducible evidence of our senses can only be expressed in words or conceived in mind, and therefore the "never-ending meditation" begins, an endless attempt to qualify and understand our sense impressions.

> Of this,
> A few words, an and yet, and yet, and yet—
>
> As part of the never-ending meditation,
> Part of the question that is a giant himself . . . (I)

It is all very well to say that the "eye's plain version" is the "vulgate of experience," but without a gloss it is obscure: only words can provide that gloss, and they constantly decay. The houses of the city are "difficult" objects, constantly washing away into "dilapidate" shadows and appearances unless our sense of their reality is refreshed. Every meditation upon the "vulgate of experience" creates a giant of the mind, an almost mythological form, who soon loses his force and identity unless "a second giant kills the first—"

> A recent imagining of reality,

Much like a new resemblance of the sun,
Down-pouring, up-springing and inevitable,
A larger poem for a larger audience.

As if the crude collops came together as one,
A mythological form, a festival sphere,
A great bosom, beard and being, alive with age.

The poem issues out of our need to refresh the world with "new resemblances." "Reality is the beginning not the end," as the second section declares, but "hierophant Omega"—our dense structures of resemblances—cannot live without it. Reality and Imagination both claim to be the "immaculate interpreters of life," but each is really dependent on the other: "Alpha continues to begin. / Omega is refreshed at every end." Therefore "We keep coming back and coming back / To the real: to the hotel instead of the hymns / That fall upon it out of the wind" (III). We seek the "poem of pure reality, untouched / By trope or deviation": a view of New Haven without resemblance or reflection. But such a view is impossible, since we hanker after the metaphysical as well as the physical to complete our minds. "In the metaphysical streets of the physical town / We remember the lion of Juda and we save / The phrase . . . " (IV). It is an outworn phrase, weak in the face of present fact, but it suggests our need for some majesty, "A minimum of making in the mind."

Since "The poem is the cry of its occasion, / Part of the res itself and not about it," words offer a temporary relief from the "casual litter" of the world: the poem unites "the whole psychology"—the self, the environment, and the moment in time ("the weather"). Thus the poem of today creates a "venerable mask" which speaks both of present vitality and its inevitable loss. An image of contemporary autumn, plain and unadorned, can be "tragedy's most moving face."

It is a bough in the electric light
And exhalations in the eaves, so little
To indicate the total leaflessness. (VI)

Sections VII and VIII push the role of the imagination to its ultimate power. The search for reality is a process of re-creation, and New Haven in its plainness is less "real" than the imagined city. The act of the mind is an "endlessly elaborating poem" which displays "the theory of poetry, / As the life of poetry."

> A more severe,

> More harassing master would extemporize
> Subtler, more urgent proof that the theory
> Of poetry is the theory of life,

> As it is, in the intricate evasions of as,
> In things seen and unseen, created from nothingness,
> The heavens, the hells, the worlds,
>   the longed-for lands. (VIII)

But Stevens is no such "harassing master," and the next section—perhaps the most moving of the entire suite—returns from "the intricate evasions of as" to the concrete particulars of autumn's end. Like the description of Oley in "Credences of Summer," it is the mind of the season made visible.

> The last leaf that is going to fall has fallen.
> The robins are là-bas, the squirrels, in tree-caves,
> Huddle together in the knowledge of squirrels.

> The wind has blown the silence of summer away.
> It buzzes beyond the horizon or in the ground:
> In mud under ponds, where the sky used to be reflected.

> The barrenness that appears is an exposing.
> It is not part of what is absent, a halt
> For farewells, a sad hanging on for remembrances.

> It is a coming on and a coming forth.
> The pines that were fans and fragrances emerge,
> Staked solidly in a gusty grappling with rocks.

> The glass of the air becomes an element—
> It was something imagined that has been washed away.
> A clearness has returned. It stands restored.

It is not an empty clearness, a bottomless sight.
It is a visibility of thought,
In which hundreds of eyes, in one mind, see at once. (IX)

The shorter version of "An Ordinary Evening in New Haven" now rounds to its close with the alternate endings (X and XI), which form a composite image of the ceaseless and necessary interchange between sight and insight, sense and language, fact and fiction. The entire movement of the poem is reflected in these stanzas: not a logical progression of thought, but a meditation "resembling the presence of thought" (V). As Joseph N. Riddel comments in his excellent analysis of the longer version: "This poem, perhaps more than any other of Stevens' long poems, is man thinking, the act of continual self-creation through poetry. . . . A 'visibility of thought' is not thought itself, but neither is it creation *ex nihilo*." [107] "An Ordinary Evening in New Haven" is thus the quintessential modern poem, since it speaks to our common experience while apparently speaking only of itself and its creator.

◡

The similarities and differences between the two halves of Stevens' poetic life are nowhere more evident than in his last poems of winter and the minimal imagination. In the poems of *The Rock*, which often embody the mind of winter even when winter is not the ostensible setting, Stevens seeks the absolute clarity of a world purged of all that could possibly be false. If "To an Old Philosopher in Rome" dramatizes the "celestial possible," as in the image of a "light on the candle tearing against the wick / To join a hovering excellence," these poems of winter reject the consolation of symbolism. In "The Course of a Particular" (1951) Stevens declares where all his ladders start: in the purity of particular things.

Today the leaves cry, hanging on branches swept by wind,
Yet the nothingness of winter becomes a little less.
It is still full of icy shades and shapen snow.

The leaves cry . . . One holds off and merely hears the cry.
It is a busy cry, concerning someone else.
And though one says that one is part of everything,

There is a conflict, there is a resistance involved;
And being part is an exertion that declines:
One feels the life of that which gives life as it is.

The leaves cry. It is not a cry of divine attention,
Nor the smoke-drift of puffed-out heroes, nor human cry.
It is the cry of leaves that do not transcend themselves,

In the absence of fantasia, without meaning more
Than they are in the final finding of the ear, in the thing
Itself, until, at last, the cry concerns no one at all. (OP 96–97)

"The Course of a Particular" invites comparison with earlier poems of the desolate seasons, such as "The Snow Man" (1921) and "Autumn Refrain" (1931).[108] Although these three poems are linked together by a common tone and obvious similarities in theme, each develops in a way characteristic of one stage in Stevens' poetic life; and the differences between the late poem and its predecessors illuminate the special qualities of Stevens' final poetic. At first glance "The Snow Man" (CP 9–10) appears to be a companion poem to "The Course of a Particular." Each poem develops through five controlled tercets, each speaks of "immense clarity and intense poverty, an abandonment to pure content of consciousness unrefracted by convention or individuality." [109] But the place of "The Snow Man" in the world of *Harmonium*, as well as its individual structure and diction, make it at bottom a very different poem from "The Course of a Particular." Within *Harmonium* it marks out one limit of the poet's sensibility, one of the poles between which he fluctuates, and is not—like "The Course of a Particular"—part of an integrated design encompassing a whole array of poems. Nor does it have the intense impersonality of "The Course of a Particular": the whimsical title serves to tame the poem's raw subject, and the "listener" of the final stanza is a more human variant of the impersonal opening voice ("One must have a mind of winter . . ."). The single complex sentence which is "The Snow Man," like the single sentence of Frost's "The Silken Tent," forms an image of intense personal thought. Only in the final line, where the three-beat verse is stretched into a bare Alexandrine, does the poem approximate the desolation of "The Course of a Particular." "The Snow Man" is a quintessential Imagist poem in that it establishes a central image (the winter landscape), relates that to an observer (the "listener"), and then defines the interaction.

"Autumn Refrain" (CP 160), which was written ten years later at the outset of Stevens' work on *Ideas of Order*, depends like so many of Stevens' earlier poems on our sense of its place in a tradition. The "skreaking and skrittering residuum" which the poem cherishes is another variant on Stevens' persistent theme: the escape from poetic falsity. The poem is more aggressive than "The Snow Man" in rejecting the pathetic fallacy; its target is outworn poetic diction, the "evasions of the nightingale." The form of "Autumn Refrain," a mock sonnet,[110] and the substitution of the grackle for the nightingale, make the poem a complex exercise in tradition and the individual talent. Like so many of the poems in *Ideas of Order*, "Autumn Refrain" tells of Stevens' own struggle to forge a personal and fluent speech.

"The Course of a Particular," by contrast, is a poem of almost unbearable impersonality. The long verse-lines, which stretch Stevens' normal pentameter units toward the extreme limit of leaden "fourteeners," contribute to a sense of exhausted finality, as do the end-stopped lines in the first three tercets. The abstract title announces the theme of impersonality: the "particular" is the "cry" of the leaves, which is repeated nine times as the poem unfolds. The course of this particular is one of gradual depersonalization. At the beginning there is a temptation to humanize the cry, as the shades and forms of winter make the landscape seem a bit more than "nothingness"; but "One holds off and merely hears the cry," and in doing so "One feels the life of that which gives life as it is." In the fourth tercet of the poem all traditional interpretations of the cry are rejected ("It is not a cry of divine attention, / Nor the smoke-drift of puffed-out heroes, nor human cry"), and the poem rises to its conclusion in a complex sentence which describes the final irreducible reality.

> It is the cry of leaves that do not transcend themselves,
>
> In the absence of fantasia, without meaning more
> Than they are in the final finding of the ear, in the thing
> Itself, until, at last, the cry concerns no one at all.

All our attempts to make nature part of us have been excluded in a desire to record "the final finding of the ear," [111] which is all that is left of the observer's annihilated personality. "The Course of a Particular" reminds us of the heavy price Stevens had to pay for his final verse, which is essentially a poetry of exclusions.

The major difference between "The Course of a Particular" and the earlier poems, however, does not lie in its diction and design, but in its relation to the other poems of Stevens' late career. The experiences of the seasons, part of the ground-tone in the earlier verse, have been turned into reference-points within a closed system of imaginative belief, so that the "nothingness of winter—like the "unimaginable Zero summer" of T. S. Eliot's "Little Gidding"—has a specific significance both within the structure of the poem and within the general structure of Stevens' poetic. The harmonies and resemblances between poems in the earlier volumes have been replaced by a more rigorous pattern, in which "One poem proves another and the whole" (CP 441). The pattern is one that was discovered, not imposed, as *Notes toward a Supreme Fiction* makes clear:

> But to impose is not
> To discover. To discover an order as of
> A season, to discover summer and know it,
>
> To discover winter and know it well, to find,
> Not to impose, not to have reasoned at all,
> Out of nothing to have come on major weather,
>
> It is possible, possible, possible. It must
> Be possible. It must be that in time
> The real will from its crude compoundings come,
>
> Seeming, at first, a beast disgorged, unlike,
> Warmed by a desperate milk. To find the real,
> To be stripped of every fiction except one,
>
> The fiction of an absolute—Angel,
> Be silent in your luminous cloud and hear
> The luminous melody of proper sound. (III. vii)

The great temptation is to impose the unity and archetypal patterns of the later verse on the poems of 1914–37, glossing the experiments of *Harmonium* and the tentative orders of mid-career with the vocabulary of the final poetic. Such a method not only falsifies the earlier poems, but obscures the voyage of discovery which led to the great achievements of the 1940's and 1950's. It would be more true to say that the earlier poems are essential to an appreciation of the later: that they supply a feeling for the poet's personality and his place in the development of modern poetry which counteracts the austerity and isolation of much of the later verse. Each phase of Stevens' poetic life has its moments of greatness. The job of the reader is to identify them, and to see them for what they are: sustaining fictions which make bearable for a moment the irremediable poverty of our lives.

Notes to Part II

1. *Letters*, p. 243.
2. *Letters*, p. 320. WS to Ronald Lane Latimer, 6 May 1937.
3. *Letters*, p. 79. WS to Elsie Moll, *c*. 1904–5.
4. *Letters*, p. 680. WS to Thomas McGreevy, 1 June 1950.
5. "Metropolitan Melancholy" (OP 32) is assigned the date 19 June 1928 by the editor.
6. Unpublished letter from WS to R. P. Blackmur, 18 October 1930. Princeton University Library.
7. WS sent the poem to Untermeyer on 11 June 1929 (*Letters*, p. 252).
8. *Letters*, p. 786. WS to Renato Poggioli, 1 July 1953.
9. *Letters*, p. 261 (WS to Lincoln Kirstein, 10 April 1931) and p. 262 (WS to Harriet Monroe, 5 August 1932).
10. *Letters*, p. 260. WS to Harriet Monroe, 26 December 1930.
11. Published in *Contempo* for 15 December 1932.
12. *Letters*, p. 262. WS to Harriet Monroe, 5 August 1932.
13. Samuel French Morse, *Wallace Stevens: Poetry as Life* (New York, 1970), p. 143. Mr. Morse and I came independently to the conclusion that these poems are part of an abandoned sequence, which is not surprising in view of their obvious similarities in content and verseform.
14. *Letters*, p. 263. WS to William Rose Benét, 6 January 1933. Benét included "The Emperor of Ice-Cream," along with Stevens' note on the poem, in *Fifty Poets: An American Auto-Anthology* (New York, 1933).
15. See *Letters*, pp. 291–92, where "A Fading of the Sun" is described as a variation on the theme of "Mr. Burnshaw and the Statue" (Part II of *Owl's Clover*). WS to Ronald Lane Latimer, 5 November 1935.
16. *Letters*, p. 295. WS to Ronald Lane Latimer, 21 November 1935.
17. *Letters*, p. 274. WS to Ronald Lane Latimer, 8 January 1935.
18. *Letters*, p. 291. WS to Ronald Lane Latimer, 5 November 1935.
19. *Ibid.*, p. 292.
20. *Letters*, p. 288. WS to Ronald Lane Latimer, 31 October 1935.
21. *Letters*, p. 370. WS to Hi Simons, 28 August 1940.
22. The poems which can be assigned to 1934–35, either from date of publication or internal evidence, may be found on pp. 35–42, 74–77 of *Opus Posthumous*: "Secret Man," "The Drum-Majors in the Labor Day Parade," "Polo Ponies Practicing," "Lytton Strachey, Also, Enters into Heaven," "Table Talk," "A Room on a Garden," "Agenda," "Five Grotesque Pieces."
23. *Letters*, p. 279. WS to Ronald Lane Latimer, 26 March 1935.
24. *Letters*, pp. 348–49. WS to Hi Simons, 9 January 1940.
25. *Letters*, p. 272. WS to Morton D. Zabel, 6 December 1934.
26. Helen Vendler, *On Extended Wings* (Cambridge, Mass., 1969), pp. 69–70.
27. *Letters*, p. 349. WS to Hi Simons, 9 January 1940.
28. *Letters*, p. 293. WS to Ronald Lane Latimer, 15 November 1935.
29. *Letters*, p. 348. WS to Hi Simons, 9 January 1940.

30. This source was first pointed out and discussed by Ramon Guthrie in "Stevens' 'Lions in Sweden,'" *The Explicator*, 20 (December 1961), item 32.

31. When Stevens sent "The American Sublime" to Ronald Lane Latimer on 5 March 1935, he asked that it be returned if Latimer could not use it in *Alcestis*, since "I am thinking of using [it] elsewhere" (*Letters*, p. 276).

32. *Letters*, p. 277. WS to Ronald Lane Latimer, 12 March 1935.

33. "I am pro-Mussolini, personally," Stevens remarked in an aside when writing to Ronald Lane Latimer about the futility of a poetry of ideas based on fixed concepts (*Letters*, p. 289. 31 October 1935). For his attitude toward the Spanish Civil War, see "The Men That Are Falling" (CP 187–88), where the death of the Spanish Republican is given a sympathetic treatment reminiscent of "The Death of a Soldier." When Stevens sat down to write a "war poem" his politics fell away, and he became concerned solely with the drama of death and violence.

34. *Letters*, p. 293. WS to Ronald Lane Latimer, 5 November 1935.

35. See *Letters*, pp. 291–92. WS to Ronald Lane Latimer, 5 November 1935.

36. Richard A. Macksey claims that Stevens mocks Shelley's "Ode" in "'Mozart, 1935' and in the central section of *Notes toward a Supreme Fiction*" ["The Climates of Wallace Stevens," in *The Act of the Mind*, ed. Roy'Harvey Pearce and J. Hillis Miller (Baltimore, 1965), p. 211]. The "Bethou me, said sparrow" of *Notes toward a Supreme Fiction* (CP 393ff.) is clearly more ironic than the echo in "Mozart, 1935," but neither allusion is completely mocking.

37. Louis Martz, "Wallace Stevens: The World as Meditation," in *Wallace Stevens: A Collection of Critical Essays*, ed. Marie Borroff (Englewood Cliffs, N.J., 1963), p. 138.

38. *Letters*, p. 279. WS to Ronald Lane Latimer, 26 March 1935. The planned publication in England never materialized, and Stevens ultimately gave the poem to Latimer for The Alcestis Press.

39. The lecture (OP 216–29), delivered at Harvard in early December 1936 (*Letters*, p. 313), contains a discussion of "The Old Woman and the Statue" and was accompanied by a reading from parts of *Owl's Clover*.

40. *Letters*, p. 368. WS to Hi Simons, 27 August 1940.

41. Stanley Burnshaw, "Turmoil in the Middle Ground," *New Masses*, 17 (1 October 1935), 41–42.

42. *Letters*, p. 340. WS to Henry Church, 1 June 1939.

43. *Letters*, p. 286. WS to Ronald Lane Latimer, 9 October 1935.

44. *Letters*, pp. 291–92. WS to Ronald Lane Latimer, 5 November 1935.

45. See *Letters*, p. 296 (WS to Ronald Lane Latimer, 21 November 1935) and p. 306 (WS to Ronald Lane Latimer, 24 January 1936).

46. *Letters*, p. 311. WS to Ronald Lane Latimer, 16 May 1936.

47. *Ibid.*

48. *Letters*, pp. 366–75 (27–30 August 1940). In these comments Stevens follows the 1937 revised text; conversions from this text to the original

text printed in *Opus Posthumous* may be found in the footnotes to the letters and in Appendix C.

49. *Letters*, p. 370. "Whether or not what I have said is implicit in the text, it is the basis of the poem, or, to say the thing a little more neatly, it establishes the poem in its perspective."

50. *Letters*, p. 311 (WS to Ronald Lane Latimer, 16 May 1936). "The statue is a variable symbol; it is not always society, but it always has a social aspect, so to speak."

51. The terms are drawn from Stevens' own paraphrase; see fn. 40.

52. *Letters*, p. 366.

53. *Letters*, p. 295. WS to Ronald Lane Latimer, 15 November 1935.

54. *Letters*, p. 295. WS to Ronald Lane Latimer, 21 November 1935.

55. *Letters*, p. 370. Stevens' gloss on the last section.

56. *Letters*, pp. 289–90 and 295 (WS to Ronald Lane Latimer, 31 October and 21 November 1935).

57. *Letters*, pp. 307–8. WS to Ronald Lane Latimer, 6 February 1936.

58. *Letters*, p. 370.

59. *Letters*, p. 373.

60. *Letters*, p. 374.

61. *Letters*, pp. 411–12. WS to Henry Church, 2 July 1942.

62. Published in *The Nation* for 24 October 1936, "The Men That Are Falling" was the *Nation* Prize Poem for that year.

63. "A Thought Revolved" appeared in *New Directions in Prose and Poetry*, ed. James Laughlin (November 1936). It and "The Men That Are Falling" were included in *The Man with the Blue Guitar and Other Poems* (1937).

64. *Letters*, p. 316. WS to Ronald Lane Latimer, 17 March 1937.

65. *Letters*, pp. 359–64 (WS to Hi Simons, 8 August-10 August 1940); pp. 783–94 (WS to Renato Poggioli, 25 June-22 July 1953).

66. *Letters*, p. 793. WS to Bernard Heringman, 21 July 1953.

67. *Letters*, p. 359. WS to Hi Simons, 8 August 1940.

68. *Letters*, p. 788. WS to Renato Poggioli, 12 July 1953.

69. Christian Zervos, "Conversation avec Picasso," *Cahiers d'Art*, 7–10 (1935), 173. Source noted in Ronald Sukenick, *Musing the Obscure* (New York, 1967), p. 91.

> Auparavant les tableaux s'acheminaient vers leur fin par progression. Chaque jour apportait quelque chose de nouveau. Un tableau était une somme d'additions. Chez moi, un tableau est une somme de destructions. Je fais un tableau, ensuite je le détrius. Mais à la fin du compte rien n'est perdu; le rouge que j'ai enlevé d'une part se trouve quelque part ailleurs.

70. *Letters*, p. 793. WS to Renato Poggioli, 22 July 1953.

71. *Letters*, p. 785. WS to Renato Poggioli, 29 June 1953.

72. *Letters*, p. 362. WS to Hi Simons, 9 August 1940.

73. *Letters*, p. 790. WS to Renato Poggioli, 12 July 1953.

74. *Letters*, p. 363. WS to Hi Simons, 10 August 1940.

75. *Ibid.*, p. 364.

76. The phrasing of Poem XXII echoes Stevens' gloss on "The Old Woman and the Statue" (*Letters*, p. 368): ". . . one more confrontation of reality (the depression) and the imagination (art). A larger expression than confrontation is: a phase of the universal intercourse. There is a flow to and fro between reality and imagination."

77. See Helen Vendler's analysis of the poem's movement from apparent opposition to apparent resolution (*On Extended Wings* [Cambridge, Mass., 1969], pp. 135–36).

78. *Letters*, p. 23, fn. 1; and p. 457 (WS to Hi Simons, 11 October 1943).

79. "The Noble Rider and the Sound of Words," NA 8–12.

80. *Letters*, p. 784. WS to Renato Poggioli, 25 June 1953.

81. *Letters*, p. 364. WS to Hi Simons, 10 August 1940.

82. Stevens' gloss on Poem III. Quoted in *Mattino Domenicale Ed Altre Poesie*, trans. Renato Poggioli (Torino, 1954), p. 174.

83. *Letters*, p. 783. WS to Renato Poggioli, 25 June 1953.

84. Ezra Pound, *ABC of Reading* (London, 1951), p. 19.

85. *Letters*, p. 789. WS to Renato Poggioli, 12 July 1953.

86. *Ibid.*, p. 791.

87. *Letters*, p. 831. WS to Herbert Weinstock, 6 May 1954.

88. R. P. Blackmur, "Lord Tennyson's Scissors: 1912–1950," in *Language as Gesture* (New York, 1952), p. 422.

89. George Santayana, *Interpretations of Poetry and Religion* (New York, 1922), p. 178.

90. Helen Vendler, *On Extended Wings* (Cambridge, Mass., 1969), p. 205.

91. See *Letters*, p. 370. WS to Hi Simons, 28 August 1940.

92. Reprinted in *The Palm at the End of the Mind*, ed. Holly Stevens (New York, 1971), p. 206.

93. *Letters*, pp. 481–82. WS to José Rodríguez Feo, 4 January 1945.

94. *Letters*, p. 637. WS to Bernard Heringman, 3 May 1949. Stevens' sonnet appeared in the *Harvard Advocate* for May 1899 (reprinted in Buttel, pp. 17–18). Santayana's reply was printed in *A Hermit of Carmel and Other Poems* (New York, 1901), p. 122.

95. Comments on Santayana's probable influence on Stevens may be found in many studies, especially Joseph N. Riddel's *The Clairvoyant Eye* (Baton Rouge, 1965) and Frank Doggett's *Stevens' Poetry of Thought* (Baltimore, 1966), but the subject needs further definition.

96. Edmund Wilson, "A Reporter at Large: Santayana at the Convent of the Blue Nuns," *The New Yorker*, 22 (6 April 1946), 59–67.

97. *Letters*, p. 637. WS to Bernard Heringman, 3 May 1949.

98. On 29 September 1952 Stevens wrote to Barbara Church: "I grieve to hear of the death of George Santayana in Rome. Fifty years ago, I knew him well, in Cambridge" (*Letters*, p. 761).

99. *The Palm at the End of the Mind*, p. 403. The third line reads: "Of a common maker, not divine, as if . . ."

100. *Letters*, p. 820. The occasion was the reprinting of "The Auroras of Autumn" in *Perspectives USA* for Summer 1954.

101. *Letters*, pp. 636–37. WS to Bernard Heringman, 3 May 1949.

102. *Letters*, p. 719. WS to Charles Tomlinson, 19 June 1951.

103. *Letters*, p. 782. WS to Renato Poggioli, 18 June 1953.

104. *Letters*, p. 719. WS to Charles Tomlinson, 19 June 1951.

105. *Letters*, pp. 721 (WS to Barbara Church, 25 July 1951) and 619 (WS to Thomas McGreevy, 7 October 1948).

106. The sections of the shorter version printed in *Selected Poems* were incorporated into the longer version as follows: I (I), II (VI), III (IX), IV (XI), V (XII), VI (XVI), VII (XXII), VIII (XXVIII), IX (XXX), X (XXXI), XI (XXIX). The text followed in this chapter is that of the shorter version as reprinted in *Poems by Wallace Stevens*, ed. Samuel French Morse (New York, 1959—Vintage paperback).

107. Joseph N. Riddel, *The Clairvoyant Eye* (Baton Rouge, 1965), p. 258.

108. See Richard A. Macksey's excellent article on Stevens' poems of winter, "The Climates of Wallace Stevens," in *The Act of the Mind*, ed. Roy Harvey Pearce and J. Hillis Miller (Baltimore, 1965), pp. 185–223.

109. *Ibid.*, p. 188.

110. When "Autumn Refrain" was first published in the *Hound and Horn*, Winter 1932, it was fifteen lines in length. The eighth line ("The stillness that comes to me out of this, beneath") was cut from all subsequent printings, presumably because Stevens wished the poem to resemble a sonnet. The earlier form is reprinted in *The Palm at the End of the Mind*, pp. 94–95.

111. "Ear" was misprinted as "air" in *Opus Posthumous*, thereby destroying the poem's consistency. The correct reading is restored in *The Palm at the End of the Mind*.

Appendix A

When, in 1930, Alfred A. Knopf decided to reprint *Harmonium*, Stevens chose to omit three poems (all three are now available in *Opus Post-humous*):

"The Silver Plough-Boy"
"Exposition of the Contents of a Cab"
"Architecture"

He then added fourteen poems which had either been published or composed sometime before 1925:

"The Man Whose Pharynx Was Bad"
"The Death of a Soldier"
"Negation"
"The Surprises of the Superhuman"
"Sea Surface Full of Clouds"
"The Revolutionists Stop for Orangeade"
"New England Verses"
"Lunar Paraphrase"
"Anatomy of Monotony"
"The Public Square"
"Sonatina to Hans Christian"
"In the Clear Season of Grapes"
"Two at Norfolk"
"Indian River"

This group of fourteen poems was inserted before the last two poems of the 1923 edition, "Tea" and "To the Roaring Wind."

The 1931 edition of *Harmonium* is the definitive text, and I have drawn my quotations from it. The text of *Harmonium* found in *Collected Poems* contains several errors in wording, punctuation, and stanzaic form (see William Heyen, "The Text of *Harmonium*," *Twentieth Century Literature*, XII [October 1966], 147–48).

Appendix B

1. Poems from *The Trend*, 1914

The "Carnet de Voyage" sequence was published in *The Trend*, VII (September 1914); "Two Poems" appeared in *The Trend*, VIII (November 1914). Poems III–VII of "Carnet de Voyage" are found in the manuscript "Little June Book" of 1909; Poem II of "Two Poems" was included in the "Little June Book" of 1908.

"CARNET DE VOYAGE"

I

An odor from a star
Comes to my fancy, slight,
Tenderly spiced and gay,
As if a seraph's hand
Unloosed the fragrant silks
Of some sultana, bright
In her soft sky. And pure
It is, and excellent,
As if a seraph's blue
Fell, as a shadow falls,
And his warm body shed
Sweet exhalations, void
Of our despised decay.

II *One More Sunset*

The green goes from the corn,
The blue from all the lakes,
And the shadows of the mountains mingle in the sky.

Far off, the still bamboo
Grows green; the desert pool
Turns gaudy turquoise for the chanting caravan.

The changing green and blue
Flow round the changing earth;
And all the rest is empty wondering and sleep.

III

Here the grass grows,
And the wind blows.
And in the stream,
Small fishes gleam,
Blood-red and hue
Of shadowy blue,
And amber sheen,
And water-green,
And yellow flash,
And diamond ash.
And the grass grows,
And the wind blows.

IV

She that winked her sandal fan
Long ago in gray Japan—

She that heard the bell intone
Rendezvous by rolling Rhone—

How wide the spectacle of sleep,
Hands folded, eyes too still to weep!

V

I am weary of the plum and of the cherry,
And that buff moon in evening's aquarelle,
I have no heart within to make me merry.
I nod above the books of Heaven or Hell.

All things are old. The new-born swallows fare
Through the Spring twilight on dead September's wing.
The dust of Babylon is in the air,
And settles on my lips the while I sing.

VI

Man from the waste evolved
The Cytherean glade,
Imposed on battering seas
His keel's dividing blade,
And sailed there, unafraid.

The isle revealed his worth.
It was a place to sing in
And honor noble Life,
For white doves to wing in,
And roses to spring in.

VII *Chinese Rocket*

There, a rocket in the Wain
Brings primeval night again.

All the startled heavens flare
From the Shepherd to the Bear—

When the old-time dark returns,
Lo, the steadfast Lady burns
Her curious lantern to disclose
How calmly the White River flows!

VIII   *On an Old Guitar*

It was a simple thing
For her to sit and sing,
    "Hey nonino!"

This year and that befell,
(Time saw and Time can tell),
    With a hey and a ho—

Under the peach-tree, play
Such mockery away,
    Hey nonino!

"TWO POEMS"

I   *From a Junk*

A great fish plunges in the dark,
Its fins of rutted silver; sides,
Belabored with a foamy light;
And back, brilliant with scaly salt.
It glistens in the flapping wind,
Burns there and glistens, wide and wide,
Under the five-horned stars of night,
In wind and wave . . . It is the moon.

II   *Home Again*

Back within the valley,
Down from the divide,
No more flaming clouds about,
O! the soft hillside,
And my cottage light,
And the starry night.

2. "Phases," 1914

In September 1914 *Poetry: A Magazine of Verse* (Chicago) announced that a prize of one hundred dollars had been offered for the best war or peace poem "based on the present European situation." Stevens submitted a series of eleven poems, which arrived so late (the November "War Number" was already in proof) that Harriet Monroe, the editor, could only find room for a two-page spread of four poems. On 21 October 1914 she wrote to Stevens:

I was heartbroken that we could not use more of your poem, especially the first section. But our war number is terribly crowded—I could give you only two pages—and II–V seemed to me about the best of it. Also it stands well without the rest.

Section VI seems to me the weakest, and I don't feel that you quite got what you wanted out of VIII and IX. . . . (*Stevens* MSS; *partially quoted in Buttel, p. 231*).

The typescript of "Phases" now in the Harriet Monroe Library of Modern Poetry, University of Chicago Library, is incomplete, and some verses other than those published in *Poetry* were apparently lost in the process of preparing the text for the printer. However, it is possible to reconstruct the sequence sent to Miss Monroe with some certainty by conflating the surviving typescripts and manuscripts, and that sequence is printed below. The series of poems reproduced and discussed by Robert Buttel (pp. 235–37) must date from a later time, since Poem VII bears the title "Belgian Farm, October, 1914" and the original order has been revised in an attempt to fill the gaps left by the four poems published in *Poetry*. The duplications and alternate numbers in the series reproduced by Buttel show that Stevens was still experimenting, and had not yet found a satisfactory order for the poems Miss Monroe could not print.

Of the eleven poems in this sequence, II through V appeared in *Poetry*, V (November 1914), 70–71, and were reprinted in *Opus Posthumous* as numbers I–IV. The editor of *Opus Posthumous* also printed Poems VII and I "to give a sample of the rest," renumbering them V and VI.

"PHASES"

"La justice sans force est contredite, parce qu'il y a toujours des méchants; la force sans la justice est accusée."

—PASCAL

I

There was heaven,
Full of Raphael's costumes;
And earth,
A thing of shadows,
Stiff as stone,
Where Time, in fitful turns,
Resumes
His own . . .

A dead hand tapped the drum,
An old voice cried out, "Come!"
We were obedient and dumb.

II

There's a little square in Paris,
Waiting until we pass.

They sit idly there,
They sip the glass.

There's a cab-horse at the corner,
There's rain. The season grieves.
It was silver once,
And green with leaves.

There's a parrot in a window,
Will see us on parade,
Hear the loud drums roll—
And serenade.

III

This was the salty taste of glory,
That it was not
Like Agamemnon's story.
Only, an eyeball in the mud,
And Hopkins,
Flat and pale and gory!

IV

But the bugles, in the night,
Were wings that bore
To where our comfort was;

Arabesques of candle beams,
Winding
Through our heavy dreams;

Winds that blew
Where the bending iris grew;

Birds of intermitted bliss,
Singing in the night's abyss;

Vines with yellow fruit,
That fell
Along the walls
That bordered Hell.

V

Death's nobility again
Beautified the simplest men.
Fallen Winkle felt the pride
Of Agamemnon
When he died.

What could London's
Work and waste
Give him—
To that salty, sacrificial taste?

What could London's
Sorrow bring—
To that short, triumphant sting?

VI

[fragment]
The crisp, sonorous epics
Mongered after every scene.
Sluggards must be quickened! Screen,

No more, the shape of false Confusion.
Bare his breast and draw the flood
Of all his Babylonian blood.

VII

[Belgian Farm, October, 1914]
The vaguest line of smoke, (a year ago),
Wavered in evening air, above the roof,
As if some Old Man of the Chimney, sick
Of summer and that unused hearth below,

Stretched out a shadowy arm to feel the night.
The children heard him in their chilly beds,
Mumbling and musing of the silent farm.
They heard his mumble in the morning light.

Now, soldiers, hear me: mark this very breeze,
That blows about in such a hopeless way,
Mumbling and musing like the most forlorn.
It is that Old Man, lost among the trees.

VIII

What shall we say to the lovers of freedom,
Forming their states for new eras to come?
Say that the fighter is master of men.

Shall we, then, say to the lovers of freedom
That force, and not freedom, must always prevail?
Say that the fighter is master of men.

Or shall we say to the lovers of freedom
That freedom will conquer and always prevail?
Say that the fighter is master of men.

Say, too, that freedom is master of masters,
Forming their states for new eras to come.
Say that the fighter is master of men.

IX

Life, the hangman, never came,
Near our mysteries of flame.

When we marched across his towns,
He cozened us with leafy crowns.

When we marched along his roads,
He kissed his hand to ease our loads.

Life, the hangman, kept away,
From the field where soldiers pay.

x

Peace means long, delicious valleys,
In the mode of Claude Lorraine;
Rivers of jade,
In serpentines,
About the heavy grain;
Leaning trees,
Where the pilgrim hums
Of the dear
And distant door.
Peace means these,
And all things, as before.

xi

War has no haunt except the heart,
Which envy haunts, and hate, and fear,
And malice, and ambition, near
The haunt of love. Who shall impart,

To that strange commune, strength enough
To drive the laggard phantoms out?
Who shall dispel for it the doubt
Of its own strength? Let Heaven snuff

The tapers round her futile throne.
Close tight the prophets' coffin-clamp.
Peer inward, with the spirit's lamp,
Look deep, and let the truth be known.

—PETER PARASOL

3. Poems from *Others*, 1916–17

"The Florist Wears Knee-Breeches" and "Song" were first published in
Others, II (March 1916); "Meditation" first appeared in *Others*, IV (December 1917).

The Florist Wears Knee-Breeches

My flowers are reflected
In your mind
As you are reflected in your glass.
When you look at them,
There is nothing in your mind
Except the reflections
Of my flowers.
But when I look at them

I see only the reflections
In your mind,
And not my flowers.
It is my desire
To bring roses,
And place them before you
In a white dish.

Song

There are great things doing
In the world,
Little rabbit.
There is a damsel,
Sweeter than the sound of the willow,
Dearer than shallow water
Flowing over pebbles.
Of a Sunday,
She wears a long coat,
With twelve buttons on it.
Tell that to your mother.

Meditation

How long have I meditated, O Prince,
On sky and earth?
It comes to this,
That even the moon
Has exhausted its emotions.
What is it that I think of, truly?
The lines of blackberry bushes,
The design of leaves—
Neither sky nor earth
Express themselves before me . . .
Bossuet did not preach at the funerals
Of puppets.

4. "Lettres d'un Soldat," 1917–18

This sequence of "war poems," composed in the summer of 1917, may originally have contained seventeen poems (Poem XIII below, "Death was a reaper . . . ," is numbered XVII in the manuscripts). On 14 March 1918 Stevens and Harriet Monroe met in the *Poetry* office in Chicago and selected nine poems for publication (*Poetry*, XII [May 1918], 59–65). Three of the poems published in *Poetry* were included in the revised edition of *Harmonium*, but without the epigraphs from Lemercier's *Lettres d'un Soldat*. Another poem from the manuscripts, "Lunar Paraphase," was included in the 1931 edition of *Harmonium*. All the extant poems are printed below, arranged in the chronological order of the epigraphs. Information concerning publication and important manuscript variants is supplied in the footnotes.

"LETTRES D'UN SOLDAT"

"*Combattre avec ses frères, à sa place, à son rang, avec des yeux dessillés, sans espoir de gloire et de profit, et simplement parce que telle est la loi, voilà le commandement que donne le dieu au guerrier Arjuna, quand celui-ci doute s'il doit se détourner de l'absolu pour le cauchemar humain de la bataille. . . . Simplement, qu'Arjuna bande son arc avec les autres Kshettryas!*"

PRÉFACE DE ANDRÉ CHEVRILLON

I

7 septembre

. . . *Nous sommes embarqués dans l'aventure, sans aucune sensation dominante, sauf peut-être une acceptation assez belle de la fatalité.* . . .

Common Soldier

No introspective chaos . . . I accept:
War, too, although I do not understand.
And that, then, is my final aphorism.

I have been pupil under bishops' rods
And got my learning from the orthodox.
I mark the virtue of the common-place.

I take all things as stated—so and so
Of men and earth: I quote the line and page,
I quote the very phrase my masters used.

If I should fall, as soldier, I know well
The final pulse of blood from this good heart
Would taste, precisely, as they said it would.[1]

II

27 septembre

Jamais la majesté de la nuit ne m'apporta autant de consolation qu'en cette accumulation d'épreuves. Vénus, étincelante, m'est une amie.

In an Ancient, Solemn Manner

The spirit wakes in the night wind—is naked.
What is it that hides in the night wind
Near by it?

Is it, once more, the mysterious beauté,
Like a woman inhibiting passion
In solace—

The multiform beauty, sinking in night wind,
Quick to be gone, yet never
Quite going?

She will leap back from the swift constellations,
As they enter the place of their western
Seclusion.[2]

III

22 octobre

Ce qu'il faut, c'est reconnaître l'amour et la beauté triomphant de toute violence.

Anecdotal Revery

The streets contain a crowd
Of blind men tapping their way
By inches—
This man to complain to the grocer
Of yesterday's cheese,
This man to visit a woman,
This man to take the air.
Am I to pick my way
Through these crickets?—
I, that have a head
In the bag
Slung over my shoulder?
I have secrets
That prick
Like a heart full of pins.
Permit me, gentlemen,
I have killed the mayor,
And am escaping from you.
Get out of the way!
(*The blind men strike him down with their sticks.*) [3]

IV

31 octobre

Jusqu'à présent j'ai possedé une sagesse de renoncement, mais maintenant je veux une Sagesse qui accepte tout, en s'orientant vers l'action future.

Morale

And so France feels. A menace that impends,
Too long, is like a bayonet that bends. [4]

V

7 novembre

Si tu voyais la sécurité des petits animaux des bois, souris, mulots! L'autre jour, dans notre abri de feuillage, je suivais les évolutions de ces petites bêtes. Elles étaient jolies comme une estampe japonaise, avec l'interieur de leurs oreilles rose comme un coquillage.

Comme Dieu Dispense de Graces

Here I keep thinking of the Primitives—
The sensitive and conscientious schemes
Of mountain pallors ebbing into air;

And I remember sharp Japonica—
The driving rain, the willows in the rain,
The birds that wait out rain in willow leaves.

Although life seems a goblin mummery,
These images return and are increased,
As for a child in an oblivion:

Even by mice—these scamper and are still;
They cock small ears, more glistening and pale
Than fragile volutes in a rose sea-shell.[5]

VI

26 novembre

J'ai la ferme espérance, mais surtout j'ai confiance en la justice éternelle, quelque surprise qu'elle cause à l'humaine idée que nous en avons.

The Surprises of the Superhuman

The palais de justice of chambermaids
Tops the horizon with its colonnades.

If it were lost in Übermenschlichkeit,
Perhaps our wretched state would soon come right.

For somehow the brave dicta of its kings
Make more awry our faulty human things.[6]

VII

29 novembre au matin, en cantonnement

Telle fut la beauté d'hier. Te parlerai-je des soirées précédentes, alors que sur la route, la lune me dessinait la broderie des arbres, le pathétique des calvaires, l'attendrissement de ces maisons que l'on sait des ruines, mais que la nuit fait surgir comme une évocation de la paix.

Lunar Paraphrase

The moon is the mother of pathos and pity.

When, at the wearier end of November,
Her old light moves along the branches,
Feebly, slowly, depending upon them;
When the body of Jesus hangs in a pallor,
Humanly near, and the figure of Mary,
Touched on by hoar-frost, shrinks in a shelter
Made by the leaves, that have rotted and fallen;
When over the houses, a golden illusion
Brings back an earlier season of quiet
And quieting dreams in the sleepers in darkness—

The moon is the mother of pathos and pity.[7]

VIII

7 décembre

Bien chère Mère aimée. . . . Pour ce qui est de ton coeur, j'ai tellement confiance en ton courage, qu'à l'heure actuelle cette certitude est mon grand réconfort. Je sais que ma mère a atteint à cette liberté d'âme qui permet de contempler le spectacle universel.

There is another mother whom I love,
O chère maman, another, who, in turn,
Is mother to the two of us, and more,
In whose hard service both of us endure
Our petty portion in the sacrifice.
Not France! France, also, serves the invincible eye,
That, from her helmet, terrible and bright,
Commands the armies; the relentless arm,
Devising proud, majestic issuance.
Wait now; have no rememberings of hope,
Poor penury. There will be voluble hymns
Come swelling, when, regardless of my end,
The mightier mother raises up her cry;
And little will or wish, that day, for tears.[8]

IX

15 janvier

La seule sanction pour moi est ma conscience. Il faut nous confier à une justice impersonelle, indépendante de tout facteur humain, et à une destinée utile et harmonieuse malgré toute horreur de forme.

Negation

Hi! The creator too is blind,
Struggling toward his harmonious whole,
Rejecting intermediate parts,
Horrors and falsities and wrongs;
Incapable master of all force,
Too vague idealist, overwhelmed
By an afflatus that persists.
For this, then, we endure brief lives,
The evanescent symmetries
From that meticulous potter's thumb.[9]

X

4 février

Hier soir, rentrant dans ma grange, ivresse, rixes, cris, chants et hurlements. Voilà la vie!

John Smith and his son, John Smith,
  And his son's son John, and-a-one
  And-a-two and-a-three
  And-a-rum-tum-tum, and-a
Lean John, and his son, lean John,
  And his lean son's John, and-a-one
  And-a-two and-a-three
  And-a-drum-rum-rum, and-a
Rich John, and his son, rich John,
  And his rich son's John, and-a-one
  And-a-two and-a-three
  And-a-pom-pom-pom, and-a

Wise John, and his son, wise John,
　　And his wise son's John, and-a-one
　　And-a-two and-a-three
And-a-fee and-a-fee and-a-fee
　　And-a-fee-fo-fum—
Voilà la vie, la vie, la vie,
　　And-a-rummy-tummy-tum
　　And-a-rummy-tummy-tum.[10]

XI

5 mars

La mort du soldat est près des choses naturelles.

Life contracts and death is expected,
As in a season of autumn.
The soldier falls.

He does not become a three-days personage,
Imposing his separation,
Calling for pomp.

Death is absolute and without memorial,
As in a season of autumn,
When the wind stops,

When the wind stops and, over the heavens,
The clouds go, nevertheless,
In their direction.[11]

XII

17 mars

J'ai oublié de te dire que, l'autre fois, pendant la tempête, j'ai vu dans le soir les grues revenir. Une accalmie permettait d'entendre leur cri.

In a theatre, full of tragedy,
The stage becomes an atmosphere
Of seeping rose—banal machine
In an appointed repertoire . . .[12]

XIII

26 mars

*Rien de nouveau sur notre hauteur que l'on continue d'organiser. . . .
De temps à autre la pioche rencontre un pauvre mort que la guerre tourmente jusque dans la terre.*

Death was a reaper with sickle and stone,
Or swipling flail, sun-black in the sun,
A laborer.

Or Death was a rider beating his horse,
Gesturing grandiose things in the air,
Seen by a muse. . . .

Symbols of sentiment . . . Take this phrase,
Men of the line, take this new phrase
Of the truth of Death—

Death, that will never be satisfied,
Digs up the earth when want returns . . .
You know the phrase.[13]

1. Printed as Poem I in *Opus Posthumous*.
2. II in OP; I in *Poetry* (without the title).
3. III in OP; II in *Poetry*.
4. IV in OP; III in *Poetry*.
5. V in OP; IV in *Poetry*.
6. Published in the revised edition of *Harmonium* as "The Surprises of the Superhuman"; Poem V in *Poetry*.
7. Published for the first time in the revised edition of *Harmonium* as "Lunar Paraphrase." I have supplied as an epigraph the passage from *Lettres d'un Soldat* which Stevens must have had in mind.
8. VI in OP; VI in *Poetry*.
9. Published in the revised edition of *Harmonium* as "Negation"; Poem VII in *Poetry*.
10. VII in OP; VIII in *Poetry*.
11. Published in the revised version of *Harmonium* as "The Death of a Soldier"; Poem IX in *Poetry*.
12. Poem VIII in OP; numbered XVI in the MS. This poem is preceded in the MS by another Poem XVI, with the same "17 mars" epigraph. The alternate poem is printed below, with cancellations indicated in brackets.

> The cranes return. The soldier hears their cry.
> No: not as if the jades of willow-tree
> Or river-fern came coloring the sky.
> But still the cranes return.
>
> The soldier hears their cry. He knows the fire
> That touches them—knows that he must not know
> Nor burden his endurance with desire.
> [But still the cranes return.]
>
> Endurance that grows heavy from despair,
> Drowsed with the oblivion of oblivions—
> The chant of spring becomes an obsolete air—
> [But still] the cranes return.
>
> [Grows heavy from despair, too much alone
> To feel the spring infusing its relief
> In sleepiness, to resist that weight of sky.
> But still the cranes return.]

13. IX in OP.

316

Appendix C

The first version of *Owl's Clover* was published in a limited edition by the Alcestis Press in November 1936. Parts of this version were extensively cut and revised when the poem was reprinted in the first edition of *The Man with the Blue Guitar* (New York: Alfred A. Knopf, October 1937). *Opus Posthumous* reprints the original Alcestis Press text on pages 43–71. The major changes between this text and the revised version of 1937 have been recorded below.

   I. *The Old Woman and the Statue*. Reprinted without change.
  II. *Mr. Burnshaw and the Statue*. Retitled *The Statue at the World's End*.
      Parts I–III: reprinted without change.
      Part IV: omitted entirely.
      Part V: reprinted as Part IV with the first line (OP 49, l. 3) omitted.
      Part VI: reprinted as Part V.
      Part VII: omitted entirely.
 III. *The Greenest Continent*
      Part I: reprinted without change.
      Parts II and III: condensed into Part II. The revised Part II opens as follows:

> The heaven of Europe is empty. But there was
> A heaven once, a heaven all selves. It was
> The spirit's episcopate, hallowed and high . . .

      and continues from OP 53, l. 29. The intervening lines are omitted.
      Part IV: reprinted as Part III with minor changes.
      Part V: reprinted as Part IV.
      Part VI: reprinted as Part V.
      Part VII: omitted entirely.
      Part VIII: reprinted as Part VI.
  IV. *A Duck for Dinner*
      Part I: lines 1–6 ("The Bulgar said . . . and without wine.'") reprinted without change, remainder omitted.
      Parts II and III: extensively cut and revised. The 1937 text is printed below.

II

Buckskins and broad-brims, crossers of divides,
For whom men were to be ends in themselves,

317

Are the cities to breed as the mountains bred? For you
Day came upon the spirit as life comes
And deep winds flooded you; for these, day comes,
A penny sun in a tinsel sky, unrhymed,
And the spirit writhes to be wakened, writhes
To see, once more, this hacked-up world of tools.
In their cadaverous Eden, they desire
The same down-dropping fruit in yellow leaves.
The scholar's outline that you had, the print
Of poets, the Italian lives preserved
For poverty are gaudy o to these.
Their destiny is just as much machine
As death itself. It will, it will be changed,
Time's fortune near, the sleepless sleepers moved
By the torture of things that will be realized,
Will, will, but how and all of them asking how.
These lives are not your lives, O free, O bold
That rode your horses straight away.

III

                              Again
The acrid Bulgar said, "There are more things
Than poodles in Pomerania. These men,
Infected by unreality, rapt round
By dense unreason, irreproachable force,
Are cast in pandemonium, flittered, howled
By harmonies beyond known harmony.
These bands, these swarms, these motions, what of them?
Of what are they thinking, of what, in spite of the duck,
Are they being part, of what are they feeling the strength,
Seeing the fulgent shadows upward heaped,
Spelling out pandects and haggard institutes?
Is each man thinking his separate thoughts or, for once,
Are all men thinking together as one, thinking
Each other's thoughts, thinking a single thought,
Disclosed in everything, transcended, poised
For the syllable, poised for the touch? But that
Apocalypse was not contrived for parks,
Geranium budgets, pay-roll water-falls,
The clank of the carrousel and, under the trees,
The sheep-like falling-in of distances,
Converging on the statue, white and high."

Part IV: reprinted with OP 63, ll. 9–17 condensed as follows:

As the man the state, not as the state the man.
But man means more, means the million and the duck.
It cannot mean a sea-wide country strewn
With squalid cells. It means, at least, this mob.

The man in the band-stand could be orator,
Some pebble-chewer practiced in Tyrian speech . . .

Parts V and VI: reprinted without change.

V. *Sombre Figuration*

Part I: reprinted without change.

Part II: reprinted with OP 67, l. 2 ("Playing a . . . in bleats.") omitted.

Part III: reprinted with OP 69, ll. 1–23 ("The churches . . . answering the worms?") and OP 69, l. 26–OP 70, l. 1 ("Poised, but poised . . . the self-same things.") omitted.

Part IV: reprinted with OP 71, ll. 14–16 ("That changed . . . the subverter, stops") omitted.

Indexes

I. WORKS BY WALLACE STEVENS

Ananke, 217, 219, 220, 223, 271
Apollinaire, Guillaume, 188
Arensberg, Walter, 10, 56, 83
"Armory Show" of 1913, 6, 10, 56
Arnold, Matthew, 44

Baird, James, 260
Beardsley, Aubrey, 27, 32
Benamou, Michel, 46
Berkeley, George, 101
Blackmur, R. P., 102, 124, 166, 257
Blake, William, 71
Bloom, Harold, 260
Botticelli, 85, 92
Burnshaw, Stanley, 204–6
Buttel, Robert, 12, 17, 108

Carman, Bliss, 12, 17
Cézanne, Paul, 151
Chevrillon, André, 72–73
Claude Lorraine, 23–24, 197
Coleridge, Samuel Taylor, 122, 245
Craig, Gordon, 56, 59
Crane, Hart, 94

Dante, 53
Davenport, Guy, 122
Dickens, Charles, 91
Dowson, Ernest, 32, 83
Driscoll, Louise, 22
Dufy, Raoul, 188

Eliot, T. S., 19, 33, 40, 42, 64, 69, 83–84, 85, 104, 217, 294
Ellmann, Richard, 97
Empson, William, 124–25

Fernandez, Ramon, 194
Ficke, Arthur Davison, 16
Fletcher, John Gould, 17, 33, 38
Flint, F. S., 19, 33, 36
Ford (Hueffer), Ford Madox, 33
Freud, Sigmund, 225, 226

Frost, Robert, 293

Goethe, Johann W., 246–47
Gombrich, E. H., 69
Graves, Robert, 75, 115

H. D. (Hilda Doolittle), 33, 116
haiku, 17, 19, 65–67, 69
Hemingway, Ernest, 229
Horace, 123
Hulme, T. E., 18, 19, 32, 33, 34–36

Imagism, 17, 18–19, 28, 32–38, 40, 41, 53, 62, 66–67, 77, 81–82, 249
Impressionism, 14, 28, 35

James, Henry, 81, 258–59, 287
James, William, 44
Johnson, Samuel, 223, 226, 252, 253
Jonson, Ben, 123
Joyce, James, 33, 120, 121
Jung, C. G., 226

Keats, John, 170, 283
Kermode, Frank, 138
Kirstein, Lincoln, 168
Kreymborg, Alfred, 10, 56

La Farge, Bancel, 55
Laforgue, Jules, 83–84, 87, 144
Latimer, Ronald Lane, 6, 165, 166
Lawrence, D. H., 46, 69
Lemercier, Eugène Emmanuel, 72ff., 309
Le Sage, Alain R., 122
Lindsay, Vachel, 116, 178
Lowell, Amy, 33, 38, 66, 105

Mallarmé, Stéphane, 69, 145
Martz, Louis, 201
Marxism, 197, 205–6, 211, 215
Matisse, Henri, 46
McGreevy, Thomas, 166

325